THE VOYAGE OF THE CATALPA

A Perilous Journey and Six Irish Rebels' Flight to Freedom

PETER F. STEVENS

CARROLL & GRAF PUBLISHERS

NEW YORK

To Peg Stevens, who first urged me to write this book
and helped keep it on course.

THE VOYAGE OF THE CATALPA
A Perilous Journey and
Six Irish Rebels' Flight To Freedom

Carroll & Graf Publishers
An Imprint of Avalon Publishing Group Inc.
161 William St., 16th Floor
New York, NY 10038

Copyright © 2002 by Peter F. Stevens

First Carroll & Graf edition 2002

Book design and ship's wheel illustration by Michael Walters

Library of Congress Cataloging-in-Publication Data is available.

ISBN: 0-7867-0974-X

Printed in the United States of America
Distributed by Publishers Group West

Contents

Prologue
Well on Her Way Now...

In the late afternoon of April 29, 1875, Captain George Anthony grimaced as the skiff cut back across the shimmering dark-blue waters of Buzzard's Bay and back toward the mouth of New Bedford, Massachusetts, Harbor. As the thirty-one-year-old shipmaster stood at the helm of the whaling bark *Catalpa* and tracked the skiff until it vanished to the east, he mentally inspected his command from bow to stern, topside and belowdecks. The sun beat down upon the whaler, illuminating her bright yellow hull. The *Catalpa*'s rigging shone with fresh tar, and her pennant flags fluttered as her pristine white canvas sails—as yet unblemished by winds, waves, and salt spray—billowed with a steady breeze rising from the southwest. Crewmen scampered along up the yards, freeing every inch of canvas to greet the wind.

As Anthony turned the helm due southeast, to anyone else's eyes the vessel appeared primed for a typical whaling voyage in the Atlantic. Her gleaming oak davits were bolted. Her new whaleboats, chase boats, glinted with fresh white paint, and spare spars were tied and stowed both on and belowdecks. In the hold beneath Anthony's oilskin boots, enough supplies and provisions for a two-year voyage were stored, everything from harpoons to tinned meats.

The handsome shipmaster had dense dark hair gathered up in his visored captain's cap and wore a blue oilskin greatcoat taut across his large shoulders and barrel chest. A whaling man nearly all of his life, he had never feared heading out to deep waters on a whaling voyage. This time, however, everything was different. His pale blue eyes stung for an instant as he thought of his beautiful wife of one year and their infant daughter.

With one hand on the oaken helm, Anthony reached into his greatcoat's breast pocket, pulled out a note, unfolded it, and silently read the light-gray notebook sheaf: *"Go gcuiridh Dia an t-a'dh ort, Captain Anthony. Go soirbh. Dia dhuit."*

The letter's writer, John Boyle O'Reilly, had translated the Gaelic for the Yankee seaman: "May God send luck to you, Captain Anthony. May God prosper you."

For several minutes, Anthony pondered his decision to take this ship and this mission. A New England Quaker and whaleman, he had signed on for a voyage across the globe to Western Australia—not to hunt whales but to attempt the rescue of six Irish rebels from Fremantle Gaol. "I was about to depart on one of the most boldly conceived and audacious expeditions against the British government ever planned," Anthony noted. At the moment, he was not even sure why he had accepted, only sure that the mission was one calculated to strike a blow at "the tyranny of John Bull." A man whose ancestors had fought in the American Revolution, Anthony liked the idea of following in their proverbial footsteps. Still, his motives remained unclear even to him. "Why," he wondered, "was I gambling all for these Irish in a cause which was not my own? To be sure, there would be profit in it if we were successful, but a British noose or a cell if we weren't. Why? I continued to ask that. The answer would come."

He tamped down a pang of depression, as he termed it, and tucked the note back in his pocket. Turning to his first mate, Sam Smith, Anthony snapped, "Take the helm, Mr. Smith, and take her out to deep waters."

Meanwhile on the skiff, headed back to New Bedford, a stocky, dark-bearded Irishman named John Devoy was perched along the port gunwale and wrote in his journal: "I have just left from seeing the ship [the *Catalpa*] 40 miles out to sea . . . . She looked splendid with every sail set, a clear sky overhead and a calm sea beneath, and the scene at parting was one we shall not soon forget . . . . We remained there till she was well out, giving three hearty cheers for the barque and her crew. Not a man but ourselves had the least suspicion of her true mission, and she is well on her way now. . . ."

The perilous voyage of the *Catalpa* was unfolding.

Part 1
Unrepentant Rebels

Desertion for Ireland's Sake

Near midnight on January 28, 1866, Private Thomas Henry Hassett stiffened at a sudden crunch of boots behind him. He pivoted, leveled his Enfield rifle, just as quickly lowered its dark steel muzzle, and slid his right index finger off the trigger. A messmate clad in the scarlet tunic of the 24th Foot Regiment waved his hands as he stumbled toward Hassett through the snow-shrouded courtyard of the Royal Army Hospital on St. John's Road West in Dublin.

Hassett, walking sentry duty, shivered—but not from the frost caking his jut-jawed features beneath the trademark black bearskin shako of the 24th. One glance at the onrushing soldier's face told the twenty-four-year-old Hassett all he needed to know even before his friend Private William Foley blurted out the words: "The guards have arrived at the picket room for you. . . ."

To warn his friend, Foley had lurched nearly a mile from the stark granite expanse of Kilmainham Barracks, his square, stolid features crimson from the gusts roaring in to lash Dublin from the nearby River Liffey. He panted, "They're going to arrest you for treason as soon as you leave your post." Nodding, Hassett thanked his comrade and urged him to return to his quarters before the guards noticed him missing. As Foley slipped away across the courtyard's slick paving stones and vanished back down St. John's West, Hassett made his decision.

At midnight, the deep-toned bells of St. Patrick's Cathedral tolled the hour, the peals a sonorous comfort to most in Dublin, but a personally momentous sound for Private Hassett, who waited for his replacement to arrive in the thickening snowfall, hoping that the man would not arrive with a squad of guards. He materialized alone. Hassett squared his five-foot, eight-inch frame and snapped a salute. After the two infantrymen exchanged the night's password and response, Hassett shouldered his Enfield and marched in the general direction of Kilmainham Barracks.

Once certain he was out of the sentry's eyeshot, Hassett veered southeast down a tiny alley, cut toward Trinity College, and tramped onto Nassau Street, where the glow of wrought-iron gas lamps reflected off the snow to nearly blind passersby. Hassett was headed to Clare Lane, a short, narrow cul-de-sac, where a nerve center of impending rebellion by Irish rebels—the Fenians—stood.

Hassett, who had sworn the secret Fenian oath, vowing to offer his life in revolt against the British Crown, walked the same route to Clare Lane as he had so many other times over the past six months. This time, however, the County Cork-born Hassett did so not as a red-coated Royal Army soldier, but as a Royal Army deserter. His failure to return from his sentry duty to the picket room at Kilmainham Barracks ensured that by morning there would be a price on his head.

With each step along Nassau Street, Hassett reflected on the hazardous choice he had made, one that he risked from the moment he had sworn the secret oath of the Fenian, the Irish Republican Brotherhood: "I, Thomas Henry Hassett, do swear allegiance to the Irish Republic, now virtually established; that I will take up arms at a moment's notice to defend its integrity and independence; that I will yield implicit obedience to the commands of my superior officers, and finally I take this oath in spirit of a true soldier of liberty. So help me God."

The words comprised treason against the Crown, and for a deserter who had taken the oath, capture ensured a swift drumhead court-martial and a noose.

As Hassett deserted the Royal Army in Dublin on that February night, he epitomized the lurking threat of Fenian rebellion against the Crown. From 1858 to 1866, Ireland's centuries-old struggle for independence materialized in the collective form of the Fenians, a body of Irish rebels on "the old sod and the new sod—America—alike." The movement posed an immense threat to the British government: in 1865, of the twenty-six thousand British Army troops garrisoned in Ireland, over eight thousand were sworn Fenians. Recruited from without by civilian agents and from within by soldiers such as asset, the Fenian Brotherhood had vowed "to free the Irish people from 700 years of oppressive British colonial rule or to die in the struggle." Failure, as every Fenian understood, carried the specter of a British noose.

The first rumblings of Fenianism began in the United States in the 1850s and soon spread to Ireland itself. A secret meeting was held in 1858 in Manhattan, where forty-two-year-old John O'Mahoney, a lanky, handsome exile from County Limerick, called to order the first gathering of a revolutionary organization. As several dozen Irishmen, immigrants all, raised their right hands, they swore a secret oath whereby they pledged to win Ireland's freedom from Great Britain by force of arms. O'Mahoney then declared the gathering the first official meeting of the Irish Republican Brotherhood, the IRB.

A Trinity College graduate and renowned Gaelic scholar, who

had translated Geoffrey Keating's seventeenth-century *History of Ireland* from Gaelic into English, O'Mahoney had taken part in the abortive 1848 revolt against British rule as a member of the Young Ireland movement and had fought in the Ballingarry Rising in Tipperary. He had escaped from the Irish defeat, one step ahead of a death sentence that would have been commuted to a life sentence of penal servitude in Australia. Having fled to Paris, he floundered there in abject poverty for four years before settling in New York in 1852.

O'Mahoney quickly immersed himself in a new revolutionary movement emerging among fellow Irishmen who had fled to New York and other American cities after the failed 1848 rising. By 1858, he had established himself as the foremost voice of the displaced Irish rebels. A contemporary noted: "A tall, gaunt figure—the mere framework of a mighty man; a large, lusterless face, with deep-sunken, introverted eyes; faded, lightish hair, worn long to the shoulders; an overcoat always buttoned, as if to hide the ravages of wear and tear on the inner garments; something of this, and something too of gentleness and knightlihood, and easily described, were in the awkward and slow-moving figure, with melancholy and abstracted gaze, so well-known to the Irishmen of New York as John O'Mahoney."

In that landmark 1858 meeting in Manhattan, O'Mahoney bestowed upon the IRB an identity that tapped into the rebels' thirst for their own nation and evoked kinship with the mythic heroes of ancient Ireland. He called them "Fenians." As one IRB member wrote, "No other word touched as deep a chord in the national consciousness of the Irish. It added to the danger of the present the glamour of the imagined past." In America the IRB was also to become known as the Clan na Gael.

As the IRB was born in New York City, a dynamic rebel named James Stephens was founding a similar organization in Dublin.

The thirty-eight-year-old Stephens, a Kilkenny-born mining engineer, had fought, as had O'Mahoney, for Young Ireland in 1848. Small in frame but an aggressive, irascible man, "who combined considerable organizing ability with knowledge of the world," Stephens's abilities launched the new revolutionary movement in Ireland, but his imperious, narrow-minded, and hot-tempered personality made him many enemies.

He and O'Mahoney established contact, and in the early 1860s, the connection deepened between the Irish Republican Brotherhood on both sides of the Atlantic. By 1865, Stephens claimed to have over two-hundred thousand Fenians in Ireland and asserted that as many as fifty thousand were well-armed. Counting on military aid from the Irish in America and also the Irish living in Britain, he planned to unleash the Fenian uprising in 1865. In addition to the eight thousand Royal Army soldiers who had sworn the Fenian oath in Ireland, he estimated that in Britain roughly fifteen thousand Irishmen serving in the Queen's regiments had taken the oath.

Stephens's right-hand man in Ireland in 1865, John Devoy, backed up Stephens's figures for Fenian soldiers stationed in Ireland: "Out of a British garrison of 25,000, some 7,000 were sworn Fenians, including 1,000 men out of a Dublin garrison of 6,000."

While informers, the age-old enemy of Ireland's ill-fated revolts, alerted the authorities at Dublin Castle that rebellion was seething in barracks throughout the country, neither the government nor the army believed that so many soldiers had sworn the Fenian oath. Still, on November 11, 1865, the police arrested Stephens in Dublin and threw him into Richmond Prison, which the Dublin constabulary had pronounced escape-proof. Among the prison staff, however, a man named John Breslin was a sworn Fenian and, with the aid of IRB operative Dennis Dugan, Devoy, and several other Fenians, whisked Stephens from the jail and put him on a ship that slipped off to France. Now a national hero in Ireland, Stephens had told Devoy and the other Fenian leaders that the rising, originally slated for 1865, would take place on an as-yet-unspecified date in 1866.

Stephens and Devoy were counting on a vast pool of Irishmen to sail from America at the appointed time and join the ranks of the "Fenian Army." By the end of America's Civil War, over three million Irish emigrants had settled in North America and as many as two-hundred thousand Irishmen had fought in the Union Army. The Fenians in Ireland believed that those combat-hardened troops would come home to fight for Ireland's freedom. With IRB membership in America surging in the weeks after the Confederate surrender at Appamattox in April 1865, Stephens's strategy seemed plausible. Both Union and Confederate veterans who had emigrated from Ireland took the Fenian oath. So great was the influx of tough, savvy soldiers eager to pit their hard-won martial skills against "the age-old redcoat foe" that a provisional Irish government blossomed in New York in October 1865. Fenian cells, or "centers," sprouted coast to coast in America, the leaders plotting to purchase ships and sail the Civil War veterans to Ireland to join their comrades there for "the grand rising" of 1866.

In February 1866, Private Hassett believed that the long-awaited moment loomed. He stopped and turned to look again and again over his shoulder as he slogged toward Clare Lane, his light-gray eyes scanning Nassau Street for any flash of red great-coats and listening for the snow-muffled thud of hoofbeats. That sound would announce cavalry horses carrying saber-wielding Royal Hussars in their blue-and-gilt tunics, red breeches, black thigh-length boots, and visored black shakos about to ride down the deserter.

On the seemingly endless three-mile trek from the Royal Hospital, Hassett not only agonized that he would be seized at any moment, he also had plenty of time to ponder the route his life and military career had taken since he first donned a soldier's uniform as a seventeen-year-old in 1859. Born on December 12, 1841, in Doneraile, County Cork, Hassett was apprenticed as a carpenter, but longing for excitement, put aside saw and adze for a musket and bayonet when he enlisted in the Papal Brigade of St. Patrick to fight in Italy for Pope Pius IX against Garibaldi's army of "red shirts."

At the Fortress of Spoleto in 1860, young Hassett had stood up to siege, incessant bombardment, and when the garrison's ammunition ran out, savage hand-to-hand fighting against the swarming red shirts. His courage and ferocity led one of the brigade's officers to laud the Cork recruit as "a born soldier."

Paroled back to Ireland with the other survivors of the siege, Hassett wasted little time in signing another enlistment paper, this time the muster rolls of the 24th Queen's Foot. Like so many Irishmen with a craving for adventure and few prospects in civilian life, Hassett put on the hated scarlet coat of the Royal Army, "the age-old oppressors of Ireland," but did so with a motive embraced by thousands of fellow Irish recruits: to learn "soldiering" and to someday apply the martial lessons in a revolt against Britain.

In 1864, Hassett took the IRB oath and proved such a committed, persuasive Fenian that he was soon selected as the regiment's centre. In private off-duty meetings in several "IRB public houses," or pubs, he had sworn 270 fellow foot soldiers of the 24th into the Fenians' ranks.

Now, as he picked up his pace on Nassau Street on January 28, 1866, he momentarily agonized that he had unwittingly recruited an informer who had fingered not only Hassett himself but the other Fenians of the 24th. He forced himself to turn his focus to the job at hand—reaching a certain house on Clare Lane where he "knew of a certain meeting of organizers [Fenians] and boys on their keeping" that was being held that evening.

Hassett cut onto Clare Lane, neared the entryway of the cul-de-sac, hesitated, and stopped. He turned to scan the snow-covered cobblestones up the back road, the way he had come. Then he ducked down Clare Lane between red-and-yellow-bricked Georgian town houses framed by wrought-iron fences and halted in front of a two-story wood-and-brick frame public house.

Nestled between a pair of town houses, its expansive ground-floor bar window reflecting the glow of the huge hearth within, Peter Curran's Public House appeared a welcome haven for any passerby seeking a warm turf fire and a draught of porter or whiskey.

However, Hassett knew that the building's appearance belied the truth of what transpired within Curran's premises. On the public house's second floor, behind windows blocked from the eyes of anyone strolling along the cul-de-sac by dense brown velvet drapes, men were plotting warfare against Great Britain. All that remained was for the leaders to issue the order—and thousands of Fenian soldiers such as Hassett would desert their British regiments and rise in revolt.

Hassett took one last look at the lane's entry, pushed open Curran's door, and scanned the crowded room for the red-bearded face and broad-shouldered frame of publican Peter Curran. Among the Fenian ranks, the phrase "Curran's of Clare Lane" meant a "safe house."

Twenty-five-year-old Peter Curran, a native of Killucan, West Meath, had come to Dublin as a boy and had gone into the family pub keeping business by his teens. A man who had been raised to loathe the sight of a redcoat or a blue-coated cavalryman and had sworn the Fenian oath in 1865, Curran now welcomed any of those British soldiers who had vowed rebellion against the Crown. A Fenian center lauded, "[Curran's] house became the rendezvous for some of the most daring spirits of the IRB and a noted center of hospitality to men in the Republican cause. Many of the north of England IRB, over in Dublin for the projected Fenian rising, were kindly received and lodged at Curran's when food ran out and cash failed."

At Curran's over the past few months, Hassett had met Colonel Thomas Kelly, who had served as a hard-charging cavalry officer in the United States Union Army, earning plaudits for daring and resourceful strikes deep behind Confederate lines. His hit-and-run approach to warfare would be perfect for a campaign in which the Fenians could not consider pitched battles against the Royal Army's weight of manpower, firepower, and materiel.

Around a scarred oak table in the public house's second-story drawing room, a dozen or so men sat. Amid acrid clouds of cigar smoke mixing with the pungent odor of a turf fire glowing in a charred brick fireplace, a dark-complexioned, stocky man spoke in low, urgent tones to the others. They all deferred to twenty-three-year-old John Devoy, his deeply set dark eyes boring into the other men, and his age belying his status as the chief organizer of the Irish Republican Brotherhood in the British Army.

A native of Kill, County Kildare, and the grandson of a United Irish Rebel of the savage Rising of 1798, Devoy embraced militant Irish nationalism as a youth and had been expelled from the public, or "national," school for refusing to sing "God Save the Queen." He was also thrashed by a school official for hurling a slate at a teacher who had derided Irish political leader Daniel O'Connell.

Simmering with hatred toward the Crown, churning out vitriolic anti-British essays in nationalist journals, Devoy joined the IRB in 1861. He enlisted in the French foreign legion a year later, determined to learn the soldier's trade but unable to stomach the notion of wearing "the Queen's red" to do so. When he returned to Dublin in late 1862, he saw so little action with the legion in Algeria that he had winced beneath a reprimand for allowing rust to cake his rifle's muzzle. His lack of combat experience notwithstanding, Devoy's keen intelligence, his daring in recruiting thousands of Irishmen in British uniforms to the Fenian cause, and his ability to sniff out potential informers made him the man who scores of hardened Irish veterans looked to for leadership. In the words of one, "he [Devoy] will fight to his last drop."

Seated alongside Devoy in the Curran's crowded parlor was a handsome man with the mustachioed and goateed mien of a man "born to the saddle." Twenty-seven-year-old John McCafferty had ridden as a cavalry officer with John Hunt Morgan's near-legendary Confederate raiders during the American Civil War. Born of immigrant Irish parents in Sandusky, Ohio, McCafferty had thrown himself wholeheartedly into the American Fenian movement within weeks of surrender at Appamattox. He sailed to Ireland, as had several other Irish and Irish American officers who wore Yankee blue or Rebel gray, to train and lead the Fenian troops in the planned rising.

From the moment in early 1866 that Devoy had introduced the Confederate cavalryman to many of the men he would command, McCafferty grasped that his new officers were not green recruits, but redoubtable riders. Irishmen such as Martin Hogan, a magnificent swordsman who had galloped into battlefields throughout the British Empire, and John Boyle O'Reilly, a dashing and daring young trooper of the elite 10th Hussars, "The Prince of Wales's Own." At meetings such as the one at Curran's on January

28, 1866, McCafferty pontificated on the necessity of hit-and-run guerilla tactics rather than the traditional "form-up-and-charge" techniques Hogan and O'Reilly had engaged in throughout their military careers.

"I believe in partisan warfare," the ex-Confederate asserted. As had Tom Kelly inside Curran's, McCafferty pointed out to Hogan that the Royal Army's sheer weight of numbers and resources dictated an "irregular" campaign for the Fenians. McCafferty added that the traditional saber fighting of the British cavalry had no place in the Fenian columns. "Nothing but the revolver," he stated.

Famed in the Royal Army as the man who had cut a dense iron bar in half with one stroke of his saber in a regimental contest, Hogan merely shook his head and smiled at the Confederate.

Unbowed by his future troopers' skepticism, McCafferty continued to preach his doctrine of partisan warfare. Now, on the nights of January 28 and 29, he, Devoy, and the other rebels gathered in the parlor discussed key Dublin arsenals they needed to seize when IRB commander James Stephens issued the order. The rebels suddenly fell quiet in unison at the crunch of soldier's boots on the stairs leading up to the parlor.

O'Reilly recalled: "We rebels sat in council upstairs; faces grew dark, teeth were set close, and revolvers grasped when they heard the steady tramp on the stairs, and the 'ground arms' [slamming down of a rifle butt] at their door."

Fingers clenched around horse-pistols' triggers, Devoy and the others believed that they had been betrayed by an informer and that British infantrymen stood ready to kick open the ponderous mahogany parlor door.

Slowly, the door swung open. The rebels, several standing now, the rest still perched around the table, leveled their pistols for chest shots.

Then, the door creaked open all the way. The rebels lowered their revolvers as a scarlet-coated soldier materialized in the doorway and strode into the room.

"All there knew him well," recounted O'Reilly. "With full equipment, knapsack, rifle and bayonet, and sixty rounds of ammunition, Hassett had deserted from his post, and walked straight into the ranks of the rebellion. He was quickly divested of his military accoutrements; scouts went out to a neighbouring clothing store, and soon returned with everything requisite for a full-fledged 'civilian.'

"The red coat was voted [into] the fire, and belt and arms were stored away with a religious hope in the coming fight for an Irish Republic."

When Hassett walked into the smoky parlor, he greeted Devoy: "Most of those who desert for Ireland's sake come to you empty-handed, but here I am ready for work."

The following evening, Devoy hid Hassett in the attic of a tiny brick home on Thomas Street. "One more was added to the group of strangely dressed men who smoked and drank their 'pots o' porter' in a certain house in Thomas Street," their fellow Fenian O'Reilly wrote.

To disguise himself from informers and Royal Army search parties—though he never left the house—Hassett shaved off his mustache and cropped his hair nearly to the nubs. Devoy noted, "He [Hassett] had the appearance of a muscular Methodist minister."

"The men there were all deserters," recorded O'Reilly, ". . . watching for the coming fight, the poor fellows lived in mysterious misery for several weeks."

During those several weeks of January and February 1866, O'Reilly still strode the barracks of the 10th Hussars and rode along the streets of Dublin with his dragoon's aplomb. As January

1866 ended, however, the young cavalryman sensed that someone was tracking him to Curran's Public House and other Fenian hideouts throughout Dublin.

In Hoey's Public House, a low-ceilinged Bridgefoot Street tavern where the oak beams overhead sagged with age and whose cramped annex served as a meeting place for Irish-born soldiers from nearby Kilmainham Barracks, the bartender, an IRB zealot named Furey, also sensed treachery. He warned O'Reilly that sworn Fenian and 5th Royal Dragoons Guard Private Patrick Foley had been seen talking to the 10th Royal Hussar's commander, Colonel Valentine Baker, on several occasions. O'Reilly, in turn, warned Devoy that unless the order for the rising came soon, they might all end up swinging by the noose.

Devoy agonized over O'Reilly's predicament and that of the so-called military Fenians who had either deserted their units already and fought fear and boredom in their hiding places or, like O'Reilly, fully expected to be rousted from their bunks some morning, trussed up with chains, and tossed into the dank, fetid cells of Kilmainham. That O'Reilly, the finest recruiter Devoy had, was begging him to act as soon as possible sparked Devoy to send several near-frantic coded letters to Stephens. From the IRB commander-in-chief came nothing but silence.

O'Reilly and Devoy alike had expected the order to arrive no later than February 1, 1866, for all during 1865, Stephens had traveled throughout Ireland and Scotland to prepare the IRB centers in the Royal Army for action. "We will be in the field by year's start," O'Reilly had said to the hundreds of soldiers he had recruited to the Fenian ranks from Kilmainham.

Devoy, O'Reilly, and other Fenian leaders spread the word throughout the movement's complex web of cells, "circles," that the anticipated moment lay near. Each of the circles filled by men such as O'Reilly was commanded by an "A," considered equal in rank to a colonel, who was outranked only by Stephens himself. Under the command of the "A" were nine "Bs," captains; following the "Bs" were nine "Cs," or sergeants. Nine "Ds," the ranks, filled out the circle. Stephens had selected the number nine because of the magical powers the Fenians of Christian Ireland had attached to it and because the ancient Fenians had fought in groups of that number. For patriotic men like John Boyle O'Reilly, the secrecy and mysticism held a deep appeal.

In the exuberant O'Reilly's view, he had surely been born for a grand purpose steeped in Irish mythology. In 1865 and 1866, as he and his brother rebels gathered at that scarred oak table in the upstairs parlor of Curran's or in the low-slung annex of Hoey's, he envisioned himself as a pivotal figure in one of the great unfolding acts of the long, bloody, and futile Irish yearning for freedom from the Crown.

The tortured history of Ireland literally lay in the ground where O'Reilly was raised. On June 28, 1844, he was born in Howth, County Meath, to a pair of schoolteachers who imbued him with nationalistic ideals. His childhood was spent hard by the banks of the River Boyne, near the site of the battle that crushed Catholic Ireland in 1690. Just a few miles away in Drogheda, Oliver Cromwell's troops had massacred twenty-five hundred Catholics.

As a youth, his fierce intelligence and love of poetry earned O'Reilly high grades and high praise from his national schoolteachers. His athleticism, especially his quick and punishing fists when he needed to rely on them, earned him the respect of his classmates.

In his teens, O'Reilly's oldest brother, apprenticed to the local newspaper, the *Drogheda Argus*, fell ill with tuberculosis, and O'Reilly's parents sent him to learn the printer's trade in his brother's place. He not only learned to set and roll type, but also convinced the publisher to let him try his hand at writing a few articles. Within a few weeks, the youth's writing skills, far beyond his years, caught the attention of the paper's readers, and their praise convinced O'Reilly that he would become a journalist, as well as a poet. He would later write however, that he first "craved the adventure and experience that I hoped would shape my prose and verse in years to come."

In 1844, when the *Argus* folded, O'Reilly's parents arranged for him to stay with relatives in Lancashire, England, and work on the *Preston Guardian* as a full-time journalist. Shortly after he arrived in the gritty coal town, he joined a company of local militia called the Preston Volunteers. He had decided to learn the soldier's trade in order to stand ready for the day when Ireland would explode again in revolt against Britain. Eventually, he realized that the "Sunday afternoon militia" comprised a poor substitute for actual military training, the brand that he knew he could receive in only one place—the Royal Army.

O'Reilly abhorred the idea of wearing the red coat that had symbolized so much misery and horror to so many Irish for over two centuries. He found a way around the prospect by enlisting at the Dundalk, Ireland, barracks of the 10th Royal Hussars, famed for their blue-and-gilt coats and their reputation as perhaps the finest cavalry regiment in the Queen's service. As he signed his name with a bold flourish to the enlistment paper, he had already taken the Fenian oath.

Having explained to his initially horrified parents his true purpose in signing the muster rolls of the Royal Army, he received their reluctant blessing—and their daily worry that he was headed on a course that could end only on a British scaffold. They grasped that they simply could not dissuade him.

O'Reilly took to the cavalryman's life, impressing his officers with his natural grace upon a charger and with his sheer physical appearance—his steely light-blue eyes, his square jaw, and his martial mustache. His charisma also caught the notice of the regiment's commander, Colonel Baker. In mid-1865, Baker wrote that O'Reilly was "officer material, a young man who will rise far in Her Majesty's service." Baker boasted, "I have succeeded in developing an extraordinary degree of efficiency and loyalty in my men." At the very time Baker wrote those words, John Boyle O'Reilly had recruited over one hundred of the 10th Hussars' Irish-born riders into the Fenian movement. The regiment revered by the Crown as "The Prince of Wales's Own" seethed with rebellion, stoked by the young Meath man singled out for plaudits by Colonel Baker.

In the fall of 1865, O'Reilly was billeted at Island Bridge Barracks on the western outskirts of Dublin. As he learned the names and reputations of the Fenian recruiters in the British barracks and bases ringing Dublin, Devoy wrote, "O'Reilly's secret, closed door efficiency was such that I had been working for several weeks on the regiment [the 10th Hussars] before I even knew of his existence."

In October 1866, Devoy asked veterinary surgeon Harry Byrne, a Fenian who treated the horses of the 10th, to set up a meeting with the enigmatic O'Reilly. Byrne was a sixty-year-old, silver-haired Irishman whose face was creased with leathery fissures testifying to years of campaigns from South Africa to the Crimea. Leaning back in a chair in Curran's parlor, drawing on a cigar, he nodded and said, "O'Reilly's the man if you want to make progress with the 10th."

The surgeon escorted Devoy to the gates of Island Bridge Barracks the following evening and introduced him as a relative of O'Reilly's. The guards scrutinized the civilian, and in deference to Byrne's rank of captain, waved them to the guardhouse, where a broad-shouldered, glowering sergeant major, the 10th's shako low on his brow, stood barring the building's studded, dense oak door, his huge arms folded. For an instant, Devoy fought an impulse to turn around.

His qualms vanished as the sergeant major smiled, saluted Byrne, and invited both men into the guardroom for a cup of tea to ward off the chill of the sodden, mist-filled night. By then, Devoy wrote, "I was convinced that the sergeant major was a bluff, hearty Englishman of the best type. He praised O'Reilly to the skies, said he was the best young soldier in the regiment, and predicted a great future for him."

Devoy added, "I regretted that we had to trick so honest a fellow."

Eager to meet the Hussar who evoked such praise from Fenians and British soldiers alike, Devoy winced when the sergeant major told them that O'Reilly was on duty that night at the Victoria Barracks, on the other side of the Liffey. Devoy and Byrne bid good-bye to the man, pulled their already wet coats closer around themselves, and trudged toward the Liffey as a steady rain and powerful gusts assailed them.

The pair finally reached the long, whitewashed granite stables of Victoria Barracks and found Trooper O'Reilly tightening the saddle girths of a sleek black stallion, the trademark mount of the 10th Hussars. Turning at the muffled treads of the two men upon the flattened mass of straw covering the stone floor, O'Reilly smiled at Byrne—and straightened up at the sight of the stranger. With his eyes fixed on Devoy, O'Reilly slipped easily into the burnished saddle and told Byrne, "I'm off for Dublin Castle with a dispatch to the Lord Lieutenant [of Ireland]."

Byrne pointed at Devoy and replied, "He's a friend. Will you meet with us at Curran's later tonight?"

O'Reilly still peered at Devoy, who waited for what seemed an interminable time. "He [O'Reilly] glared at me," Devoy noted. "He was a handsome, lithely built young man of perhaps twenty years, immaculately turned out in the dark blue uniform of the 10th Hussars, gold-braided across the chest, a shiny black busby set at a jaunty angle on his head, and the bearskin held by a linked brass chain catching under the lower lip. . . ."

O'Reilly nudged his horse forward and, as he purposely passed within inches of Devoy, said, "I can meet you at eleven." Then he clattered from the stable and galloped down the flagstones of the stable yard.

Devoy was impressed, and by February 1866, O'Reilly had proven invaluable to him. For that reason, O'Reilly's fears that the Royal Army and the police stood ready to pounce upon the Fenians alarmed Devoy more than the concerns of others.

Among those unnerved by the apparent paralysis of the Fenians' commander-in-chief were Irish soldiers Martin Hogan, James Wilson, Michael Harrington, Robert Cranston, and Thomas Darragh. Hogan, the man who had shaken his head in disbelief at McCafferty's disdain for the saber, was born in 1839 in Limerick and learned the carriage painter's trade. He had enlisted in his teens in the Royal Artillery and had transferred to the 5th Dragoons in 1857. In 1864 he had taken the Fenian oath, deserting his regiment in early 1865, and had lived in that "mysterious misery" in safe houses in Dublin ever since, chafing to fight his former army. McCafferty called the twenty-six-year-old veteran "a born soldier, finely built, with the gait and appearance of a cavalry officer."

Thirty-year-old James Wilson, also of the 5th Dragoons, had deserted with his friend Hogan in 1865. While he was known as Wilson, the dragoon's actual name was McNally. Many Irishmen who faced trouble with the police "escaped" by enlisting under a false name in the British ranks. McNally, a native of Newry, County

Down, and a hardfisted man who reportedly pummeled a constable and signed the muster rolls before he could be apprehended, served in the Bombay Artillery, and had seen heavy action in India. After he was mustered out, he drifted, living in Syria and America before heading back to Ireland, where he enlisted in the 5th Dragoon Guards and was sworn in as a Fenian in 1864. Stout, five-foot-nine, with brown hair, brown eyes, and an oft-broken nose, Wilson had proven one of the most zealous Fenians in Dublin.

Another deserter, twenty-four-year-old Robert Cranston, was a native of County Tyrone and a farmer. After eight years eking out an existence on lazy beds of potatoes in Stewartstown, he flung his spade aside in June 1863 and enlisted in the 61st Foot Regiment, a hotbed of Fenian activity with at least four hundred men having taken the oath. O'Reilly noted, "Cranston joined his fortunes with the Fenians early and industriously assisted in propagating the faith." Burly, with gray eyes and brown hair, he had a Fenian cross tattooed on his right bicep.

Michael Harrington was one of the most respected soldiers in the ranks of Cranston's regiment. Like O'Reilly, Harrington, the son of a Cork merchant, was well-educated, but longed for adventure rather than a staid existence poring over ledger books and bank slips. In 1844, he enlisted in the 61st and was shipped to Calcutta the following year. He fought in the Punjab Campaign of 1848, earning a medal and two clasps for bravery under fire; from 1850 to 1857, he had survived countless savage battles between the Royal Army and Indian rulers, his heroism at the Siege of Cawnpore winning him another medal and clasp. Harrington joined the IRB in 1864, and in January 1866, he deserted and hid in Dublin to await the order for the rising. Wounded several times, his face burned a deep brown by the Indian sun, he was just the sort of soldier who filled the Fenian ranks, spoiling to fight the army that had honed his martial skills.

Of Harrington, Hogan, Cranston, Wilson, Darragh, and Hassett, O'Reilly offered:

> These six men were typical members of the Fenian organization in the British army. As will be noted from their careers, they had given meritorious and honourable service, some of them over a long period of years. All were unmarried, career soldiers, figuring they could wed and raise families once their soldiering days ended.
>
> It cannot therefore be said of them that their adherence to the Fenian movement was a whim, conceived without serious thought, or out of a sense of grievance, or at dissatisfaction with their lot or any such unworthy or paltry motive. They were young men, but not so young and inexperienced as to be rash. The telling fact is that they joined the Fenian organization for the patriotic reason of achieving an Irish Republic. They joined a movement to fight the way out of the British Empire. With the decisive mind of the soldier, they went into this project with clear vision and with a full appreciation of the risk.
>
> They were only six out of fifteen thousand who did likewise and who considered that the call of loyalty to an Irish ideal was superior to every other consideration. Many of these men had long service and would soon leave the army on pension. They chose instead the perilous way of insurgency and threw their modest material prospects to the winds.

For O'Reilly and five of those six other military Fenians, the "way of insurgency" would indeed soon prove "perilous." For the sixth, Thomas Darragh, ruin and the Queen's justice had already arrived.

Darragh was born in 1834 in Broomhall, County Wicklow, to a Protestant farm family. When he enlisted in the 2nd Queen's Foot Regiment, Darragh held no nationalistic views—he was actually a member of an Orange Lodge, celebrating the Protestant triumph of the Battle of the Boyne. He fought for "Queen and country" in China and in South Africa, receiving the "Distinction Medal for Gallantry Displayed" and a promotion to sergeant major.

In 1864, Darragh's regimental commander recommended that the sergeant major be placed on the waiting list for an officer's commission, a rare honor for a man in the ranks. Darragh, however, had vowed his life to the Fenian cause in 1863. Like many other Protestant Irishmen in the army, he had slowly come to believe that he was merely serving as cannon fodder in the red-coated ranks and that a free republic of Ireland with room for Protestants and Catholics alike was his land's destiny. The Fenian movement was similar to the United Irishmen of the 1798 rising in that Catholics and Protestants alike were welcome so long as they vowed to fight Britain. For Darragh and many other Irish Protestants, mainly from the northern counties, the egalitarianism of the Fenian movement quelled traditional religious suspicions of "Papists."He resolved to play his part in that unfolding drama. Stationed in 1865 at the prestigious School of Musketry in Fleetwood, England, he became a Fenian "B" and recruited several hundred men to the cause.

In September 1865, guards burst into the Fleetwood barracks, hauled the muscular, red-haired, five-foot-six veteran from his blankets, clapped chains around his wrists and ankles, and dragged him to the guardhouse. Then he was tossed into the hold of a transport bound for Cork, the 2nd Queen's barracks, tried in a drumhead court-martial, and sentenced to "be hanged by the neck until you be dead." In February 1866, the highly decorated soldier languished in a Cork City cell, awaiting his day with the noose, his gray eyes rheumy from an infection bred by the bone-numbing dampness of his six-by-six-foot granite-block cell.

In February 1866, the Royal Army and squads of police, unable to downplay the evidence of informers in barracks spread throughout Ireland, England, and Scotland, pounced upon the military Fenians' cells. Scotland Yard and Dublin Castle, the seat of British rule in Ireland, were terrified by spies' reports that up to fifteen thousand trained soldiers were awaiting the order to revolt in late February or early March 1866 as soon as Stephens issued the order. From 10 Downing Street itself, a secret directive to seize the Fenian centres in every and any regiment galvanized constables, detectives, and handpicked squads of soldiers noted for their ferocious loyalty to the Crown.

On February 10, 1866, Martin Hogan and James Wilson had huddled all day in the garrett of a Fenian safe house, speaking little, starting at the slightest creak on the stairs. They were awaiting the knock of a comrade with the news that the rising had started. The friends paced and fidgeted till nearly midnight before climbing beneath the rough woolen blankets of their cots and falling into fretful sleep.

A short while later, the crunch of boots and men's shouts jerked Hogan and Wilson awake, but they were still climbing from their blankets when a squad of Dublin police kicked the door from its hinges, surged at the two men, threw them to the floor, and shackled their wrists and ankles. Then the police pummeled the pair and dragged them outside to a waiting police van and bundled them off to the grim cells of Kilmainham Gaol. Private Patrick Foley of the 5th Hussars, who had sworn the Fenian oath at Curran's and knew the whereabouts of deserters throughout Dublin, had been an informer from the start. His revelation of Hogan and Wilson's hiding place was just the start.

Though unnerved by the arrests of Hogan and Wilson and furious that Stephens still balked at ordering the revolt, Devoy continued to slip in and out of Curran's, Hoey's, and Pilsworth's public houses to meet with similarly rattled military Fenians and tell them the order to seize key bastions in and around Dublin was at hand. He told no one that he had lost all faith in Stephens.

In the afternoon of February 22, 1866, Devoy met with Colonel Thomas Kelly and other Fenian commanders in a rooming house on Kildare Street. Devoy had pleaded that they give the order to fight before the British swooped down on the barracks, but they had voted four to three to wait.

Devoy trudged from the rooming house near sunset and headed to Pilsworth's. He walked to the public house's back room, filled with the tobacco clouds from the pipes and cigars of an agitated crowd of Fenians clad in their Royal Army uniforms. They argued whether to risk a return to barracks that they suspected were full of informers or desert immediately. Standing among his fellow soldiers and wearing the gilded blue tunic of the 5th Hussars was Private Patrick Foley.

As Devoy began to speak, a man rushed into the room and warned that a pair of plainclothes Dublin detectives were watching Pilsworth's from across the street. Devoy told the soldiers to slip calmly out the back door, and a handful vanished into the alley and scattered.

Suddenly the detectives rushed into the pub with pistols brandished and burst into the back room. Devoy started to pull his revolver from his coat pocket, but one of the other Fenians shouted, "Don't fire! There are a hundred policemen outside!"

Devoy dropped his hands. The detectives twisted his arms behind his back and handcuffed him.

Dozens of uniformed police officers surged into the room and rounded up the Fenians who had not moved quickly enough for the back door. As the police started to shove the prisoners into Pilsworth's taproom and toward the front exit, an ashen-faced detective appeared in the doorway and warned his colleagues that a huge crowd had gathered outside the pub at the sight of so many police and could-be Fenian sympathizers. An officer was already riding to Kilmainham Barracks to summon soldiers to the scene; meanwhile, the police held Devoy and the other Fenians inside, warily eyeing the door and the prisoners.

Within a half-hour, red-coated infantrymen with fixed bayonets marched down the street to Pilsworth's and cleared a path through the crowd. As the police escorted the Fenians to several heavily guarded and caged vans, growls and oaths erupted from onlookers. A Royal Army officer bellowed for the crowd to move back, and for a fleeting moment Devoy and the others hoped that the mob would defy the command and overwhelm the troops. Slowly, however, the throng edged away. The police loaded the Fenians into the vans and clattered away to the Chancery Lane station house.

Later that night, Devoy and the others were trundled off to Island Bridge Barracks. John Boyle O'Reilly happened to gaze out a barracks window as guards shoved Devoy, glowering, bareheaded and coatless against the lashing rain, across the parade ground to the guardhouse.

Turning to a fellow Fenian staring slack-jawed at the procession, O'Reilly whispered, "My turn will come next."

Forty-eight hours later, on February 24, 1866, guards rushed up to O'Reilly's cot near dawn, tipped him onto the stone floor, kicked him numerous times, fixed shackles around his wrists and ankles, and prodded him barefoot with bayonets across the wet parade ground. Then they hurled him face-first into the back wall of a narrow, windowless granite cell in the guardhouse. His nose shattered, blood coursing down his face, he crumpled atop the stone floor.

From February through April 1866, the Royal Army and the police similarly rounded up several hundred Fenians in barracks and bases throughout Ireland, Scotland, and England. Riddled by informers and spies, the ranks of the soldier Fenians virtually collapsed, and with them the best hope for a full-scale rebellion. Michael Harrington and Robert Cranston were among the last of the military Fenians captured, Harrington seized in Dublin on March 10, 1866, and Cranston a few weeks later in April. The highly decorated Harrington, lauded as a soldier's soldier in the Punjab and the Siege of Cawnpore, was placed in solitary confinement in Arbour Hill Prison.

Parliament and the army realized that they could not simply arrest all fifteen thousand Fenians in the various bases, so the regiments with the heaviest numbers of Irish Republican Brotherhood recruits were shipped en masse to other sites throughout the British Empire. The government then turned to the matter of the misfortunate Fenians seized in their barracks. The Royal Army intended to deliver a harsh lesson to them and to any Fenians still hoping to sow rebellion in the Queen's regiments.

All that remained for the military Fenians were drumhead court-martials and a march up the gallows stairs.

Throughout the summer of 1866, Devoy and the other civilian Fenians were tried in Dublin Castle or the Four Courts, drawing sentences for treason from twenty years to life imprisonment. The deserters and the soldiers seized at various barracks and forts also faced their trials in the summer of 1866. The soldiers' heads were shaven to the scalp by their guards, a latticework of cuts left behind by the razor. The military Fenians wore the gray-woolen,

buttoned tunic and trousers of convicts, wrists and ankles mana-
cled. O'Reilly, Hogan, Hassett, Darragh, Wilson, Harrington, and
Cranston heard the same words in the Kilmainham barracks of
the 85th Foot, the site of the court-martial: "You have been in due
course of law, indicted, tried, and convicted after having con-
spired and contrived to levy war upon Our Lady the Queen. . . .
Thereupon it is adjudged that within the walls of the Prison in
which you shall be confined, you will be there hanged by the
neck until you are dead."

Wilson declined to mount any defense whatsoever, and
O'Reilly, Hogan, Darragh, Harrington, and Cranston had pled
"not guilty," all believing that they had committed no crime, as
they had been fighting for the cause of Irish freedom. Hassett
defiantly proclaimed himself guilty of treason against the
Crown—and proud of it.

Shortly after, another of the Curran's men, O'Reilly, was convicted. Prisoner No. 9843, he scratched a message on one of his
cell's damp Wicklow granite walls: "Written on the wall of my cell
with a nail, July 17th 1866. Once an English soldier, now an Irish
Felon; and proud of the exchange."

O'Reilly and the other Fenian prisoners soon discovered that
Dublin's general public accorded them hero status, buttressing
the convicts' spirits. In a letter from Mountjoy Prison to his parents, O'Reilly wrote: "Never grieve for me, I beg you. God knows
I'd be only too happy to die for the cause of my country. Pray for
me, pray also for the brave true-hearted Irishmen who are with
me; we are all brothers who are suffering.

"Men who do not understand our motives may call us foolish
or mad; but every true Irish heart knows our feelings, and will not
forget us."

On September 4, 1866, guards clapped chains around the
wrists and ankles of O'Reilly and two other Fenian soldiers,

Sergeant William McCarthy and Corporal Thomas Chambers, shoved them through the streets of Dublin to a transport ship at Howth, and packed them off to England. They were bound for Millbank Prison, which lay within earshot of the bells of Westminster. At about the same juncture, British ships also ferried Hogan, Hassett, Wilson, Cranston, and Harrington to various prisons in England. So, too, were Devoy and other "nonmilitary Fenians" conveyed to Millbank, Portland, and other gloomy English jails. There, no one would treat the Fenians as heroes.

In Millbank Gaol, O'Reilly immediately learned that the guards and warders deemed him "the most accurst of men, a traitor." Though conditions proved harsh for Devoy and the so-called civilian Fenians, warders and sentries accorded them slightly better treatment than rebels who had worn Royal Army greatcoats or tunics.

O'Reilly, a soldier Fenian, languished in solitary confinement in a twelve-by-eighteen-foot Millbank cell, whose stone floor and bare, whitewashed walls a prison official derisively dubbed "spacious." Sleep eluded O'Reilly on his bed, three planks raised three inches from the floor at the foot and six inches at the head, which forced him to try sleeping in a slanted position. Alongside his bed stood a lidded wooden bucket filled with rancid water for washing and, when the lid was closed, served as a stool. O'Reilly performed the mind-numbing task of picking oakum or coir for eight to ten hours a day, the drip of rainwater from the bare stone walls and ceiling upon the floor tormenting him and testifying to ceaseless hours to come. His cell contained no other furnishings besides the crude stool and bed.

In Millbank, officials believed that "seclusion, employment, and religious instruction" would serve to rehabilitate prisoners. Charles Dickens railed against the treatment accorded the military Fenians and the general population of Millbank: "I hold this slow and daily tampering with the mysteries of the brain to be immeasurably worse than any torture of the body; and because its ghastly signs are not so palpable to the eye and sense of touch as scars upon the flesh; because its wounds are not upon the surface, and it exhorts few cries that human ears can hear; therefore the more I denounce it, as a secret punishment which slumbering humanity is not roused up to stay."

Michael Davitt, one of the Fenian prisoners at Millbank and a man who would return to Ireland to bedevil the British government through political rather than military means, described the silent misery that he, O'Reilly, and the other Fenians endured in the London prison: "Oft in the lonely watches of the night, it [the sound of Westminster's chimes] reminded me of the number of strokes I was doomed to listen to and how slowly those minutes were creeping along! The weird chant of the Westminster clock will ever haunt my memory, and recall that period of my imprisonment when I first had to implore Divine Providence to preserve my sanity and save me from the madness which seemed inevitable through mental and corporal tortures combined."

For the garrulous ex-Hussar O'Reilly, both the silence and the proximity of murderers, rapists, and the hardest convicts in the British penal system chipped away at his spirit. He lost weight, and dark furrows materialized beneath his eyes. Normally a young man afraid of little, accustomed to the freedom of galloping astride a cavalry charger, O'Reilly cringed whenever he caught a glimpse of one particularly intimidating convict—nicknamed the "Corpse-man"—during the one-hour common and silent exercise period in the prison's courtyard, enclosed by walls blocking any view of the outside world.

Yet, several weeks into O'Reilly's incarceration at Millbank, an encounter with the massive, slope-shouldered prisoner changed the erstwhile Hussar's mind about his fellow inmates, reinforcing the reality that all of Millbank's prisoners, whether political or criminal, shared a common bond.

Even the exercise yard offered no respite for the prisoners, as they were all at the crank handle of a massive pump that worked Millbank's water system.

> I turned toward the center of the yard, where ran the series of cranks arranged with one handle for two men facing each other. When I got to my place, I was face to face with the Corpse-man, and when he turned sideways, I saw his left eye through the scoop in his cheekbone. The officers stood behind me. There were three of them to the gang of twenty men, and their duty was to watch so that no communication took place between the prisoners. I felt that the Corpse-man wanted to talk to me, but he kept his hidden eyes on the officers behind me, and turned the crank without the movement of a muscle in his face. Presently, I heard a whisper, "Mate," and I knew it must be he who spoke, although still not a muscle seemed to move. I looked at him, and waited. He said again, in the same mysterious mutter, "Mate, what's your sentence?"

The vigilance of the guards notwithstanding, the Fenian inmates of Millbank contrived a means of communication. At night, O'Reilly and the others knocked once on their cell walls in a signal to say a silent prayer for Ireland's freedom. O'Reilly wrote, "Men who a few months ago were careless, thoughtless soldiers, are now changed into true patriots, however humble."

In Millbank, the warders allowed only the Bible and other religious tracts for reading material, and O'Reilly immersed himself in *The Imitation of Christ,* by the mystic Thomas Kempis. Kempis's advocacy of sealing oneself away from the world at large resonated for a time with O'Reilly, a devout Catholic. He strove to find comfort from the philosopher's credos: "Thou shalt find in thy cell what thou shalt often lose abroad"; "Thy cell, if thou continue in it, grows sweet; but if thou keep not to it, it becomes tedious and distasteful."

Still, O'Reilly, a high-spirited man of twenty-three now, longed for escape and for news of the rebellion that he believed was yet imminent.

As 1867 dawned, Tom Kelly, a former Union Army officer who had been part of the Curran's crowd and had escaped to New York, and John McCafferty, still on the loose, slipped into England intent on igniting the long-awaited rising. Without consulting his fellow Fenian commanders, McCafferty mustered Fenian recruits for an intended February 11, 1867, assault against Chester Castle, a munitions depot in northern England. He planned to rush the captured arms and ammunition on a mail boat to Dublin and issue the order for a general revolt against the Crown.

But on February 11, word reached McCafferty that informers had tipped off the British, who had heavily reinforced the castle. McCafferty called off the attack in time, but police and soldiers rounded up many of the Fenians who had shown up in England for the aborted raid.

Kelly launched the Fenians' next gambit in early March 1867. The former Union Army officer believed that over fourteen thousand Fenians in Dublin and nearly twenty thousand in Cork stood ready to strike, and issued the order to attack British bastions on March 5.

Throughout the first week of the month, Fenian units unleashed successful forays against two police barracks, in Glencullen and Stepaside, near Dublin. In Cork with two thousand Fenians, former Union Army captain Michael O'Brien stormed and seized the Ballyknockane police barracks. Then the attackers ripped up local railway lines and spliced the telegraph cable.

The Fenian successes proved short-lived. With no centralized chain of command or headquarters in the field, the Irish units were soon running from British columns throughout the western and southwestern counties, the Fenians' flight impeded by sudden, heavy snowfall. At Kilclooney Wood, in County Tipperary, British troops and local police cornered the last band of rebels still in the field and overwhelmed them after a brief but spirited clash.

In a letter to a friend in America, Thomas Kelly lashed out, "Little Baldy [James Stephens] has finally given up the ghost and acknowledged that if he came to Ireland the people would be certain to make short work of him. The rascal is in Paris, taking his ease with his wife, while the destiny of Ireland is in the balance. . . . We now begin to realize fully the madness of McCafferty's attack at Chester. Now it is war to the knife. Only send us the knife."

Several weeks after the ill-conceived Fenian attacks, O'Reilly, already disheartened by rumors of the disaster that had culminated at Kilclooney Wood, was taken in chains to Chatham Prison, along the Thames in Kent. Solitary confinement had governed Millbank, but at Chatham, warders extolled harsh physical labor for the prisoners. O'Reilly dug ditches and hauled earth with his fellow inmates as part of the expansion of a naval dockyard; reportedly, he tried to escape but was quickly recaptured and punished with a diet of bread and water. He was sent to Portsmouth Prison just a few weeks later, enduring another convict labor-gang stint, this time on a harbor enlargement project. Once again, he tried to escape but failed.

In the summer of 1867, gaunt and desperate, O'Reilly was shipped to infamous Dartmoor Prison, a windswept edifice perched on a moor in Princetown, Devonshire. It was originally built in 1809 to hold French prisoners during the Napoleonic Wars. With the dark-brown stone walls of Dartmoor as a backdrop, endless days of digging drains in the boggy turf and hauling quarried stones to the moors further stoked O'Reilly's determination to escape or to die in the effort.

Of life and labor at Dartmoor, O'Reilly recorded: "Through the thick drizzle of the early morning the convicts were marched in gangs to their daily tasks; some to build new walls within the prison precincts, some to break stone in the round yard encircled by enormous iron railings fifteen feet high, some to the great kitchen of the prison, and to the different workshops. About a third of the prisoners marched outside the walls by the lower entrance; for the prison stands on a hill, at the foot of which stretches the most forsaken and grisly waste in all Dartmoor."

Invariably finding himself and the other Fenians ordered into the cutting ditches crisscrossing the moors, O'Reilly never forgot how he, McCarthy, and Chambers "toiled in the drains which were only two feet wide, and sunk ten in the morass. It was a labour too hard for brutes, the half-starved men, weakened by long confinement, standing in water from a foot to two feet deep, and spading the heavy peat out of the narrow cutting over their heads." Slowly, the effects of those days in the ditches would kill both Chambers and McCarthy.

Though exhausted and rapidly losing weight, O'Reilly did not collapse on his cell's cot when he returned soaked and shivering from the moors each night. Casting glances at the cell door's small barred window for a guard's sudden appearance, listening for the crunch of a warder's hobnailed boots against the corridor's stones, he fashioned several of his rough woolen bedsheets into a rude shirt and trousers. Every day in the ditches, he wore the garb beneath his gray prison uniform, waiting for a chance to slip away from the guards, discard his convict clothing, and make a run for freedom.

A dense fog suddenly arose late one summer afternoon and cloaked the moors before the sentries could manage a proper head count. When the guards reassembled the ditch gangs in the prison courtyard, one man was missing.

Having hidden in a fog-blanketed trench until the other prisoners had been marched away, O'Reilly splashed across the moors in his makeshift clothes toward the coast. For two days, squads of soldiers and police with bloodhounds combed the moors for him, the baying of the dogs and the distant shouts of his trackers reaching O'Reilly, lurching ever closer to the shore. They found no sign of the escapee except for his discarded convict uniform.

On O'Reilly's first night of freedom, he climbed onto a thatched cottage roof and huddled in a downpour. On the second day, as the dog's barks and the soldiers' cries pealed closer and closer, he dove into a ditch filled with frigid, neck-high sewage and for hours stood ready to submerge into the offal, hoping that the water would mask his scent from the hounds.

Still in the distance, one of the pursuit party's officers stopped, raised his field glasses, and scanned the bleak moors ahead. He spied no hint of the prisoner's shaved head bobbing in any of the dykes. Then the officer's lenses caught a ripple in one of the trenches.

Within minutes, guards dragged O'Reilly from the water, chained him, and dragged him off to spend twenty-eight days in the prison's punishment cells on meager rations of bread and water. Disconsolate, O'Reilly awaited his return to the drainage ditches, years of cutting and tossing peat looming ahead of him.

Rumors that O'Reilly and his fellow Fenians in Dartmoor and other British jails would not labor in the penal gangs for much longer began to circulate among the prisoners in late September and early October 1867. Some said that they were all to mount a scaffold. Others whispered the word "Australia."

Unaware as yet that life in an Australian road gang was just a slower form of death than the noose, O'Reilly seized upon the news as a potential delivery from Dartmoor. He and many other Fenians believed that nothing could prove worse than the prison rising from the Devonshire moors. O'Reilly also figured that a resourceful and determined man might more easily escape an Australian prison than an English one. "Australia!" he averred. "The ship! Another chance for the old dreams [escape]; and the wild thought was wilder than ever, and not half so stealthy."

He waited and prayed for deliverance to a land he knew little about, hoping that the first rumor—the hanging of the military Fenians—was false.

In the first week of October 1867, O'Reilly and other rebels who violated their sworn oath to the Queen and her army received their answer. "Down the corridor came the footsteps again," remarked O'Reilly.

> The keys rattled, doors opened, and in five minutes we had double irons on our arms, and were chained together by a bright strong chain. We did not look into each other's eyes; we had learned to know what the others were thinking of without speaking. We had a long ride to the station in a villainous Dartmoor conveyance, and then a long ride in the railway cars to Portland. It was late at night when we arrived there. The ceremony of receiving convicts from another prison is amusing and "racy of the soil." To give an idea of it, it is enough to

say that every article of clothing which a prisoner wears must at once be sent back to the prison whence it came. It may be an hour, or two, or more, before a single article is drawn from the stores of the receiving prison—during which time the felon is supremely primitive. To the prison officials this seems highly amusing; but to me, looking at it with a convict's eye and feelings, the point of the joke was rather obscure.

O'Reilly had no time to bid farewell to McCarthy and Chambers, who were left behind at bleak Dartmoor. The ex-Hussar would never see them again.

For John Boyle O'Reilly, an ordeal that would far eclipse the trials of Dartmoor lay ahead. So, too, for military Fenians Hogan, Wilson, Harrington, Darragh, Cranston, and Hassett, all of whom, like O'Reilly, had already suffered in British prisons for their collective dream of Irish freedom.

A Floating Hell

Wind and rain slashed in from the English Channel across Chesil Bank on October 12, 1867, and pounded the four-and-a-half-mile length of Portland Bill, the harbor within frothing with whitecaps. The gusts lashed at the rigging of the ships moored behind the new mole and drove giant waves against the stone quays of Portland.

Behind the limestone walls of Her Majesty Queen Victoria's Royal Prison, the crunch of sentries' boots and the groans and snores of a thousand prisoners merged in a doleful din with the wind and rain. Water seeped down the granite walls and soaked the thin cotton coverlets beneath which the prisoners lay on rough-planked pallets. The smell permeating the dim corridors and cells, wrote John Boyle O'Reilly, stank like a sour kitchen sponge soaked in excrement.

O'Reilly, Harrington, Wilson, Darragh, Cranston, Hogan, and Hassett had been shipped to Portland from Mountjoy and Millbrook Prisons in England, where they had suffered beatings and other abuse from guards for over a year. Rumors were rife that they would soon swing from the gallows in the prison courtyard.

The seven Fenians were huddled in seven double-locked and barred cells. Leg irons had torn into each man's ankles, covering them with festering sores. The warders had classified the seven Irishmen as "dangerous in the extreme not only to Queen Victoria's government, but to Her Most Gracious Majesty herself."

The fact that the Fenians still breathed did not reflect any inclination toward mercy by the Queen or by her ailing prime minister, Edward George Geoffrey Smith, 14th Earl of Derby. Nor did their survival so far owe anything to the British press, which continued to brand them as traitors and to demand that they swing from the noose. In the United States, France, and other European nations, however, public officials and newspapers demanded that the Fenians be treated as prisoners of war. The queen and her ministers realized that to hang the men would make them martyrs in Ireland and America. Throughout Ireland, those seven were already acclaimed as patriots, guilty only of love of country and hatred of tyranny. Such thoughts notwithstanding, the Crown intended to make examples of the convicted Fenians languishing in Portland.

However, the matter of retribution divided the Queen's government. George William Frederick Charles, Duke of Cambridge, Commander-in-Chief of the Queen's Armies, had pleaded to his cousin the Queen that the death sentences be carried out immediately to preserve British Army discipline. On the other side, Lord Derby and his cabinet, worried that hanging the men more than a year after their convictions would appear barbaric, hurt trade, and might reflect badly on the Queen herself.

Sallow-faced Michael Harrington and Thomas Hassett lay in adjoining cells in the early morning of October 12, 1867, their consecutive convict numbers placing them alongside each other in chain and dungeon cell. Such had been the case from Dublin's Royal Barracks to Mountjoy, to Pentonville, through the terrible solitary confinement of Millbank, and now to Portland. These two Fenians had been brought to Portland by steam train from

Millbank just twelve hours earlier. Each lay wide awake, sensing that something was about to happen.

Near dawn, guards suddenly shot back bolts, yanked iron doors open, burst into cells, and kicked the Fenian prisoners to their feet. A warden's copper-toed boot brought Harrington up from his planks snarling, and he lurched into the corridor, his chains nearly tripping him. Within seconds he was alongside Hassett, who glared at the guard who had just punched him in the stomach.

The guards rousted prisoners from row after row of cells, oaths and curses pealing through the stone corridors. Soldiers bellowed at the prisoners, and the thuds of fists and feet against the convicts' flesh echoed everywhere, as did howls and groans from the victims.

Guards pushing wheelbarrows of food forced the prisoners to eat as they were shoved toward the prison yard. They choked down a pint of cold oatmeal and potato gruel, a hunk of sour bread the size of a small boy's fist, and a mug of watery cocoa.

As Harrington and Hassett gulped their meal, a guard smirked at them and said, "We've seen the last of you—you're for Australia today."

The two Fenians gaped.

"You're for the convict ship today, all right. She's the *Hougoumont*, and she's waiting down the harbor ready to take you."

Hassett could not utter a reply. He rubbed the stubble on his head where the hair had been torn out by the roots when he was pitch-capped—his head covered with melted pitch—by English warders in the Provost's Prison in Dublin's Royal Barracks. Harrington similarly stared wide-eyed at the soldier.

Shouts of "Chains! Chains!" exploded throughout the prison. Squads of red-coated soldiers waded into the crowded, musty corridors with long strands of iron chains in tow.

Armorers and warders began shackling the wrists and ankles of screaming women in the "ladies' section" of Portland. In three chained ranks, ten women in each, they whimpered against the walls, while 260 men—murderers, thieves, pimps, and political prisoners —were chained in order of their registered convict numbers.

As always, Harrington, No. 9757, and Hassett, No. 9758, were fastened to a long chain, and then an armorer knocked off their leg manacles.

In the wind-churned harbor, the H.M.S. *Hougoumont,* a huge converted merchantman, strained at her two bow anchors at 6:30 A.M. She was a convict ship marked with the broad white-painted arrow of her "status" along 153 feet of her otherwise black hull, her teak decks awash with such a heavy rain that her topsails were barely visible from the dock. Sheets of water poured off her furled canvas.

Scarlet-coated pensioners, former British soldiers who had signed to go to Australia with their families for a lifetime government pension, lined the gunwales, holding Enfield rifles. The soldiers' wives and children were belowdecks in their cramped cabins in the stern.

Also huddled near the gunwales were four men in dark-blue caps and uniforms, their families also safe in their stern cabins from the rain, as well as from the sights soon to fill the main deck of the *Hougoumont.* James Archdeacon, Charles McGarry, William Howard, and Thomas Rowe had been appointed the ship's warders, and Rowe was handpicked by Britain's Secretary of State for the Colonies, the Duke of Buckingham, to keep watch on the Fenians for any sign of shipboard rebellion.

Born in 1839 at Tiverton, Devonshire, England, Rowe had joined London's Metropolitan Police in 1859 as a constable. He rose through the ranks quickly, garnering a reputation as a shrewd assessor of crime-scene evidence and a man whose quick wits were equalled by his quick fists. In 1861, he was promoted to the prestigious slot of Detective Sergeant of Scotland Yard and shed his "constable's blues" for the plainclothes garb of "The Yard."

When the Colonial Office decided in 1867 to transport the Fenians to Australia, the Duke of Buckingham ordered Scotland Yard Chief Sir Richard Mayne to select a detective to keep a vigilant watch on the Irish rebels. Mayne chose Thomas Rowe, but Rowe, whose wife was pregnant and who had little wish to leave England, balked. Still, he obeyed Mayne's order to see Inspector General of Prisons Sir Y.W. Henderson.

Rowe would later record:

> I was sent by Sir Richard with a letter to 10 Downing Street, which I presume was concerning my selection to accompany the Fenians where I saw Sir Y. W. Henderson . . . by whom I was sent with a letter to the Duke of Buckingham's office. His Grace informed me that I should be appointed to the Convict Service in due course.
>
> I replied that I was not aware of the contents of the letter I had brought, but that I could not accept the appointment unless my services were transferred from the Police to the Convict Service (nearly seven years' service). His Grace said there was no precedent for such a thing, and I replied, "Perhaps not, Your Grace. Is there any precedent for the Convict Authorities applying for a police officer to accompany Fenians to Western Australia?"
>
> On my remarking that I could not afford to lose my seven years' service, His Grace said he would give his

word that my services in the Metropolitan Police and Scotland Yard should not be lost on joining the Convict Service, thus saving that time with a view to seniority and in other respects and [ensuring] that I should be transferred to the Convict Service on that understanding. I therefore accepted the appointment.

Now, on that gray morning in Portland Harbor, Rowe worried that he had made the right decision for his wife, Sarah, and their three children, especially since she was due to give birth at virtually any time during the opening days of the voyage. He peered through the rain at the jail and waited.

In Portland Prison at 6:30 A.M., the chief warder's voice echoed: "Convicts! Stand! Attention! Ready! March!"

The gates of the prison swung open, and as steady drumbeats and the rasps of chains against cobblestones filled the air, a procession of 320 criminal convicts and 63 Fenian prisoners— including O'Reilly, Harrington, Hassett, Darragh, Hogan, Wilson, and Cranston—trudged out the gates. Soldiers with fixed bayonets led every third chain.

O'Reilly, disconsolate, recalled, "Scant mercy—we were bound for the Establishment. Better we were given the noose."

By "the Establishment" O'Reily meant Fremantle Gaol, in Western Australia. Evidently, the Fenians' sentences had been commuted to a life of penal servitude in the most godforsaken, escape-proof prison in the Empire. In reality the broiling sun and the life of convict road gangs in the outback of Fremantle ensured a slow death sentence for many.

A crowd had gathered to get a last look at the convicts headed to "the dry arse of the earth." In the drenched throng were many who had come for a last glimpse of a loved one. The convicts trudged down the cobbled hill, the women first in line, followed by twenty-six ranks of chained men. Every so often a shriek erupted from an onlooker who would rush up to a chain to touch or speak to a prisoner, only to be greeted by the butt of a soldier's musket.

A young Irish girl whose brother, Thomas Dunne, was among the Fenian prisoners burst toward him from the throng. O'Reilly would later write, "Poor Dunne could only stoop his head and kiss his sister—his arms were chained; and that loving heart-broken girl, worn out by grief, clung to his arms and chains as they dragged her away; and when she saw him pushed rudely to the gangway, she raised her voice in a wild cry: 'Oh, God! Oh, God!' as if reproaching Him who willed such things to pass. We saw her watching tirelessly, and we tried to say words of comfort to that brother—her brother and ours. He knew she was alone and had no friends in wide England."

Harrington and Hassett, in the twentieth chain and within sight of the heartrending scene, looked at each other and cried, "Erin Go Bragh!" From the other chains some sixty voices roared back in unison the identical words.

Tears ran from Harrington's eyes, eyes that had faced down men on battlefields across the Empire. Then a sentry rushed over to him and slammed a fist into his face. "Quiet, goddamn you!" the soldier roared. "If you speak again, I'll stick you through!"

As the procession neared the quayside, soldiers, warders, and sailors shoved and cursed the convicts aboard a small paddle-wheel steamer. The horror of what lay ahead gripped many of the convicts, and a chorus of cries and screams reverberated along the docks.

When the 320 criminal convicts and 63 Fenians were finally jammed aboard the steamer, it puffed low in the murky water to the massive black-hulled convict ship. Sailors made her fast to the *Hougoumont,* and the bayonet-wielding redcoats forced rank after rank of prisoners up the gangway stairs.

On the vessel's deck, prisoners who had been chained for hours and barred from using a privy pleaded with the guards for relief. One of the Fenians recalled:

> In the bustle and confusion preceeding [sic] the removal of the handcuffs, the sights presenting themselves on the deck of the *Hougoumont* were sickening beyond all description. For the especial relief of the demands of nature, hurried appeals come from all sides only to fall in vain on the ears of the warders, and for the few close enough to command attention the remedy is found to be as mortifying as the disease. In a union of chains, he, who, is not in immediate needs is forced to accompany him who is, and in a stooping posture keep guard and witness the revolting spectacle till all manner of shame ceases to be a virtue. It is an occasion never to be forgotten, an occasion of loathing, barbarous brutality, from whose indecent gaze the savage might turn in sickening disgust.

The Fenians and the others stared almost uncomprehendingly as the soldiers struck off their chains, and stood dumbly on the deck, staring about them as their shackles came away. O'Reilly peered along the ship's decks, his eyes finding a roofed-over, V-shaped section just behind the bowsprit. His gaze fell on the wide end of the "V," which was latticed with inch-thick iron bars—the convict ship's punishment cell. Attached to the foremast, a black gaff with two iron rings that were set as wide apart as a man's outstretched arms was set up. On the deck immediately below the apparatus stood another iron ring, just as far apart and bolted down—the "triangle," for flogging. Dangling from the foremast, above the triangle, was a thick noose dubbed "the hempen halter."

Two of the main cargo hatches, an iron cage with a barred door atop each, were flanked by Royal Marines and warders. They shouted out the registered convict numbers, and as each man and woman replied, he or she joined a line that entered the cages and descended down narrow ladders into the dark holds of the ship.

To O'Reilly, the journey into the vessel's "bowels" was terrifying:

> As I stood in that hatchway, looking at the wretches glaring out, I realized more than ever before the terrible truth that a convict ship is a floating hell. The forward hold was dark, save the yellow light of a few ship's lamps. . . . There swelled up a hideous diapason from that crowd of wretches; the usual prison restraint was removed, and the reaction was at its fiercest pitch. Such a din of diabolical sounds no man ever heard.
>
> We hesitated before entering the low-barred door to the hold, unwilling to plunge into the seething den. As we stood thus, a tall, gaunt man pushed his way through the criminal crowd to the door.
>
> He stood within, and stretching out his arms, said, "Come, we are waiting for you." I did not know the face—I knew the voice. It was my old friend and comrade, Keating.

The sixty-three Fenian soldiers and civilians descending into the hold of the *Hougoumont* were the last political prisoners Britain would ever pack off to Australia. All sensed the torments awaiting them in the dim hold and in the penal colony at voyage's end.

"Only those who have stood within the bars," O'Reilly noted, "and heard the din of devils and the appalling sounds of despair, blended in a chorus that made every hatch-mouth a vent of hell, can imagine the horrors of the hold of a convict ship."

Crouched in a corner of that hold was Thomas McCarthy Fennell, a twenty-five-year-old County Clare Fenian who had been wounded leading rebels against a coast guard station at Kilbaha, Clare, in March 1867, convicted of treason in July 1867, and sentenced to ten years' hard labor in Fremantle. A stocky, well-educated man with thick auburn hair, he had stood up to imprisonment in Mountjoy well and thought of himself as a man who feared little—until he saw his "shipmates."

"Here then," he observed, "huddled together is an impenitent brood of human creatures representing every shade of crime and wickedness and whose equals the world never saw. An assemblage of vilest criminals composed of thieves, blacklegs [cardsharps], forgers, murderers and fiendish despoilers of character and virtue, with a handsome sprinkling doomed to oblivion— indulgent victims in the abominations of Onan and Sodom."

Fennell immediately learned that the Fenian prisoners, particularly the seventeen soldiers, held a special "status" onboard the convict ship: "Their [*sic*] is another mixture amongst the doomed ones of the *Hougoumont* . . . they are political prisoners. Their aspirations were not of that order that would merit classification with thieves and murderers, no, for history fails to record where a liberty-loving patriot has been put on a par with a common desperado by any nation of modern times."

From the moment that the men who had once served in Her Majesty's regiments stepped onto the deck of the prison ship, their captors singled them out for harsher treatment than that administered to the criminals. "Right along," Fennell noted, "they [the ex-soldiers] were made the objects of constant reflection, abuse and ridicule by the warders in charge, who took advantage of every occasion to tell them, and make them feel, they were no better than common criminals. The government has instructed them [the warders and guards] to persecute them [the seventeen soldiers] as far as the physical frame could endure without causing instant death, till evidence of decline was to become apparent and dissolution in the near future made certain. Abuse, annoyance, and ill-treatment has been the order of the day."

By 11 A.M., the guards had forced every prisoner into the hold. The sudden screeches of the massive anchor chains through the hawsepipes and the jarring bumps of the ascending anchor conjured screams and cries from the hold. O'Reilly and the other Fenians felt the strain of rigging that was tightening. The ship's very decks creaked as the vessel began to move. The *Hougoumont* shuddered and slipped toward the narrow opening of Portland Mole.

The convicts fell mostly silent, the quiet pierced only by the occasional sob or moan. Slowly, the tide lifted the convict ship toward the English Channel and out into the Atlantic.

In Exile and Chains

S carcely out from Portland, military prisoner John Boyle O'Reilly agonized: "The first few days of the voyage are inexpressibly horrible. The hundreds of pent-up wretches are un-used to the darkness of the ship, strange to their crowded quarters and to each other, depressed in spirits at their endless separation from home, sickened to death with the merciless pitch and roll of the vessel, alarmed at the dreadful thunder of the waves, and fearful of sudden engulfment, with the hatches barred. The scene is too hideous for a picture—too dreadful to be described in words."

At 6 A.M. on October 13, 1867, Captain William Cozens allowed the Fenians on deck of the *Hougoumont* for Mass. Father Bernard Delany, a thirty-three-year-old Dubliner who harbored Fenian sympathies and had volunteered to accompany the rebels to Australia, lay belowdecks, retching, so Cork-born Fenian John Sarsfield Casey, a deeply religious young man with penetrating eyes, held an impromptu service near the main hatchway. Throughout the voyage, Father Delany would celebrate Mass, hear confessions, and bestow the sacraments, with Casey serving as acolyte. Dr. William Smith, Surgeon Superintendent, presided over Church of England services at a much larger space near the mizzen mast. There, according to one of the Fenians, "the

Protestants sang themselves hoarse with song and canticle . . . the doctor's sermons are to be greatly feared."

The Catholic Masses abovedecks gave O'Reilly and the sixteen other military Fenians a welcome respite from their berths in the main convict hold. Though men such as Harrington, Darragh, and Hogan had gone to war, they feared the horde of criminals who thrashed about in rude, two-tiered "deal-board" beds near and above the soldiers' berths those first few nights. The military prisoners craved a move to the guarded quarters of the civilian Fenians, who did not have to mingle with the bonafide criminals. Denis Cashman, a handsome, twenty-five-year-old clerk from Waterford and one of the nonmilitary rebels, wrote, "Of course, we did not associate or scarcely speak to the unfortunates [convicts], although I believe a portion of them had been very respectable and well-educated."

Captain William Cozens, a ship's master of four decades and a man whose stout, ruddy-cheeked appearance and congenial demeanor belied his ability to deal out harsh and swift shipboard discipline, had assigned the "unfortunates" and everyone else aboard to their specified quarters. One of the Fenians described the arrangements: "On the elevated poop deck in silks and broad cloth the prison magnets [magnates] occupy position; on and around the forecastle, in greasy pilot, lounge the bulk of the sailors; amidships, wedged together, soldiers in blue and red, warders in blue and gold, and sad-looking, dejected convicts in ill contrasting costumes, brown smocks, knickerbocker breeches, long stockings, and a four-hand high cap of the same material and crossbarred red, the entire suit beautified with quaint broad arrow stamps of different paints to contrast in color with the garments."

No one, least of all a prisoner, was supposed to question his or her assigned quarters. But as the seventeen military Fenians envisioned countless nights of fretful sleep among the murderers and rapists amidship, James Wilson decided on the morning of the third day that he would not endure the quarters that the *Hougoumont*'s officers had assigned him and his comrades. Shoving his way through the convicts, determined to find a berth where "we only needed to face the convicts from the front and not the rear," Wilson staked out a spot in the fore hold for the ex-soldiers, and they slung hammocks there. Guards who had served with Wilson or other Fenians in the Queen's regiments allowed the move.

At night, Wilson and his comrades posted "sentries." Even though they no longer had to watch their backs at night, battle-tested veterans such as Hassett, Darragh, and Harrington remained as wary of the murderers just a few yards away as the soldiers had once been of Sikhs and other foes on the battlefields of the Empire.

Several of the guards with whom Wilson had soldiered gave the Fenians a few whale-oil lamps, the guttering whitish light allowing them to spot any criminals stealing toward the soldiers' "encampment." The faint light also allowed the prisoners to thumb through Bibles and books borrowed from the civilian Fenians, who were accorded more privileges and hands-off treatment from their captors.

The former soldiers took heart in a rumor that a heavily armed Fenian ship from the United States was bearing down on the *Hougoumont,* the prisoners pointing to the starboard presence of the gunship H.M.S. *Earnest* ever since the convict ship sailed from Portland Harbor. O'Reilly and the others peered at the western horizon for a "Fenian raider" during their daily exercise period topside. Captain Cozens also studied the waters to the west, worried that an American rescue vessel was, in fact, racing his way.

On the *Hougoumont*'s fifth day out of Portland, Cozens observed dense, dark clouds gathering above the Bay of Biscay and ordered the crew to batten down the vessel. The prisoners packed belowdecks huddled as the ship began to pitch, some groaning with each roll, many fingering rosary beads.

As roaring gusts tore at the ship's rigging and giant gray waves thudded against and over the hull, screams erupted from the hold. Sailors raced up the ratlines to sheaf the ship's sails. Suddenly a deafening crack echoed from above—the vessel's sail had split in half from the force of a wave. The wind ripped several holes in the topsails and jib before the crew finally furled the canvas. As the waves swelled, the *Hougoumont* bobbed and dipped in the frothing water.

In the convict holds, sobs mingled with the screams. Buckets of slop tipped over, the reeking contents pouring across the planks. The ship's lurches tossed prisoners across the timbers of the hold, opening gashes and breaking bones.

The seventeen military Fenians huddled in their perch near the bow with terrified murderers, thieves, arsonists, and worse, all sharing in the misery. Although none of the soldiers, men who had gotten their proverbial "sea legs" on British troop transports, threw up their guts like the convicts all around them, the soldiers quickly grasped just how severely the storm was hitting.

As the gale's battering continued, a shout from topside cut through the roaring gusts and reached the prisoners: "Sail Ho!"

The cry set off near-pandemonium among the Fenians. They prayed that the anticipated "Fenian ship" had arrived. On the *Hougoumont*'s quarterdeck, Captain Cozens braced himself against the rail and trained his telescope on the approaching vessel's mainmast. He grimaced—he could not make out an ensign.

As word spread into the hold that the strange ship flew no

colors, the Fenians shouted curses at the Crown and cheered on the rescuers they prayed had arrived. Then, another cheer—from the main deck—pierced through the wind. The prisoners' hopes plummeted. The other ship had run up the Union Jack. It was a merchant ship carrying a cargo of rice from Charleston, South Carolina, to Liverpool, not "the Fenian cruiser" of the prisoners' hopes. Meanwhile, the storm did not abate. Gloom enveloped O'Reilly and Hogan, who for a time, cared little if the convict ship foundered or rode out the gale.

Even as the storm continued to batter the *Hougoumont*, Cozens tossed a midshipman into the roofless punishment cell on the main deck for his refusal to take his position on the swaying mainmast. Several hours later, the man was found dead from "exposure and ingestion of a quantity of sea water." Crewmen hurled his corpse, wrapped in a tied canvas shroud, into the monstrous waves. The message was clear to sailors and prisoners alike: any breach of shipboard discipline would result in the stiffest consequences.

As Cozens delivered his message, a far different delivery was taking place in one of the warders' cabins. While the *Hougoumont* reeled and pitched in the storm, Sarah Rowe was in labor. The wife of Assistant Warden James Archdeacon, not ship's surgeon Smith, tended to Sarah as the gale buffeted the vessel, and somewhere in the Bay of Biscay, off the coast of France, an infant's cry rose from the stern. The parents named their new daughter Hougoumont Archdeacon Rowe.

The *Hougoumont* rode out the three-day storm, and early the following morning, as the clouds broke and the sun poured down, Cozens ordered the crew to set all canvas—topsails, topgallants, royals, skysails, jib, and staysails—and steered due south. To starboard, the H.M.S. *Earnest*'s captain called out a good-bye through his "speaker-horn" to Cozens and turned back for

England. Now the Fenians faced the mind-numbing daily routines of life aboard a convict ship that was expected to take at least three months to drop anchor at its destination.

As the *Hougoumont* plowed through deep waters, crewmen pried open the main hatch to let fresh air into the hold, which reeked of feces, vomit, urine, and sweat. The soldier Fenians were handed brushes and ordered to scrub their quarters. They sprinkled lime on the planks and lit sulfur candles to quell the stench.

The prisoners were reminded on the same morning that Captain Cozens would brook no discipline. At 10 A.M., guards dragged several convicts who had broken the ship's rules, and tied them in turn to the triangle. A boatswain's mate read the offenses, which included theft of food from the galley and brawling, and Cozens handed down the sentences. As the Fenians and the other prisoners were forced to watch, the cat-o'-nine-tails ripped open the backs of the misfortunate offenders. Then, groups of prisoners scrubbed the bloodstained deck beneath the triangle.

For many who had been flogged, more punishment remained. They were shoved into the main deck punishment cell, open to searing sun and icy rainfall alike, and behind the cell's inch-thick iron bars, forced to twist oakum, coarse hemp fiber, into caulking for the ship's seams. The offenders' rations of bread and water proved just enough to keep them alive. Some of the prisoners spent weeks in the main cell and emerged as walking skeletons.

Except on days when storms assailed the ship, guards armed with rifles, repeating pistols, and sabers escorted O'Reilly, Hogan, Cranston, Wilson, Harrington, Hassett, Darragh, and the other military Fenians abovedecks. They marched at a fast, hard pace around the fore and main hatches for an unbroken half-hour, the convicted soldiers making a point to march with the crisp precision they had learned on Royal Army parade grounds and earning the frank admiration of several of the ship's officers.

Already chafing beneath the boredom of the voyage, yet fearful of what their passage's end would bring, the Fenians sought means of diversion. Denis Cashman, an aspiring writer, and other civilian political prisoners came up with the idea of "concert parties" to entertain any prisoners, as well as crew, who might have an interest in music, theater, literature, and even comedy.

On October 25, 1867, with Cashman serving as the company's "president," he and Joseph Noonan sang duets, and twenty-seven-year-old Corkman and carpenter John Edward Kelly—captured in the brief and desperate clash in March 1867 at Kilclooney Wood, where he had survived grave wounds to his thigh and testicles—showed a flair for reciting verse. Eloquent John Kenealy rendered Shakespeare and such patriotic poems as "Remember Fontenoy," which prisoners cheered as he boomed out the stirring exploits of the eighteenth-century Irish Brigade. Captain Cozens, recognizing that the concerts offered the prisoners an outlet, even allowed them to end each performance with an emotional rendition of the patriotic ballad "Let Erin Remember."

The Fenian prisoners rose to their feet, tears coursing down many faces, as they sang the unofficial Fenian anthem:

Let Erin remember the days of old,
Ere her faithless sons betrayed her;
When Malachi wore the collar of gold
Which he won from her proud invader;
When her kings with standard of green unfurled
Led the Red-Branch Knights to danger;
Ere the emerald gem of the western world
Was set in the crown of a stranger.

One of the most literate Fenians evinced no interest in the first two concerts, dismissing Cashman's entreaties that the man write and read verse for the other prisoners. John Boyle O'Reilly brooded along the ship's bow rails and in his hammock, dismayed by his conversations with sailors who contended that the *Hougoumont*'s destination, Fremantle Gaol, was escape-proof.

Resigned to the reality that no Fenian raider would swoop down on the convict ship to pluck the prisoners from British hands, O'Reilly devised a plan to seize the *Hougoumont*. He first approached Cashman and several of the military prisoners in private shortly after the first concert and was heartened that the idea of taking the ship appealed to them. "A number of us secretly consulted," Cashman noted, "and decided to try the experiment [O'Reilly's plan], provided we could get the greater part of our associates to determinedly enter the project. . . . O'Reilly would have attempted it like a thunder-clap. . . and Flood was a first-class navigator."

Cashman, who yearned for freedom but balked at the thought of never seeing his wife and three children again, agonized about the plot. Another civilian also sworn to secrecy by the military Fenians in the scheme's early stage, Thomas McCarthy Fennell, embraced the idea of O'Reilly, Keating, and company at first.

"For some time," Fennell wrote, "the idea of expediting a change and throwing off the yoke is lurking and gaining strength in the bosoms of a good many aboard, it is now [early October 1867] pretty well ripened and lacks only the hand to guide, the mind to dictate and the nerve to give it shape and form to set the ball a rolling." O'Reilly, Hogan, Hassett, Keating, Wilson, Darragh, Harrington, Cranston, and the other nine former soldiers spoiled to strike at their captors.

As the soldiers, in a blunt and ruthless manner, outlined their plan to the civilian Fenians, many who were initially attracted

to the plot blanched. Fennell related that the erstwhile caval-
rymen and foot soldiers of the Queen now frightened their
civilian counterparts, "fierce and swift the vengeance in each
glance of the soldiers, the eye, meanwhile, reflecting that horrid
fiery glare. . . ."

Fennell also preserved the details of the simmering plot:
"Capture and disarm the officers and guards is the terrible
intent. Signaled for simultaneous action and general assault, the
watchword is fire every brand, use every weapon, strangle all
adversaries, stiffle [sic] every opposition and give no quarter. To
fail would be eternal disgrace, would entail death most shocking
to the survivors, therefore, let no man shrink from duty till life
is dearly sold, the gore complete and the last one dead at his
post. Be victory or death the motto, for it is far better to perish
in the unequal strife than await strangulation from the yardarm
another day."

On October 27 or 28, 1867, with Hogan and Hassett posted as
lookouts to warn of approaching guards or sailors, O'Reilly held
a meeting in the front of the hold, the wan light of tallow candles
flickering across the tense, haggard faces of the sixty-three military and civilian Fenians. In hushed, tense tones, the ex-Hussar
outlined his scheme to the entire contingent. Immediately, several men with families and shorter sentences bristled at the proposal, pointing out that even if a mutiny succeeded, they could
never return to their loved ones in Ireland. Others asserted that
even if they overpowered the guards, the problem of what to do with
the warders' and guards' families who were onboard remained.
Then, assuming that the Fenians managed to capture the ship and
sail it to New York, would American authorities even allow the
landing of a ship packed with over two hundred convicts—many of
them bonafide and brutal criminals?

Near the bow and almost directly above the corner where the

Fenians pondered O'Reilly's plan, the price to pay for a failed mutiny stood. The noose and halter would be affixed to plotters, and they would be swung blindfolded and bound into the water and eternity.

O'Reilly paced among the others, his handsome face haggard, with dark hollows beneath eyes red-rimmed from fitful sleep since the voyage's start. He scrutinized their faces as the men huddled, and listened to their murmurs. A glance at the tight-jawed countenances of Hogan, Darragh, Hassett, Wilson, Harrington, Cranston, Keating, and most of the other soldiers confirmed that they craved a fight. However, as O'Reilly passed knots of the civilian Fenians, they averted their eyes.

O'Reilly demanded that a vote be taken. As each man either raised his hand, the "yes" signal, or laid his palms on his trousers, the "no" vote, O'Reilly's face flushed and his breathing quickened. Glowering at the majority of men with their hands pressed against their thighs, he muttered something and lurched to the oaken base of the bowsprit. Then he leaned against the wooden column and sagged to the deck.

Cashman, Keating, and Harrington rushed to O'Reilly, crouched over him, and clutched his heaving shoulders. The civilian Fenians began to shuffle back to their quarters, amidship, and had to pass Hogan and Hasset. As most averted their eyes from the glares of the dragoon and the foot soldier, who stood with their arms tightly folded, lips clenched, the pair wondered how men who had committed treason against the Crown in near-hopeless attacks in Ireland could be cowed by the prospect of mutiny aboard one of the Queen's ships. Throughout that night, Cashman, Harrington, and other cooler heads assuaged the disconsolate O'Reilly and convinced him to delay any escape plans until they reached Fremantle. No one, Harrington assured him, wanted to escape more than he did, and, like O'Reilly, Harrington professed his willingness to die in the attempt.

Still worried about O'Reilly's state of mind, Cashman implored him to find some measure of solace from his literary talent. Rather than wither from despair and lose any chance for escape, he urged O'Reilly to keep his hopes alive. Along with Cashman's ministrations, gunwale admonitions from Hogan, Harrington, Keating, and other soldiers for O'Reilly to "buck up manfully" took effect quickly. As Cashman and his makeshift theatrical troupe readied their third concert, on October 29, 1867, O'Reilly approached them with a fistful of his handwritten poems and asked if he might read them at the upcoming performance.

From the moment that O'Reilly stood in front of the prisoners, guards, crew, and even officers gathered for the concert, the power of his lines riveted his listeners. The sentimental verses of his poem "Farewell," which he read on a night when the light of countless stars illuminated the crowded deck of the *Hougoumont*, captured the emotions churning within all of the Fenian prisoners, as well as many of the convicts aboard:

Farewell! Oh, how hard and how sad 'tis to speak
That last word of parting—forever to break
The fond ties and affection that cling round the heart,
From home and from friends and from country to part.
'Though it grieves to remember, 'tis vain to regret.
The sad word must be spoken, and memory's spell
Now steals o'er me sadly. Farewell! Oh farewell!

Farewell to thy green hills, thy valleys and plains,
My poor blighted country! In exile and chains
Are the sons doomed to linger. Oh God, who didst
  bring

Thy children to Zion from Egypt's proud king,
We implore Thy great mercy! Oh stretch forth Thy hand,
And guide back her sons to their poor blighted land.

Never more thy fair face am I destined to see;
E'en the savage loves home, but 'tis crime to love thee.
God bless thee, dear Erin, my loved one, my own,
Oh! how hard 'tis these tendrils to break that have
   grown.

Round my heart. But 'tis over, and memory's spell
Now steals o'er me sadly. Farewell! Oh, Farewell!

In early November 1867, as the *Hougoumont* slid within view of the Spanish coast, the prisoners lined the gunwales beneath dazzling sunshine for a glimpse of the shore and the mountains rising behind it. O'Reilly reflected years later on the emotions that those glimpses of Spain had evoked about Ireland's plight: "I felt as if I would never weary of admiring the grand majesty of those noble mountains, and while I inwardly cursed the power which held my own dear land in bondage, I sighed for the time when her sons would emulate the example of the chivalrous Spaniard."

Anguish over the failed rising tore at the thoughts of O'Reilly and his fellow Fenians day and night. The concerts, while furnishing a distraction from the ennui of life on the *Hougoumont,* could do nothing to allay the harsh conditions of the overcrowded ship or the constant threat of flogging or worse for the smallest infractions. Although several modern accounts of the convict ship's voyage have related that the shipboard discipline was not unduly harsh, the diary of Thomas McCarthy Fennell and the letters and recollections of John Boyle O'Reilly, Martin Hogan, and James

Wilson paint a starkly different version. Warders routinely beat convicts for offenses real and imagined; black eyes, broken noses and bones, missing teeth, and massive bruises became the emblems of the ham-fisted and billy club-wielding guards.

For sport, warders pitted convicts against each other in belowdecks boxing matches, promising favors of increased rations or extra time on deck to the winners. The guards wagered on the outcomes and, on the frequent occasions when "the chums and followers of the principal combatants [started] taking up the fight," allowed them to pummel each other before wading in with clubs and musket butts, slamming them against the convicts' skulls. None of the Fenians took part in either the matches or the brawls. As O'Reilly noted, several warders tried to goad the "harder cases among the pugilistic miscreants" into "starting something" with the former soldiers, but none of the brawlers cared to square off one-on-one against them, especially Harrington, Darragh, or Hogan. Word had spread in the convict hold that the trio had likely killed more men in battle than the aggregate victims of the murderers infesting the hold.

Harrington, Darragh, Hogan, and the other Fenians sweltered as the convict ship sailed past the Cape Verde Islands in early November, having covered some four thousand miles from Portland. "It was disagreeable on deck with the hot sun pouring down its molten rays day after day upon the heads of the unfortunate passengers, who were stretched in every conceivable fashion on the forecastle," Cashman wrote in his journal. "Imagine how much worse it was in the hold, where the air was stifling and oppressive. There was no draught through the barred hatches. The deck above was blazing hot. The hot pitch dropped from the seams, and burned flesh as it fell. Water was the one thought in all our minds."

At Funchal, the Portuguese fortress and harbor on the island of Madeira, the *Hougoumont* docked to take aboard casks of fresh water, barrels of potatoes and other vegetables, limes and lemons to ward off scurvy, and bottles of pricey Madeira wine for the officers and cheap red wine for the crew, the guards, and the convicts. Funchal was the last stop that Cozens planned to make, as he was concerned about running into any U.S. Navy vessel whose captain might hold Fenian sympathies. On the open seas, where passing ships often stopped for a "gam"—officers and crews would meet on one or the other of the vessels to swap any news and to chat over a measure of wine or rum—Cozens knew that most ships spotting the white "convict arrow" on the *Hougoumont*'s hull would give her a wide berth. He set a course that would take the converted frigate past Ascension Island, St. Helena, and Capetown and across the Indian Ocean to Fremantle.

The *Hougoumont* had passed many other ships in the opening month of the long voyage. But once she cleared the Cape of Good Hope and sailed into the Indian Ocean, fourteen thousand miles from Portland, nothing but vast water—four thousand more miles to Fremantle—winds, and clouds greeted her. Discomfited by the eerie feeling that he was aboard a ship that seemed so alone as to be a "spectral vessel" and unnerved that she was carrying him to a land similarly isolated, O'Reilly composed a poem entitled "The Flying Dutchman." Likening the Fenians' evolving ordeal to that of Coleridge's legendary ship, O'Reilly wrote, "Go wretch, accurst, condemned. . . ."

As the days dragged on, blistering heat and sudden storms sapped the prisoners' strength and spirits. Still, the Fenians found small ways to subsist. Michael Harrington, who had learned the workings of a regimental mess during his campaigning days, talked his way into a slot as an assistant in the ship's galley. He smuggled scraps of food under his shirt to his friends in the fore hold, aware that if caught, a cat-o'-nine-tails would tear his back into bloody stripes at the triangle.

Harrington and the other Fenians assembled around Father Delany every night on the foredeck or below it to bow their heads and utter a communal prayer loudly enough for the crew and officers to hear: "O God, who art the arbiter of the destiny of nations and who rulest the world in Thy great wisdom, look down, we beseech Thee, from Thy holy place on the sufferings of our poor country. Scatter her enemies, O Lord, and confound their evil prophets. Hear us, O God, hear the earnest cry of our people, and give them strength and fortitude to dare and suffer in their holy cause. Send her help, O Lord, from the holy place. And from Zion protect her. Amen."

The Dragon of Despair

In mid-November 1867, Captain Cozens learned that despite the Fenians' long months of imprisonment and ravaged physical straits, the rebels still seethed with defiance. Days of soaring heat had spoiled the meat slopped onto the prisoners' trenchers, and the chief galley cook was using rancid water for the Fenians' daily morning ration of hot chocolate. Harrington, Hogan, Darragh, and four other Fenian "mess captains" demanded to see the ship's surgeon superintendent, Dr. William Smith. He refused.

Glowering and silent, the seven mess captains climbed from the hold on the following morning with their mugs of hot chocolate and plates of rank beef in hand, brushed past startled guards, and in full view of Captain Cozens, who stared down from the quarterdeck, flung the rations overboard. Onlookers tensed, waiting for Cozens to order the Fenians clapped in irons and hurled into the punishment cell to await a turn at the triangle.

For several minutes, arms folded, Cozens peered down at the men, who glared back at him from the starboard rail. Only the creaks of the ship's masts and rigging broke the quiet enveloping the deck. In his four decades at sea, including years in the Royal Navy, the shipmaster had honed the necessary knack of reading men, of deciding instantaneously whether or not a man could be cowed. A careful look at the set jaws and hard eyes of veteran soldiers Harrington, Darragh, and Hogan made up Cozens's mind. The captain called out the surgeon's name, and Smith scampered to the quarterdeck, his narrow, pockmarked face crimson. A few muttered words by Cozens sent Smith over to the prisoners to negotiate a resolution.

A half-hour or so later, the seven Fenians climbed back down the ladder to the fore hold and informed their nervous comrades that no longer would they be served rotten meat, no longer would their hot chocolate be tainted, and from now on, their daily water ration, previously a scant pint per man, would be increased to fourteen pints per eight men.

Those adjustments notwithstanding, the meager fare doled out to the Fenians and the other prisoners continued to strip pounds from already gaunt frames. For the seventeen soldiers, hard bisquit and "salt horse," a chunk of salted beef or pork, choked down with bitter hot chocolate or sour red wine, comprised the bulk of their diet. One of them complained,

> Two ounces of hard, mouldy [sic] dried-out bisquit for the day per adult on which to chew the entire time. That is the slim morsel on which the poor convict is to live. To offer so meager a quantity to eight able-bodied men as their quota to live on for twenty-four hours would be an insult under any circumstances except where the intention backed by force was to starve and kill.
>
> The salt horse has been packed in the ship's hold for so long, months and months and mayhap years, that it has shed its third and last coat of maggots and that with

them dissolved its entire substance and solidity, virtually leaving but a spongy tissue of what might have been once good meat.

Harrington, Hogan, Hassett, and Darragh had encountered rock-hard bisquit and rancid meat in their campaigning, but never anything like the "beef, pork, or pea soup" spooned from a filthy wooden tub into their bowls by "the cook togged all in white." One of the men fumed,

> To grapple with this variety on a rough day is more than one man can attend to. . . . To the beef broth, if it deserves the designation, is added a very slim sprinkling of pea powder that forms a compound when stirred up and mixed and to which every convict is entitled to a pint and no more. It is sudsy and dark colored with hard offensive scales floating on the surface and steams to the nostrils like odor from the gutter wash. . . . [A] cruel method of killing and yet so artful that the responsibility can be placed no where [sic] but at the door of the government and that is safe against attack from manacled criminals.

Although the skimpy rations weakened all of the prisoners, the military prisoners' constitutions tolerated the gruesome fare better than their civilian counterparts. Still, the diet ravaged the seventeen soldiers: "All aboard look wilted pictures of death and starvation, the feeling which predominates is for more bread, for something to eat and drink, something to fill up, to appease the craving appetite, to allay and conquer in some way the stinging greed of hunger and thirst."

In the early stages of the voyage, Hogan, suffering from acute indigestion, staggered into the office of ship's surgeon Dr. Smith and quickly learned the extent of medical services that the "military traitors" could expect. "In this cubbyhole," wrote the patient,

> he [Dr. Smith] is as surly as a bear, his manner austere, forbidding and cold as a corpse, and treats his Fenian callers with insolence and contempt instead of with kindness and sympathy. No man knows the dastardly prison doctor but the wretch who is forced to deal with him. Of all the officials he alone has the least feeling, the least humanity and the least manhood. From the doctor there is always something expected besides ugliness and brutality, and when the sick man is turned away without a look to cheer, or a word to console, he is sadly disappointed and feels there is not a kindly face within the walls for him, wherewith his soul burns with increased misery.

Smith's demeanor proved no kindlier when he made his required daily visits to the convict hold. Thomas McCarthy Fennell charged:

> Indifferent to vomit and groan and all the appalling scenes of those strangling in convulsions and the plague-stricken aspect of the entire cargo, the cold-blooded, callous-hearted Doctor Smith . . . unfeelingly performs his forenoon visits with all the sullen indifference of an unpitying, fiendish brute in human form. Never stops in consultation, never enquires into the cause, or never prescribes a remedial dram to a living soul, but in curtest language tells any who accost him, report his case to an officer and go to the hospital, a

comical dormitory hid under some stairway amidships, where any variety and quantity of empty vials, glass bottles, jars, and drugs are on exhibition—a kind of drug store without drugs.

Even as the Fenians realized they were not welcome in the ship's surgery, and battled for more food and water from their captors in November 1867, the rebels continued seeking another form of sustenance—that of mind and soul. Having launched their theater troupe, they wanted to create a handwritten news and literary magazine entitled the *Wild Goose*. The term referred to Ireland's famed Wild Geese, soldiers flung to the far corners of the world and forced to fight "in every army save our own," whether in the British army or those of other European nations, and the venture offered an outlet well-suited to the talents of O'Reilly, Cashman, Kelly, and John Flood, a friend of O'Reilly and a civilian Fenian.

With thirty-year-old Father Delany, whose blue eyes glimmered with an intelligence, humor, and force that offset his pale, freckled features and thin frame, eagerly supplying paper, pens, and ink, the Fenians went to work on their first issue. As with all seven weekly issues that the Fenians produced, the "staff" wrote by hand on both sides of four long white sheets of paper, the sheafs folded in the center to make an eight-page booklet and each page double-columned.

Cashman decorated the front page with delicately rendered shamrocks and ivy wreaths and subtitled the paper "A Collection of Ocean Waifs." In a caustic piece called "Australia," John Edward Kelly wrote: "That magnanimous government [Great Britain] in the kindly exuberance of their feelings, have placed a large portion of that immense tract of country [Australia] at our disposal, generously defraying all expenses incurred on our way to it, and providing retreats for us there. . . ." He signed the commentary "Laoi," Gaelic for "K."

O'Reilly similarly used a nom de plume, his articles and poetry signed with the name "Boyne," his birthplace and the site of the battle that gutted Catholic Ireland's hopes for centuries. On the pages of the weekly, O'Reilly published poems and articles ranging from the humorous, to the patriotic, to the dark. His poem "The Green," in the second issue, radiated love and longing for his homeland:

> Oh! Fairest and best of the colours on earth,
> How I love thy gentle smile!
> Thy bright warm hue in my heart gives birth
> To dreams of my own Green Isle.
> To my childhood's home my memory runs,
> O'er every well-known scene,
> Ah! Deep in the hearts of her exiled sons
> Is the love of their beautiful green.
>
> 'Tis never extinguished. It never decays.
> It came with their earliest breath;
> 'Tis a light that is holy and pure, whose rays
> Are vanquished alone by death.

On Saturday evenings in November and December 1867, the Fenians, all sixty-three of them, gathered in their corner of the hold, the taste of their salt pork and hardtack dinner lingering blandly, their smocks and breeches baggy on bony frames. Smoking hand-rolled cheroots, or cigars, from a handful of Irish-born guards and former Royal Army soldiers who secretly sympathized with their ex-comrades' cause, the Fenians sat knees-up on the pitching planks and waited for O'Reilly or Flood to perch himself on a three-legged stool in front of the group. One of the men crouched next to the stool with a sputtering whale-oil lamp. As always, the soldiers sat together. Then, as the Fenians fell silent, O'Reilly or Flood began to read the latest edition of the *Wild Goose*. O'Reilly would never forget the scene: "Amid the dim glare of the lamp the men, at night, would group strangely on extemporized seats. The yellow light fell down on the dark forms, throwing a ghastly glare on the pale faces of the men, as they listened with blazing eyes. . . ."

The Fenians' eyes shone with a second act of defiance on Sunday, November 10, 1867, the morning after the reading of the first *Wild Goose*. At 11 A.M., the Fenians assembled on the main deck with the other convicts for open-air Mass. Father Delany, his chasuble and vestments soon dripping from a tropical deluge that burst upon the ship at the beginning of his sermon and rose back from the warm planks in clouds of steam, spoke of how men must submit to God's will, no matter how difficult one's life became.

O'Reilly and the other Fenians shook the priest's hand as usual at the service's conclusion and waded into the line for their daily ration of wine. A youthful ship's officer sat behind a mess table flanked by blue-coated Royal Marines who cradled muskets with long bayonets. The officer held a ladle, poised to slosh cheap red wine, cut with water, into a wooden bowl that each man drank from in turn. Before a prisoner could gulp his often sour measure, he was required to call off his name and shout, "Sir!" or "Here, Sir!" to the officer on duty. On this particular Sunday, James Wilson stepped up to the table, glared at the officer, and refused to call him "Sir." O'Reilly, Harrington, Hogan, Cranston, Darragh, and Hassett—the man who had defiantly proclaimed his treason at his court-martial—and all of the other Fenians likewise refused to acknowledge the officer. The officer slammed his fist against the table, sprang from his stool, and roared at the

Fenians to address him with proper respect. They stared at him, saying nothing. From the quarterdeck, Captain Cozens shouted for the guards to remove the Fenians to the hold, and as soldiers swarmed around the Irishmen and prodded them with bayonets down the foredeck hatch, O'Reilly and the others complied without a word.

The spluttering officer followed them down the ladder and once again ordered the Irish to address him as "Sir." Once more, only their silence greeted him. Waving a fist in their faces, his other hand clamped around the hilt of his naval cutlass, he shrieked curses and threatened to clap every man in irons, flay every one at the triangle, and toss them into the punishment cell. Silence still met his oaths.

Finally, he wheeled around, still cursing and vowing revenge, and stormed out of the hold, followed by the guards. The Fenians argued whether to resist when the Marines and warders swarmed down the ladder with shackles ready. At every heavy footfall from the direction of the main hatch, fists clenched and breaths came in bursts.

From the quarterdeck, a sailor called out "twelve bells"—midnight—and still no guards stormed into the hold. The Fenians slept little in the following hours, waiting to be dragged from their hammocks and hurled into the punishment cell.

As the first faint rays of sunlight seeped into the fore hold between tiny gaps in the deck planks overhead, the Fenians began to hope that they would be spared the triangle and the punishment cell. By noon, when the military prisoners were allowed to mingle with the civilian Fenians on the main deck, the soldiers realized that, for the moment, they were safe. They had no idea why.

Despite his officers' protests, Captain Cozens allowed the Fenians' defiance to go unpunished. What the craggy shipmaster would tell no one at the time was that he had developed a dual measure of respect for the way that the rebels, particularly the military Fenians, comported themselves, along with a fear that the ex-soldiers, if hopeless enough, would try to seize the ship. Cozens had received no hard information about O'Reilly's vetoed plot, as the Fenian leaders had maintained a tight secrecy about it and would-be informers were too terrified of Harrington, Hogan, and Darragh to take the risk. The captain, however, did not want to hand the Irishmen an issue with which they could sway their comrades into open mutiny. He tolerated their refusal to address the ship's officers, except the captain himself, with the title "Sir." Tempering his decision was his knowledge of what awaited the military prisoners in Fremantle.

On December 16, 1867, with a relentless rain pelting the *Hougoumont,* several of the Fenians were unsettled by news that they interpreted as a harbinger of what lay ahead in the penal colony. Guards had discovered an indigent Irishman named Thomas Corcoran, sentenced to transportation to Australia for petty thievery, dead in his berth at 6 A.M. Dr. Smith was summoned and barely gave the corpse a glance before pronouncing Corcoran dead from unspecified natural causes. At Father Delany's request, Captain Cozens allowed the Fenians and the convicts to attend Corcoran's funeral service, slated for 6 P.M.

The ship was rolling sharply when the Fenians took their place on the starboard rail with the other prisoners. Father Delany, draped in white funerary vestments, stumbled along the heaving deck with six convicts, who shouldered a canvas sack containing Corcoran's body. Just as they reached the rail, they nearly dropped the sack as the planks rose and fell beneath them. The Union Jack that covered the Irishman's sack elicited low growls from several convicts and Fenians. Father Delany raised his hand for silence, and the prisoners' mutters soon ebbed.

Splashing a tiny vial of holy water on the shroud, the priest intoned several prayers, and a choir of prisoners Father Delany had formed delivered the somber strains of the "Miserari" and the "Te Deum." The six pallbearers then tipped the sack, open at the far end, at the rail, and Corcoran's body, weighed down with several sandbags, slid into the churning water and vanished.

No one aboard could have grasped the significance of the petty thief's end —Thomas Corcoran was the last transported prisoner to die aboard a ship bound for Australia.

Although the Fenians had known Corcoran only in passing, his death filled O'Reilly, Cashman, Hogan, and Wilson with foreboding each of them voiced in their writings. O'Reilly brooded: "He sinks immediately in consequence of weights attached to his feet. Cannot but meditate on the certainty of death and the uncertainty of life. Cannot think without emotion of dying in a far distant land away from friends, home and kindred without a single hand to soothe and comfort me in my last moments."

During the evening of the service for Corcoran, O'Reilly and Cashman were deep in melancholy analysis of the larger meaning, if any, of his death. Suddenly they turned their heads toward the tramp of heavy boots. A warder in his blue-and-gilt coat smirked at the pair and informed them that the next issue of the *Wild Goose* was to be the last. The prisoners were ordered to surrender any remaining paper, pens, and ink to Dr. Smith. Sneering, the warder added, "Everything in the following few weeks is to be set in order for arrival at Fremantle."

O'Reilly and the others determined that the final edition, their "Christmas issue," would be "the best number yet" and would be read to the prisoners on the holiday itself.

Christmas dawned with the *Hougoumont* bobbing amid massive, foam-laden swells kicked up by a gale. Unable to celebrate Mass on deck, Delany sloshed through ankle-deep water in the hold to administer communion, which all of the military Fenians except the Presbyterian and Orangeman Darragh received. Yet his Catholic comrades thought nothing of it, for in the Fenian movement, a man's religion mattered little. His conviction to the cause of Irish freedom did.

In honor of the holiday, Captain Cozens ordered that sweet-loaf—"rather a delicacy"—be served with "salt horse and plum duff" to the prisoners, as well as a double ration of wine at 2 P.M. Later that afternoon, the convicts, the Fenians, and most of the crew and officers packed the fore hold as O'Reilly cleared his throat, sat on his stool, and began to read the pages of the final *Wild Goose* aloud, the ship still pitching wildly.

He read three of his own poems, and a line from "Christmas Night" summed up the terror that every prisoner in the hold grappled with amid increasing urgency as the ship pushed ever closer to Australia. Imagining the "old north wind" as a congenial traveler blowing around Christmas celebrations over an idyllic countryside, O'Reilly read of how the wind came suddenly across "a prison, all massive, and silent and stern, its darkening shadows cast, and the old north wind saw not a sign of mirth."

Instead of the applause his work usually evoked from the audience, silence met that last verse, some listeners in their convict caps, smocks, and breeches biting their lips to maintain their composure, others including "brutish miscreants" brushing away tears.

O'Reilly concluded with Cashman's farewell letter as editor of the *Wild Goose:* "The end of your passage quickly approaches, and already your hearts are beginning to quicken with anticipation at what may be your future in the new land you are fast nearing. I know not what may be in store for you. I cannot pierce the inexorable veil of the future, drawn alike for me and for you; but bidding you a long farewell most likely, however we may wish it, never to meet again, I say to you—Courage, and trust in Providence."

As a keepsake, Cozens and several of his officers, all of them impressed in spite of their abhorrence of Fenianism by the literary talents of the paper's editors and writers, asked Cashman and O'Reilly to make them copies of the Christmas issue, and ensuring that O'Reilly's final two weeks aboard the ship would prove more tolerable, the captain permitted him to move from the convict hold to the separate quarters of the civilian Fenians. O'Reilly slung his hammock in Number 6 Mess, where Kelly, Flood, and the rest of the *Wild Goose* staff had spent their nights separated from the convicts whose presence had cost the military Fenians so much sleep. With his fellow writers, he was granted permission to stay until 7:30 P.M. in good weather.

Worried about O'Reilly's bouts of melancholia, Keating, Hogan, and the rest of the military Fenians welcomed his reprieve from "the close company of the convicts" amidship. As Hogan wrote, however, O'Reilly's respite, such as it was, would not last long.

On Sunday, January 6, 1868, Cozens laid a course due west, the *Hougoumont* now less than five hundred miles from Western Australia. The prisoners' thoughts roiled with eagerness to leave the prison ship behind, yet with anxiety over the unknown hardships to come in the penal colony. Cashman and many other civilian Fenians, whose sentences generally ranged from seven to ten years, held out hope that good conduct at Fremantle would earn them a "ticket-of-leave," which would force them to serve the rest of their sentences in Australia, but would allow them to live outside the prison. To Cashman, that meant his wife and three sons might someday be able to join him in Australia.

The military Fenians harbored no such hopes. They held a

special status—traitors to the Crown and to the Royal Army—
and expected merciless treatment from their new set of warders
ashore. Fennell noted the increased worry on the faces of the seventeen soldiers:

> The sails are set in full and the vessel speeds on over
> the silken sheen that strokes the prow-beating tide. . . .
> Soon again their [the military Fenians'] evidences of
> fresh fears are apparent, the dragon of despair is felt
> knocking at the sore-tried bosom for it is now a naked
> fact that a few more brief days will bring the gaunt cargo
> to an inhospitable shore, perhaps to face a more rigid
> system of servitude, harder labor and a sterner
> taskmaster than those . . . aboard ship. Brooding over
> such hapless prospects diminish [*sic*] heart and soul
> and pray [*sic*] most acutely on the mind and body of the
> shattered convicts .

As if confirming the ordeals to come at Fremantle, a bosun's
pipe screeched in the languid air as the *Hougoumont* tacked just
a few days away from the colony. Guards burst into the main hold,
drove all of the prisoners on the main deck, and at bayonet point
formed them into columns. As they waited, sweat pouring from
them in the broiling sun, O'Reilly, Cashman, and several other
Fenians lit cigars, silently defying the order that no convict was
to smoke when assembled to view punishment. Cozens strode
from his cabin to the quarterdeck, halted near the helm with his
arms clasped behind his back, and shouted an order. A brace of
warders appeared from the main hatchway with a young, scraggly
bearded convict caught stealing food from the galley. They
dragged him to the triangle, chained him to the device, and tore
off his shirt to expose a frame so thin that his spine and ribs

seemed about to push right through the thin flesh. A towering sailor with cat-o'-nine-tails in hand stepped behind the prisoner.

Cozens nodded, and the sailor snapped the tails against the convict's back. Again and again the lash cracked, turning his back into a bloody latticework, the ship's first officer counting the strokes aloud. O'Reilly and Cashman turned away from the spectacle, but the other Fenians watched. Murmurs rippled among the prisoners—the man had endured thirty strokes without so much as a grunt. Hogan nodded almost imperceptibly in approval of the convict's toughness. Six more times the cat ripped the man's back. He remained silent.

As the guards unchained him from the triangle, the deck at his feet awash in his blood, the massed convicts and Fenians alike let out a raucous cheer for the man's grit. The convict looked at his guards "with sheer disdain."

The nameless prisoner's bravado proved the last bit of defiance aboard the *Hougoumont*.

Robert Cranston started in his hammock. Mopping sweat from his brow with his rough woolen sleeve, he slid to the damp deckboards and stood motionless in the clammy fore hold for several moments. Something felt wrong—the ship was not moving forward. She swayed lightly, the muffled creak of her yards seemingly the only sound.

Cranston stepped up to the adjoining hammock and nudged Hassett. Sputtering, he thrashed about for a moment, opened his bleary eyes, and rubbed the brown stubble on his skull, which was still scarred in several patches where English warders had doused his head with boiling pitch in Kilmainham Barracks.

As Hassett peered at Cranston and adjusted his eyes to the darkness of the hold, years of sentry duty and night marches told him that the time was about 3 A.M. In the hammock next to

Hassett, Wilson sat bolt upright, glared at the other two men, and growled, "Why did you wake me?"

Cranston, sweating again, but this time from combined fear and excitement, replied, "The ship's stopped. I think we've come to Australia."

In their hammocks or deal-board beds, the other military Fenians stirred. Harrington, Hogan, and Keating, veterans of troop transports, did not need Cranston to tell them the ship had halted. They, too, had felt it in their ragged sleep. The prisoners then waited over three hours for the guards to open the hatch and take them up for their first look at Australia, the land where they fully expected to perish in a road gang and be buried in an unmarked grave somewhere in the wilderness.

"Few words were spoken those last few hours in the hold," recounted Hogan. "What was there for any of us to say?"

Around 7 A.M., the deck above pealed suddenly with sailors' shouts and the thumps of their feet. A deafening metallic rasp shook every corner of the convict ship as the crew dragged the vessel's cable chains from a locker on the main deck and muscled the *Hougoumont*'s pair of ponderous anchors into their settings on both sides of the bow. The chains screeched, and two thunderous splashes startled young Cranston. Grimly, Harrington and Darragh nodded at each other.

At 8 A.M., sailors unlocked the hatches' iron gates as heavily armed Royal Marines lined the deck from hatches to gangway, sweat already staining their scarlet coats in the sultry air. Warders brandishing pistols climbed down the iron ladders and formed the prisoners into two long columns. First, the guards prodded the women two at a time up the ladder. Next, the civilian Fenians and O'Reilly were sent topside, followed by the general mass of convicts.

Eyes probing for any sign of a fight, index fingers close to pistols' triggers, the warders finally surged into the foredeck, where the sixteen military Fenians waited. The guards, keeping a safe distance, ordered the military prisoners up the ladders. Wordlessly, they obeyed. When they reached the opening of the hold, they blinked in the dazzling sunlight. Marines stepped up to them and prodded them to the starboard rail, where they stood separated from the other convicts.

The Fenians took their first look at Australia. O'Reilly wrote, "From morning light they leant on the rail, looking away over the smooth sea to where the land was yellow with heat above the unseen continent. . . . The shore of Western Australia is quite low, and the first sight of land is tall mahogany trees in the bush."

A few miles to the lee side of the *Hougoumont,* a whitewashed lighthouse jutted from a long, low outcrop called Rottnest Island. Somewhere beyond the lighthouse lay Fremantle, shrouded by a steamy mist.

From the crow's nest atop the mainmast came a shout: "Boat ahead!"

A low, dark silhouette materialized from the haze, puffs of gray smoke spilling from a single black funnel. From the *Hougoumont*'s rails, the prisoners stared at the oncoming ship. Fennell turned to look first at O'Reilly, near him, and then farther down the gunwales at the sixteen soldiers surrounded by Marines and warders. "Every eye is anxious," he noted. "Every heart beats as she draws nearer. . . ."

The Penalty of
Which Is Death

S hip ahoy!"

The words rang from the bow of the low-hulled steamship drawing near. The speaker, a man peering beneath the visor of a battered 1840s-issue Royal Navy officer's cap, cupped his hands again to his mouth and shouted: "Want a pilot?"

From the *Hougoumont*'s helm, Captain Cozen's calm voice easily carried the hundred yards still separating the two vessels. "Yes. Slack, port your helm. Pilot come aboard!"

The steamer's crew lowered a skiff to the glassy water, and the pilot leaped nimbly down into the craft. Within a few minutes, he sidled the skiff alongside the *Hougoumont*'s long black hull, its painted prison arrow faded in spots from the pounding of the eighteen thousand-mile voyage, and climbed the rope ladder that had been lowered down the starboard side.

Without so much as a sideward glance at the prisoners—he had seen their thousands of predecessors arriving in similar transports for eighteen years—the jack-tar walked straight for Captain Cozens in the quarterdeck. The man's tobacco-stained teeth nearly as brown as his sun-bronzed skin, the pilot handed his license to Cozens. The captain did not even glance at the paper but pointed to the *Hougoumont*'s helm. The pilot nodded, slipped behind the giant wheel, and cried, "Raise anchors!"

Near the bow, bare-backed sailors grabbed the long arms of a massive crank and pushed, their grunts and muttered oaths filling the steamy air. The *Hougoumont* shook again as the groaning crank tugged at the chains and the anchors inched upward from the floor of the bay. Once the anchors pulled free from the sandy bottom's grip, the work went faster. Minutes after they broke the water's surface in a gush of foam, the sailors secured the anchors in their slots along the bow.

The pilot ordered sailors arrayed along the spars to set "short sail," just enough canvas to catch any hint of a breeze. Turning the wheel to port, trailing the steamer, he started to take her in with the tide to the rim of the Swan River Estuary. As the *Hougoumont* slipped past the jagged tip of Rottnest Island, several of the Fenians gaped. On the beach below the lighthouse, white men whose blue coats identified them as warders even from a distance snapped knotted cat-o'-nine-tails across the black backs of naked Aborigines enslaved in government work crews.

On the land the haze dissipated. Dolphins sped alongside and leaped in front of the ship as if urging her into the port. Farther away from the vessel's hull, gray fins knifed through the water. Fremantle Gaol's unofficial waterborne guards, sharks infested the bay and the ocean beyond.

The prisoners craned their necks along the ship's rails, few words spoken, everyone bracing for their first glimpse of the penal town where so many would meet their ending. Slowly, awash in the sunlight ahead, the Australian shoreline and vast open tracts stretching ever inland filled the convicts' eyes. Fennell, with O'Reilly and a knot of civilian Fenians, blanched at the unfolding scene: "From the deck of the *Hougoumont,* it appears a crude, uninhabitable country marked with perfect universal desolation . . . half-grown bushes sun-browned [and] stunted underbrush is all to be seen."

In the distance, the dark contours of thick forests and the Darling Mountains hinted at terrain every bit as harsh as the barren acreage stretching inland from the sandy shore. The Fenians squinted as stark white shapes began to appear. The sandstone and limestone buildings of Fremantle reflected the sunlight so harshly that some of the prisoners covered their eyes. They would see the town soon enough.

O'Reilly wrote that "nothing is seen but white," a jarring sight to those prisoners who had been raised amid Ireland's rural greenery.

Adjusting his eyes to the brightness ahead, Hassett grimaced as he spotted another structure. "The Establishment," whose dark and bloody reputation eclipsed even the horrors of Millbank and Portland, loomed atop a slope just to the east of the town. Shivering despite the ninety-degree heat, Hassett studied the high limestone walls and twin octagonal towers that flanked a barred gateway. Behind the walls rose two long, multistoried and blocklike structures bisected by another building, a complex whose sheer whiteness was almost blinding. Hogan mumbled to Wilson that Hell itself could not be as painful a shade of white as The Establishment.

As the prisoners wondered at what lay behind those alabaster walls, the *Hougoumont* glided into the crystalline waters of the inner harbor, a warm offshore breeze combining with the sun and glare to make dozens of convicts swoon. Those who clutched the rail to prop themselves up against the heat spotted another steamship cutting through the calm waters toward the *Hougoumont*. Double lines of white-coated pensioner guards, all former British soldiers, were arrayed along the steamers' gunwales. Their bayonets sparkled in the sunlight. Amidships, water police in their dark tunics and rakish black caps carried carbines and revolvers.

A half-mile to the steamer's stern, the presence of two red-coated companies of the 14th Regiment, rushed from Tasmania to Fremantle, testified to the special nature of the *Hougoumont*'s cargo. So, too, did the sight of a lanky man on the steamer's quarterdeck. Doctor John Stephen Hampton, the Governor of Western Australia, cut an imperious and imposing figure in his dark-blue tunic adorned with gold epaulets and two rows of gold buttons, immaculate white breeches, and shiny black riding boots. Stylish long sideburns, dense eyebrows, and pale blue eyes framed his face beneath a cocked and yellow-plumed commodore's cap.

Hampton approached the convict ship with a reputation tainted by a penchant for the lash and corruption. In 1857, Hampton, a physician who specialized in the treatment of tropical diseases, and a career foreign service man, had been accused of financial and moral irregularities as head of the Van Dieman's Land convict department. A court of inquiry found substantial evidence to support the charges.

Drawing upon his many contacts in the service, Hampton avoided a trial and wrangled an unofficial sentence of exile at half-pay to Canada. In 1862, relying upon the same contacts in the Colonial department, he became Governor of Western Australia. In this role the capable doctor with little regard for the Irish, whom he deemed convicts and traitors as a whole, oversaw the operation of Fremantle Gaol.

Under Hampton's stewardship, chains, whip, and noose reigned within the walls of the prison. He personally ordered ninety-six Irish convicts tied to the triangles for the slightest infraction, real or imagined, the cat-o'-nine-tails' strokes ripping into the men's collective backs 6,559 times. In pitch-black, solitary punishment cells, forty-pound leg-and-body chains affixed so tightly that oozing sores soon appeared on the men's limbs comprised one of Dr. Hampton's "curative measures."

Now, as the steamer closed the distance to the *Hougoumont,* Hampton worried not about the latest batch of "common prisoners," even though the British government had packed the last convict ship to Australia prior to the *Hougoumont* with some of the worst criminals from English jails. Instead, he brooded about the potential menace posed by the Fenians aboard the frigate. He had read again and again a dispatch regarding the *Hougoumont*'s cargo that had arrived on October 17, 1867, at the governor's mansion in Perth. Emblazoned with the official seal of the prime minister, the missive stated: "Some of the Fenian prisoners to the number of _____ should be included."

The specter of highly trained and rebellious military Fenians combined with the prime minister's "oversight" in failing to list their number in the ship's hold alarmed Hampton and other Australian officials. They knew that in the penal colony, a wellspring of sympathy for the Fenians flowed through the many locals. Some feared that the convicted soldiers could ignite a rebellion in Western Australia, rumors rife that a "Fenian privateer" was already sailing to Fremantle to sack the port and flee with the prisoners.

In panicky statements to the *Fremantle Herald,* George Leake, the Crown Solicitor (top legal official) of Western Australia, had further stirred up local fears that a Fenian strike against Fremantle loomed. Captain Charles Manning, commander of the Fremantle Company of the Western Australian Volunteers, also known as the Enlisted Pensioner Guards, had warned Hampton that the territory was "a community where the Irish element largely prevails, and where about three fifths of the military at my disposal are Irishmen." The stout, middle-aged Manning, his sunburned face and hands startling red against his white tunic and trousers, inspected his similarly white-coated troops. Many of them were Irishmen who had served in the same regiments as the arriving Fenians, and he suspected that some harbored Fenian sympathies.

Both Manning and Hampton hoped that the H.M.S. *Brisk,* a sixteen-gun corvette that had been dispatched to Fremantle from the Sydney Royal Navy Station in late December 1867, would show along the horizon to secure a smooth transfer of the prisoners, but only the *Hougoumont*'s black hull, with its painted convict arrow, and the pilot's skiff stirred the waters ahead of the steam tug. Another official, a small, thin veteran of the Colonial Service, stood behind Hampton. Freshly appointed to the post of Comptroller-General of Convicts, fifty-year-old Henry Wakeford would deal on a day-to-day basis with the Fenians of Fremantle Gaol.

The *Hougoumont*'s anchors screeched from their casings and sank into the soft, sandy ocean floor near the Swan River Estuary, several hundred yards from the Fremantle jetty. The tug churned alongside the frigate and dropped anchor, the two hulls bumping each other. Sailors at the starboard rail of the frigate lowered a gangplank with rope-and-pulley railings, and Hampton ascended. Behind him Manning, Wakeford, several other prison officials, and the port doctor, who was sent aboard every anchored ship to determine if any crewmen or convicts displayed symptoms of contagious disease, climbed the swaying gangplank. Last in the procession clambered water police with carbines unslung and volunteers toting Royal Army-issue Enfield rifles.

As Hampton stepped onto the main deck, he scanned the silent throng of convicts for the Fenians, as if the rebels might somehow appear different than the rest of the male prisoners. But all of the convicts had achieved the same deplorable appearance.

The sweat and grime of three months spent largely in the dank, fetid hold of the *Hougoumont* had stained their once-gray smocks and ragged knickers nearly black. Skeletal wrists and hands hung from sleeves. Unkempt, lice-filled beards cloaked the prisoners' jaws and cheeks, and matted hair lay lank against glistening brows. Through dark-circled eyes fearful, sullen, or malevolent, the convicts measured Hampton and the other men surging from the gangplank onto the ship. "The colonial magnets [*sic*] . . . for protection [were] accompanied by a detachment of water police or coast guards. . . . Up the pendant they nimbly climb on deck," noted Fennell.

> Appear puny and sun-smitten and tread the deck of the great transport with that suspicion of unsafety that an elephant does a shaky bridge. They look anything but kind-hearted, generous-minded specimens of humanity and it could not be expected that they would, for they are evil geniuses, overseers, and methodical torturers of their kind. . . . On the dried out face is a laconic sneer that could be mistaken for a smile did it not gradually increase to contempt while some who are not so afflicted carry such an air of self-assurance as to once convey their knowledge and familiarity with cargoes of this kind . . . content with their haughty superiority.

Hampton's fears of the potential threat posed by the Fenians somewhere among the ragged pack of convicts mirrored those of Colonial authorities from Sydney to Perth and Fremantle. On the front page of the *Fremantle Herald*, an editor assessed: "The town was in a state of great excitement, and pretty equally divided between those who sympathized with [the Fenians] and those who from fear or a principle were determined to find that they had attempted some desperate deeds during the voyage."

The man who could answer Hampton's concerns about the Fenians' conduct throughout the voyage descended from the quarterdeck to the main deck and strode toward the governor general. A reporter from the *Fremantle Herald* who had accompanied the Colonial entourage burst past Hampton and dashed up to Captain Cozens. Halting, Cozens glanced down at the reporter, a diminutive man wearing a floppy, white sunhat and an ill-cut white linen suit.

"How had the Fenians behaved on the journey?" the reporter asked.

Cozens replied: "Well."

Then Cozens brushed past him and met Hampton, Manning, and Wakeford near the main hold to answer the same question. With the reporter on Cozens's heels, the captain informed the officials: "They [the Fenians] expressed themselves pleased at being forwarded to Western Australia . . . and they determined to conduct themselves so as to merit, what in all probability will be extended to them—Fenianism being stamped out—the royal prerogative of mercy."

Cozens assured, "The conduct of the Fenian convicts during the voyage has been good in every respect."

The military Fenians would find doses of mercy in Fremantle. Perhaps Cozens, well aware of what lay ahead for the men who had sworn and then broken the Royal Army's oath of loyalty to the Crown, chose not to add to the prisoners' coming hardships by failing to inform Hampton and Wakeford of the defiance the ex-soldiers had hurled his way during the long voyage. Whatever his motive, the Captain's report made no mention of the truculent demeanor of the military prisoners now glaring at their new jailers. That attitude was a distinguishing feature of the Fenians, according to Fennell, "as patriots their [the Fenians'] past record forbid [*sic*] them yield like crawling cowards or play the part of other subservient slaves and dance to every tune struck up by the organs of impudent gaolers."

Warder Thomas Rowe, having donned for the occasion his dark-blue dress helmet and uniform, the emblems of a detective sergeant of Scotland Yard, was entrusted with the official delivery of the civilian and military Fenians. He marched up to Hampton with a satchel under his left arm and saluted.

Rowe recalled:

> The Fenian convicts were safely landed under my charge on the 10th of January 1868 and handed over to the officers at Fremantle. Following my handing to Governor Hampton of the Colonial Despatches and at the conclusion of the formalities the Governor's conversation with me went as follows:
>
> "'Well, Rowe. What do you intend to do now?'
>
> "'Sir, I intend to have some months' holiday before returning to England.'
>
> "Would you consider remaining here and pursuing your previous vocation?"

Rowe's decision would ensure that he would match wits and wills with the Fenians again.

As Rowe spoke with Hampton, the port doctor studied the crowd of convicts, discerning no signs of any disease that could harm the residents of Fremantle. He reported to the governor that no quarantine of the prisoners was necessary. Hampton then ordered that the prisoners be deposited onto several long, flat barges lumbering up to the *Hougoumont*'s hull.

The water police herded the convicts onto the foredeck, the

guards' eyes darting toward the sixty-three Fenians several times. As sailors lowered another gangplank, this one thumping against the first barge as the other flat-bottomed craft awaited their turn, squads of police and soldiers clambered down the gangplank. They deployed along each barge, ready to rake the prisoners with carbines and Enfields if resistance erupted.

One of the Fenians recounted: "The half-starved felons are ordered unloaded. With their stock in trade, the canvas bag, they are, in accord with official desire, assembled . . . and as the register number and name of each is announced he is bade to step forward and in a woebegone melancholy the old bag is slung recklessly on the shoulder and proceeds slowly as directed out the gangway and scrambles into the barge."

As the police shouted out prison register numbers 9702, 9707, 9757, 9758, and 9767 among the long litany of convict identifications, Robert Cranston, Thomas Darragh, Michael Harrington, Thomas Hassett, and Martin Hogan shouldered their canvas knapsacks in turn and headed down the gangplank with their faces taut. The realization that they had been condemned to life sentences of penal servitude, that they would likely perish in road gangs beneath the harsh Western Australia sun and be pitched into plots in the prison graveyard or unmarked holes in the bush country hit each of the military Fenians full bore.

The fact clutched Imperial Convict Number 9843 when a policeman barked out the number. John Boyle O'Reilly stepped front and center from the throng at the rail, called out "present," and marched down the gangplank to the barge with the ramrod straight bearing of a Hussar. Pushing his way into the jostling crowd of convicts on the craft, guards' fingers poised close to triggers, waiting for the slightest sign of trouble, he did not look back up at the *Hougoumont*. Escape already roiled O'Reilly's thoughts as he waited for the barge to lurch toward the Fremantle jetty.

Fennell remembered: "Batch by batch as they load and depart a thrill of fear and mortal horror of the shore pierce each breast, which steadily increase in proportion as the distance diminishes, drawing irrepressible sighs as now and again a lingering look is cast behind at the wistful old ship that bore them from afar. . . . A sail anywhere in any boat with any wind fair or foul before facing that frowning Bastille [Fremantle Gaol]."

James Wilson, number 9915, stepped onto the last of the barges. When it was loaded and under way, Hampton and the other officials shook hands with Cozens and boarded the steam tug again. The steamer, puffs of smoke rising from the funnel, pulled away from the *Hougoumont,* churned ahead of the lumbering barges, crammed with so many prisoners and guards that the waters of the harbor lapped over the low decks, and docked at the jetty, Victoria Quay. Along the stones of the jetty, a white-coated contingent of the Enlisted Pensioners Reserve waited with rifles at shoulder-arms.

The barges lumbered up to the jetty and thumped against the stones. At bayonet point, guards prodded the prisoners in pairs onto the quay, and the waiting pensioners lined the stumbling convicts into a single-file line stretching the entire expanse of the jetty. As always, prisoners 9757 and 9758—Harrington and Hassett—stood together.

To the surprise of O'Reilly, the soldiers did not clamp manacles around the Fenians' ankles and wrists. The guards had orders to march the convicts to the prison as rapidly as possible, and affixing chains would take too much time. Besides, one look at the twitching jaws of the menacing guards convinced all of the convicts to follow orders.

One of the Fenians assessed those first moments on the jetty, the prisoners' first moments in Australia:

'Tis now midsummer heat, multitudes are surging to and fro on the wharf, conspicuous among them are horse police in snow-white uniforms mounted on caparisoned steeds prancing along the creaking planks [on top of the jetty's stone base] to arrest the onward march of the pressing crowd whose sinewy necks like those of cranes stretch out one behind the other anxious to catch a glimpse of the hunger smitten transports now crowded to suffocation by uncouth savage gangs of prison officials, supported by a detachment of "old fogies," pensioned soldiers, drawn hither more for ornament than real use, for cadaverous and beat as the transports look, these old fogies appear frightened out of countenance for fear anything might arise that would provoke a skirmish.

The Fenians recognized the show of force for what it was: "To give the newcomers a practical idea of the importance of this military post, strike them with fear and trembling and be to them in the future a standing menace against any effort of theirs to rebel."

The guards made no attempt to assemble the prisoners by number, and the Fenians gathered together near the front of the line, squinting in the sunlight at the town in front of them and at the prison crowning it.

"Forward, march!" The shout rang above the jetty. The crowd pressing in front of the jetty parted as the soldiers leading the convicts stepped from the quay and onto High Street. Behind them, the long, single-file line of prisoners, flanked by guards and with the Fenians in front, shuffled onto the road.

Patrick Walle, a civilian Fenian who had been born and raised near Drogheda like O'Reilly, noted: "The little town of Fremantle presents to the immigrant eye a rather strange appearance—the houses are constructed in an old-fashioned style, of all white sand-stone, nothing is seen but white . . . the streets are covered with white sand, which floats about with the wind most abundantly; prison all white, yards white, people dressed in all white. . . ."

Hassett allegedly scoffed, "Well, 'tis no Dublin and that's a fact."

As the sun poured down, the prisoners reeled up High Street, the searing sand ankle-deep in spots, and passed several shops and houses. The Fenians all noticed a two-story wood-frame structure whose sign proclaimed in gilded green letters "Emerald Isle Hotel." On the long, shaded veranda, a middle-aged man with a bristling mustache and brawny forearms poking from rolled-up white sleeves scrutinized the Fenians. Pat Maloney, the proprietor of the Emerald Isle, a native of County Clare and an erstwhile Dublin constable, counted himself among Fremantle's Fenian sympathizers.

With their bayonets the guards nudged the convicts along at a brisk pace, eager to shove them behind the walls of the prison as soon as possible. Staggering along just behind O'Reilly and the other ex-soldiers, Fennell would always remember the scene: "[T]hrough the dusty streets they move and up the heights deep in drifted sands. Are pushed on in hot haste through clouds of suffocating heat. . . ."

Climbing in that heat, wiping at the endless, stinging stream of sweat that poured from their brows into their eyes, the prisoners noticed the well-built stone homes of Colonial officials and prosperous merchants. O'Reilly spied another building, a Gothic edifice with two huge wings and steep roofs. He was looking at the town's asylum, for prisoners who lost their sanity in the jail or the penal work gangs.

Suddenly, at the front of the line the Fenians gaped. Two octagonal stone towers flanked a gateway that conjured images of a medieval portcullis. Atop the tower, sentries stared down rifle barrels at the prisoners. A huge clock with a black face greeted the prisoners from a round pediment above the gate, a reminder of how slowly time passed in Fremantle Gaol, of how the clock's slow hands would measure the seemingly endless seconds, minutes, weeks, months, and years of the military Fenians' sentences.

With a ponderous creak, the studded wooden gate swung open. The convict line snaked through the gate and into a sprawling parade ground covered by white sand and enclosed by high white walls. At the far end of the courtyard, a pair of four-story barracks blocks towered from both sides of a two-floor neoclassical portico that fronted the prison officials' offices, the complex's storehouses, and the commissariat building. Large Georgian windows shone in the sunlight, and a handful of scraggly trees cast faint shadows across the sand and the crushed limestone walls. From a lofty staff, the Union Jack dangled in the dead air.

With guards ringing the parade ground, the water police and pensioners who had guided the convicts from the jetty ordered them to halt in front of the commissariat, where Hampton and his fellow officials waited. A guard roared, "Fall in double!"

Though exhausted, Hogan, Hassett, Harrington, Cranston, Wilson, Darragh, and O'Reilly instinctively obeyed with the precision of men who had followed orders on the Queen's parade grounds. The civilian convicts all around them had a harder time responding to the command: "Slowly they muster on the call as if each one breathed a silent desire for death."

A second order rang out: "Right dress!"

Again the soldier Fenians instantaneously complied. The other prisoners also obeyed, but with little élan: "Poor wretches . . . (they are in full possession of the faculty of hearing the greasy sleeves of their filth-coated jackets grate on the ear as in most awkward effort they stammer into line). . . . Each joint and chord is stiff, it is a torture to move. . . . Three hundred despicable broken down forms toe the mark . . . like moving mummies. . . ."

Another command echoed across the parade ground: "Right face, march!"

With guards' curses booming and the ever-present bayonets steering the double line of convicts past the portico, the prisoners stumbled as if on a regimental review, and were ordered to salute the officials. With his practiced doctor's eye, Hampton scanned each of the convicts, speculating on their fitness and physical weaknesses and making comments that a clerk jotted down in a black ledger. The governor had numerous roadways and buildings under construction throughout the colony and needed bodies for the road gangs and the quarries that furnished the stone for all of his public works. As Hampton noted aloud any wounds, scars, moles, and all other physical characteristics from the color of eyes and hair to tattoos, the clerk's pen scratched across the pages. From their days in the Royal Army, the military Fenians knew the reason for such detail: the distinguishing marks would be used on a death certificate as proof of a man's identity.

In the prison register, the clerk described the scar made by an Afghan warrior's scimitar on Hogan's left cheek. "He has the gait and appearance of a cavalry soldier," read his file. The clerk noted Darragh's red hair and square shoulders, as well as several moles. Harrington, already showing the effects of his ordeal, had a sallow visage. The prison officials noticed Hassett's clear complexion, marred only by a scar across his left upper lip, a wound incurred in the service of the Papal Brigade at the Siege of Spoleto. On Cranston's right arm was emblazoned a tattoo in the shape of a Fenian, or Celtic, cross. Wilson stood five feet, eight inches, taller than most of his comrades.

When the medical inspection finally ended, the guards once

again shoved the convicts into a ragged double line and ordered them to stand in the middle of the parade ground in front of a limestone block serving as a makeshift podium. Officials crossed from the portico and halted behind the rostrum. As a guard cried, "Attention!" Comptroller-General Henry Wakeford, clad in a tall "castor hat," a hunting frock, buff-hued knee breeches, and black patent-leather boots, climbed onto the rostrum. He stared for a minute or two down at the long lines of prisoners.

As the perspiring, exhausted prisoners fought to stay standing in the heat, Fennell would summarize the Fenians' initial, as well as later, impressions of the official: "The hon. Henry Wakeford is an appointee from home with a big salary and with nothing on earth to do to earn it but practice horseback riding when it suited his whims to visit convict stations along the highway through the extensive bush. . . . Very unprepossessing, of short stature, brown eyes, sunburnt face full of sand-colored bushy beard character-istic of the Saxon. . . . On the whole, an odd, ungainly genius, his style, appearance, and costume resembling the aesthetic para-phernalia of an actor in comic opera more than a high government functionary."

The prisoners would dub him "Boots," but there was nothing comic in the words he uttered after clearing his throat loudly. His voice rose above the parade ground: "To you men it is needless to mention the fact that by your lawless conduct and behavior in the mother country, you incurred the anger and indignation of law-abiding subjects . . . and the justice of the courts to punish and deprive you of exercising the rights of free men. On this account you have merited your present fate, banishment from society, your native home and country to penal exile in a foreign land. . . ."

Standing sullenly among the prisoners, O'Reilly and Wilson seethed at Wakeford's use of the words "free men." Neither they nor the other military Fenians accepted that they had ever, as

Irishmen, been free. O'Reilly bristled inwardly at the notion he had committed any "lawless" act or that England was his "mother country": "No treason we bring from Erin—nor bring we shame nor guilt, the sword we hold may be broken, but we have not dropped the hilt."

Wakeford discerned the defiance staring back at him from the grimy faces of the Fenians and launched into a thinly veiled series of warnings: "You must therefore, from the onset, consider yourselves nothing more than what you really are in the eyes of the law, criminal transports without a voice in your own personal preference or disposition, cast here to endure incarceration with the thousands of your class and kind sent hither to expiate their sins and misdeeds. . . ."

As Hogan looked at the genuine criminals in the yard, he seethed at the thought that he and his comrades shared anything in common with them.

"It is a stern duty," Wakeford harangued,

> but I am obliged to warn [that] you stand prepared for the worst, for each and all of you must without hope of relaxation spend the remainder of your unexpired sentences in durance as your commitments call for. . . . You are in reality the joint property of both British and Colonial governments. . . . I earnestly advise and recommend you to do [the sentences] quietly and submissively. . . .
>
> Obey your superior officers is the golden rule, trespass on no injunction, avoid insolence and insubordination, do as you are bade cheerfully and willingly and your good conduct will be one day rewarded by getting your sentences remitted as provided by prison rules and regulations.

Many of the civilian Fenian prisoners took a measure of solace in the word "remitted." For the military Fenians, however, the word meant nothing: they had received life sentences for treason, and even Fremantle inmates convicted of manslaughter stood a better chance of reduced sentences than the former soldiers. For O'Reilly, Harrington, Hassett, and the others who had sworn the oath of the Royal Army, death loomed as the only certain escape from The Establishment—particularly as Wakeford began to read the long litany of prison rules.

"If you do not obey orders," Wakeford said to the silent throng, "you will discover that we have in this prison colony a code which provides the most severe penalties. You will learn that I do not hesitate to carry out these penalties to the utmost."

> For refusal to obey any order of a prison official, the punishment is flogging, extension of sentence, and solitary confinement.
>
> For refusal to perform any task while on work detail, the punishment is flogging, extension of sentence, and solitary confinement.
>
> For attempt to escape from a work party engaged in lawful prison activities outside the walls of the prison, the punishment may be death or extension of sentence, flogging and solitary confinement.
>
> Attempt to escape from the confinements of the prison—the penalty for which is death.
>
> Theft of any article whatsoever in Her Majesty's storehouses, buildings, and camps—the penalty for which is death.
>
> Any attempt, whether successful or not, to destroy by fire the property of Her Majesty—the penalty for which is death.

The killing of a prison official—the penalty for which is death.

Barely a cough or any other sound but Wakeford's voice rose from the parade ground. He continued: "If you are accused of any infraction of the rules or of discipline in this prison, I am the judge and I am the jury. I will hear the charges brought against you and I will render the verdict. There is no appeal from my judgment. "

The rules of "The Establishment" read, Wakeford turned to the matter of escape.

Many of you say to yourselves, 'Those penalties will never apply to me. I will escape.

There is no doubt you will have plenty of opportunities to escape. If you are not being punished—and we have dungeons in which to pen you up when you are being punished—you will often be assigned to work parties outside the walls. You may work on the jetties, or you may be assigned to a road gang or a timber gang. You will think it easy to get away. But, if you do run away, you will be caught or you will perish.

I repeat, you will be caught or you will perish.

There are two ways to escape from this prison. . . by the sea or by the land."

As Wakeford described the terrain confronting the prisoners beyond the prison's walls, any thoughts of escape among the civilian Fenians dissolved. They figured that their chances of regaining their freedom were better in serving their five to seven years with hopes of early remittance rather than in risking the near-certain death depicted by Wakeford. The largest barriers to successful escape lay not in the guards' weapons nor the solitary cells of The Establishment, but in the very nature of the land and sea beyond Fremantle's environs:

> On the landward side there was a vast expanse of bush, an uncharted wilderness, without tracks, food or friendliness, a hostile steppe which wore down the resistance of anyone blind enough to trust to its mercy. For the man who evaded capture, it meant a slow but certain death, for the man who was recaptured from its pitiless wastes it meant the burning slavery of the chain-gang. To seaward there was the vast expanse of the Indian Ocean, which invited no prisoner to escape that way. Or so it was thought. Thus Nature was the most powerful jailer that presided over the Imperial Convict Establishment of Fremantle.

A slow death by the sting of poisonous snakes and insects in the arid bush, a grisly end in the shark-infested waters off Fremantle, or one's last moments spent chained to a murderer or worse—a trio of agonies awaited any man who "made a dash for it." Wakeford added: "And I will start searching for you the moment you are posted as missing. While you are wandering, confused, thirsting, starving, dying, I will have trackers on your trail. These trackers are Aborigines. They are natives of the bush country. They can trace the spoor of a man through forests, over barren ground, over sun-baked rocks. They will find you. If you are still alive, they will drag you back. If you are dead, you will not be worth dragging back, and they call to the carrion birds to feast on your carcass."

If the sight of ships anchored off Fremantle lured prisoners to escape by sea, Wakeford warned, most of the ships were British, and no captain in his right mind would conceal a convict—particularly a Fenian with a price on his head. He also reiterated that giant sharks would tear apart any escapee so naïve as to believe he could swim twelve miles into international waters and be picked up by a foreign vessel. O'Reilly and the rest of the Fenians had already seen those fins knifing the waters off Fremantle from the gunwales of the *Hougoumont*.

Still, O'Reilly leaned toward Darragh and whispered, "There'll be a way. There has to be a path to liberty. I swear it, Red, I swear I'll find that path."

Wakeford shouted, "Officers, file them off!"

Officially, the indoctrination of The Establishment's newest inmates—now part of Western Australia's penal population of 3,220, nearly one-sixth of the colony's 20,000 souls—had begun.

The warders and pensioner guards thrust the two lines of convicts into motion again, this time across the parade ground and into the "reception block." Now forcing them into a single column, the guards led them down a lengthy, dim corridor and into the bath house, where twenty to thirty long wooden troughs holding a foot-and-a-half of water each were partitioned into scores of stalls. The convicts were ordered to strip and toss their clothing onto the cold stone floor. Heaps of the soiled, lice-ridden smocks and breeches the men had worn since the *Hougoumont*'s departure from Portland greeted a work party of inmates too elderly for the road gangs anymore. They were judged strong enough to shovel the foul garments into carts, haul them under guard outside the prison walls to a pit, burn them, and cover anything left with lime.

The warders arranged the naked convicts in "teams" according to the numerical order of the men's prison register numbers, and the Fenians took their turn immersing their grime-coated limbs in the troughs with the other convicts. Fennell grumbled:

An economic construction [the troughs] that gives a chance to the filth to defuse without obstruction through the whole bed, giving the cleanest person every opportunity to benefit from the dirt of his neighbour, who by continual tumbling and splashing keep the water rolling along the walled aqueduct. It is a most unenviable place to be. The pent-up stagnant fluid in this long trough is . . . cold and for the first plunge or two makes the teeth chatter and chills the vapid blood in the body through and through. Although badly needed, 'twere far preferable stay the operation altogether but that the rules are arbitrary and bathe they must, for to disobey orders would be to incur the severest punishment.

As the prisoners emerged from the muddied water, the warders pointed at several piles on the floor, one of towels and the others the convicts' new uniforms, the infamous emblems of The Establishment. Standing in front of the clothing, the prison doctor, with Hampton, Wakeford, Superintendent of Fremantle Henry Maxwell Lefroy, and other officials, looked each convict up and down before waving him past to collect his uniform. Fennell and O'Reilly rendered nearly identical accounts of the humiliating scene:

Under optic as well as microscopic observation of the functionaries . . . the convicts scramble in and out in batches 'till the three hundred have washed and scoured themselves in the same water without change. With derisive side glances they are under the scrutiny of the doctor, who, after limited consulation and interchanges of opinion with the rest of the magnates, agrees as to their "good condition" and pronounces the outcasts of the *Hougoumont* as fit to resume duty on hard labor.

Not here alone but in the penitentiaries of old England is the pernicious rule enforced, that crawling about is sufficient guarantee of physical ruggedness for the examining doctor to consider convicts capable of performing prison labor, or any other drudgery the unscrupulous wretch takes a notion to assign to them.

In turn, the convicts were issued their Drogheda-linen summer garments: a dark gray jacket, a vest, three shirts—two of cotton, one of flannel—two handkerchiefs, two pairs of socks, two pairs of trousers, one pair of boots, and a soft white hat. A red stripe ran down the jacket and pants, and all over the clothing appeared the wide, crow-footed, multihued "convict arrows" of The Establishment. One of the Fenians railed: "Scarce a square inch of . . . this incomparable suit is not daubed over with broad arrow stamps of different paints. It is no strange thing to count as many as fifty of these offensive looking stamps on a single suit besides the register number of the convict in the most conspicuous spots. . . . In paints that make the brightest contrast with the goods worn, the felons are stamped all over, moving curiosities."

For O'Reilly and Hogan, men who had worn the jaunty shakos and gilded tunics of the Queen's cavalry, the mere act of putting on the garish Drogheda linens galled. Harrington, Darragh, and Hassett, all of whom had fought and bled in soldiers' uniforms, wrestled with emotions tinged by equal parts rage and shame. None of the Fenians viewed themselves as common criminals who should have to wear felons' garb, but with each already interminable minute they spent in Fremantle, awareness that their jailers thought otherwise seeped into the prisoners' thoughts. For some of the Fenians, hopelessness began to surface even at this initial phase of their incarceration.

The despair increased for many of the rebels moments later with another rule spouted by Wakeford: "By one's register number and not his lawful name, the convict is known and addressed during the entire period of his incarceration."

"Fall in!" the warders yelled. "Right about face, march!"

Automatically, the military Fenians obeyed, though Hogan and O'Reilly glowered at the guards. The long procession wound once again to the parade ground, the men cleaner than before, but quickly sweating as the noon sun bore down on them. "On this occasion," Fennell noted,

> the victims of the *Hougoumont* present a gayer aspect than they have been blessed with for a long time before, dressed in bright new suits as compared to when clad in greasy brine-steeped smock and breeches.
>
> Despite the qualities of repelling of heat claimed in behalf of [their] apparel it don't seem to avail much now, for the sun of this southern mid-summer day is simply stifling on the parade ground, which is composed of dazzling white sand stone pulverized to finest dust from the steady tramp of convicts, so that the rays that beat down so fiercely reflect back from the surface with double force and much more intensely than they descend.

Summer temperatures in Western Australia could reach 120 degrees Fahrenheit. Although Harrington and Darragh had squinted in the harsh light of the South African steppes and the Indian plateaus, their eyes had never throbbed as they now did in the Western Australian sun. All around them, men lowered their eyes, grimacing, the pain coursing through their temples. Some tightly shut their lids, but found little relief. A bell suddenly tolled across the yard. Within minutes, other convicts and their guards emerged from the two massive cell blocks, and work parties with their carbine-toting escorts streamed through the main gate and plodded to the mess hall at the far end of the eastern cell block. Warders ordered the common convicts among the new arrivals to join the others, but shouted at the Fenians to stay put. They stood silently at attention, swaying from time to time in the heat.

A half-hour later, the inmates shuffled from the mess hall and passed the sixty-three men still standing in their new but already saturated Drogheda linen. Some of the sunburned, stoop-shouldered Fremantle "veterans" of the road gangs and quarries cast sympathetic glances the Fenians' way; others leered with gap-toothed grins testifying to blows from warders or other inmates. For many civilian Fenians, little in their lives had prepared them for life with convicts so murderous and depraved that Britain had dumped them a world away. Harrington, Hogan, Darragh, and Hassett had stared down death in battle and recognized that these brutes posed as much—perhaps more—of a threat than any Zulu, Sikh, or Afghan warrior.

Another cry of "fall in" yanked the Fenians from such thoughts. The prisoners followed their guards into the mess and sat on benches fronting long, scarred gumwood tables. Moments later, wizened prisoners, some of whom had arrived in the 1830s aboard the first penal transports to Australia, rolled up carts piled with wooden bowls and slapped down the Fenians' first meal in The Establishment. They washed down their dinner—an odorous portion of meat, a pound of slushy boiled potatoes, and six ounces of hard bread—with a draught of bitter, tepid chocolate.

"Instead of . . . allaying the pangs of hunger," wrote Fennell, "the miserable collation only increases greed for more."

After dinner, the guards allowed the Fenians to mill about the parade ground and seek the relative shade closer to the shadow of the portico, many of the men slumping wordlessly against the courtyard's walls. The sentries patrolling the walls and the gateway's two towers watched every movement made by a Fenian that first day.

Late in the afternoon, warders reassembled the Irishmen and separated the ex-soldiers from their civilian comrades. The guards then led the two lines in opposite directions, marching the military men into one of the barracks blocks, the civilians into the other.

O'Reilly, Hogan, Hassett, Cranston, Darragh, Wilson, Harrington, and the other military Fenians gawked at the cavernous, four-tiered expanse of the prison block, which stretched some six hundred feet. Wan light pierced the grime of skylights set on the edges of a saddle roof arching far overhead. The guards ordered the Fenians up a spiral iron staircase to the top tier and pushed each prisoner within the dingy whitewashed walls of his solitary cell. An instant later the slams of the cell's thick corrugated iron doors crashed through the block.

Once his eyes grew accustomed to the faint light of his cell's sole window, which was barred and too high to see out of, each man realized he could barely extend his arms to the limestone walls of the three-foot-wide chamber. He could not even pace about the cell, which covered only seven feet from the door to the back wall. From the floor to the ceiling, both built of native red mahogany, the nine-foot height added to the impression that he had been tossed into a narrow tower. A canvas hammock dangled from a hook near the door and another hook on the rear wall. Two unbleached cotton sheets, a ragged blanket, and a threadbare cotton rug lay atop the hammock, but no pillow was allowed the prisoner. In a corner sat a wooden water pail for washing, a scrubbing brush, and a pewter urinal. A tiny oil lamp offered nothing more than a ghostly, flickering glow to read the only books allowed: the Bible and other religious works.

For existing meals and for writing letters, an eighteen-by-fourteen-inch table was hung "by the wall till needed, when, by the aid of a transverse leg fastened underneath in the center, it is brought to a horizontal position, and the other end made to rest on a wooden block inserted in the wall." Although the prisoners were allowed to write letters to family and friends, prison officials, convinced that the Irishmen would try to "spread Fenian crime" through the mail, would pore over each line the men wrote. In time, O'Reilly, Hogan, and Wilson would find means to evade the censors.

That first evening, January 10–11, 1867, in Fremantle Gaol, the Fenian soldiers wept and prayed, cursed and sweated in their wobbly hammocks and dreamed fitfully of Ireland and of all they had lost. O'Reilly, Hogan, Harrington, and Wilson were already plotting to somehow escape, even though Nature itself seemed against them. For a few men, exhaustion brought sleep and a fleeting respite from thoughts of the days—and years—to come.

The clang of the prison bell jarred the Fenians from sleep and tormented reverie at 4:30 A.M. Warders stomped down the long corridors and roared at the prisoners to roll out of their hammocks and wash. In the small pails, the inmates splashed water on their faces. No soap was provided. Then, as instructed during Wakeford's reading of the prison rules, the Fenians unslung their hammocks, rolled them neatly, stowed them in a corner, and waited with their urinals in hand until the warders' keys grated against the iron locks and the doors opened with a metallic screech. The guards ordered the prisoners into the corridor, formed them into a single line, and led them outside, where the first golden hues hinting of another steamy morning were spreading across the gunmetal gray sky. After the Fenians dumped their chamber pots' contents into a trench filled with lime powder at the edge of the parade ground, they were marched back to their cells and locked in again. The guards returned at 5:15 A.M. to take the prisoners to the mess for a 5:30 breakfast of watery oatmeal or gruel, a chunk of stale bread, and a pint of lukewarm cocoa.

Fighting to hold down the vile mix, the Fenians were taken to a small stone chapel near the commissariat for a 6 A.M. prayer service conducted by the prison chaplain, Father Lynch. The priest, new to the post, searched the forlorn faces staring at him from the chapel's sagging wooden benches. He was looking for a dark-haired young man whom Father Delany had asked the chaplain to help. The *Hougoumont's* cleric was worried about John Boyle O'Reilly's state of mind, sensing that the emotional, once-dashing Hussar would crack under the bleak prospects of escape and the certainty of years spent among thugs and inmates gone mad. Having promised Father Delany to intercede with Hampton on O'Reilly's behalf, the prison chaplain spotted prisoner 9843 sitting among the sixteen other ex-soldiers near the front of the chapel. John Boyle O'Reilly sagged on the bench and stared ahead blankly, the dark hollows around his eyes adding years to his face.

Frowns filled most of the Irishmen's countenances. Several Fenians brushed away tears. After mumbled, automatic responses to the prayers, the men were once again herded back to their cells.

For the entire weekend of January 11–12, 1867, with the exception of dinner at noon and another parade-ground inspection followed by tea at 6 P.M., the Irishmen were confined to their cells. The warders allowed them no reading materials yet. All the prisoners could do was to brood or weep as they awaited word of their work assignments.

While the Fenians languished in the gloom of the cell block, Governor Hampton and Comptroller-General Wakeford deliberated on how to deal with the men they considered traitors to the Crown and a danger to the penal colony. Having inspected the rebels several times since the *Hougoumont*'s arrival, Hampton had decided that men such as Cashman, Fennell, Flood, and the other civilian Fenians already determined that their salvation lay not in further revolt, but in compliance with prison rules. For the civilian Fenians, obedience offered the reward of reduced sentences.

Sitting in the ornate study of the High Street mansion he had established as his temporary headquarters to deal with the "Fenian problem," Hampton dipped pen into inkwell and scratched orders for Wakefield upon official Colonial Office stationery: "As their [the civilian Fenians] conduct onboard ship and their demeanour upon landing had been so satisfactory, I considered it desirable to order the civilians to be separated from the ordinary criminal class."

He had no such mercy in mind for O'Reilly, Cranston, Darragh, Hassett, Hogan, Harrington, Wilson, and the other ten military Fenians: "The risk of such men combining together for evil purposes induced me to disperse them as widely as possible throughout the colony, not sending more than one or two of them to the same station."

Hampton was assigning them to the road gangs and quarry crews composed of some of the worst criminals in the British Empire.

The Companionship
of Desperate and
Degraded Men

Within a week of the *Hougoumont's* appearance in the waters off Fremantle, Governor Hampton dispersed the military Fenians in quarries and road gangs, where they were shackled to criminals day and night. Harrington and Hassett were separated for the first time since their arrests, forced to endure alone the company of convicts ranging from the depraved to the psychotic.

O'Reilly proved more fortunate for his first month in Fremantle, as Father Lynch had arranged to have the former Hussar assigned as a clerk to the prison library with his friends Cashman and Flood. In early February 1868, an Irish newspaper somehow smuggled into Fremantle Gaol ended up in the hands of O'Reilly, Cashman, and Flood. The front-page story graphically chronicled the hanging of three Irishmen who would be known to the Fenians as the "Manchester Martyrs." As the three men pored over the account, O'Reilly offered: "This is another evidence of their implacable hatred of the Irish race; these men are innocent."

O'Reilly had still been in Dartmoor when the events leading to the executions of the Manchester Martyrs had unfolded. On September 11, 1867, Colonel Tom Kelly was in Manchester, England, still seeking a way to ignite a Fenian revolt—if not on Irish soil, then on British. Informers revealed his wherabouts to the police, and on September 11, he and a Captain Deasy, who had fought in and escaped from the abortive rebellion in Cork in March 1867, were seized in a Manchester doorway and thrown into cells in the city jail.

A week later, the two Fenians were brought to court, formally charged with treason, and packed into a police van for the return trip to the prison. As the van clattered with a police escort beneath a railway arch on Hyde Road, a Fenian jumped into the middle of the street, aimed his revolver at the driver of the van, and ordered him to rein in the horses. Thirty Fenians then swarmed around the van and forced it to stop. The rebels, unable to force open the thick steel door, demanded that Sergeant Charles Brett, the police officer guarding the prisoners within, open it. According to several conflicting accounts, a Fenian fired his revolver either at the lock or through a ventilator shaft, and the bullet tore into Sergeant Brett. A woman prisoner inside the van grabbed the keys from the mortally wounded Brett and handed them through the ventilator to the Fenians. Within seconds the rescue party whisked away Kelly and Deasy, and as the escapees and their rescuers climbed over a wall and sprinted to safety across the railway tracks, one of the Fenians—a man named O'Brien, Allen, or Larkin—said, "Kelly, I'll die for you."

Kelly and Deasy would soon be safe on a steamer for New York and receive a hero's welcome from the city's Irish. The man who had vowed to lay down his life for Kelly would do just that.

The British police, in a fury over Brett's death, swept Fenian enclaves throughout the region and arrested five young Irishmen for murder. One, an Irishman in the Royal Marines, had no involvement and was soon released. Another suspect, an American citizen named Condon, won his freedom through the intercession of U.S. Secretary of State William Seward. For the remaining three Irishmen—ex-Union Army captain Michael O'Brien, William Allen, and Philip Larkin—the court handed down death sentences despite the fact that none of the men had fired the shot that killed Brett.

Although the American government urged Parliament to commute the three men's death sentences to life in Western Australia, the condemned were led up the scaffold stairs of Manchester Gaol on November 23, 1867, and the nooses were slipped around their necks. When the hangman pulled the trap, one of the three died immediately when his neck snapped, but the other two thrashed for two or three horrifying minutes—the executioner had misgauged the proper "fall" for the two men's weights, and they strangled to death slowly.

O'Reilly, Cashman, and Flood were "greatly excited at this shocking event." Cashman would write, "We talked the matter over in no terms of eulogy to the British power, and separated to our cells." The story of the Manchester Martyrs refueled the hatred of Britain that still seethed in the military Fenians such as O'Reilly and many of the civilian Fenians alike.

O'Reilly's unrepentant demeanor greeted Cashman the following morning. According to Cashman,

> At 6 o'clock O'Reilly came over to me in the prison yard as I was polishing the hoops of my night pail [chamber pot], a duty that meant a bright shine or solitary cells [confinement]. He said: "Denis, I have written a poem." I replied: "Jack, you have not. How could you do it in the dark, and without a means of writing?" He replied: "I have done it."

"Well," said I, "I shall believe it when I see it."

He answered: "You shall as soon as I can obtain a pen and ink."

Later on in the morning, he brought me a sheet of paper, and, holding it up in his dear, laughing way, said: "Now, old man, here it is, and tell me what you think of it?"

I read it and was astounded at the production. I knew he had no earthly means of writing anything in his three or four foot cell, there being only room for a hammock to run through it, and, besides, it was dark from the time he retired until a few moments before he made the announcement to me.

I took his hand, and while squeezing it said: "Dear Jack, wherever or whatever part of the globe you may go when these accursed chains are rent, you will make a name and become great."

A sigh was the response, and a thoughtful "Twenty years, Denis, twenty years."

Cashman and the other Fenians knew that O'Reilly, one way or the other, would not spend twenty years in Western Australia.

As O'Reilly walked away, Cashman pocketed the piece of paper. Not until decades later would "The Dead Who Died for Ireland," O'Reilly's tribute to the Manchester Martyrs, be published:

The dead who died for Ireland!
Oh, these are living words
To nerve the heart of patriots—
To steel avenging swords—
They thrill the soul when spoken,

And lowly bend the head
With reverence for the memories
of all our martyred dead.

The dead who died for Ireland—
the noble ones—the best,
Who gave their lives for Motherland,
Who poured upon her breast,
In Freedom's cause, the blood she gave—
Who with their dying breath,
Sent prayers to God to heal her woes—
Then sealed their love in death.

The dead who died for Ireland,
How hallowed are their graves!
With all the memories fresh and green,
Oh! How could we be slaves?
How could we patient clang the chain?
How could we fawn and bow?
How could we crouch like mongrels
'neath the keeper's frowning brow?

Be proud, ye men of Ireland!
Be proud of those who died;
Never men o'er all the earth
Had greater cause for pride—
Hope and strive, and league for freedom,
And again the souls will rise
Of the dead who died for Ireland
To cheer you to the prize.

On February 12, 1868, just days after O'Reilly surreptitiously penned the poem, he received an order from Comptroller-General Wakeford: "9843 John O'Reilly will be transferred hence to Bunbury for the party about to clear the new line of road between Bunbury and the Vasse. The accountant of stores will make the necessary requisition for transport."

O'Reilly's brief sojourn in the prison library was ended. There was speculation that the full record of his escape attempts in England had reached Governor Hampton's desk. As a military Fenian, O'Reilly would now suffer the same hardships of body, mind, and soul as Cranston, Darragh, Harrington, Hassett, Hogan, Wilson, and the other ten ex-soldiers. Cashman would write: "We waved him an adieu as we were bustled through the gates. Our hearts were heavy: we could not speak. A tear—well, no matter. Flood, whom O'Reilly loved, never saw him again."

From Bunbury, alongside Geographe Bay, south of Fremantle, O'Reilly was dispatched to the road gang of Deputy Warder Henry Woodman, to take his place in "the companionship of desperate and degraded men, 'the poison flower of civilization's corruption,' and the future seemed hopeless." Most of the other military Fenians were scattered in similar road gangs hacking out roads north of where O'Reilly and the thirty to forty other convicts toiled under Woodman's control.

O'Reilly had to wield shovel and pick ax for at least part of his time in the gang. The convicts worked nine or more hours per day in the heat of the Australian summer, bludgeoning rocks with sledgehammers, sawing and felling trees, hacking out dense, deep roots, breaking up rocks, and cutting down brush that lacerated their skin. Against the sun boring down, the floppy hats and linen clothes worn by the prisoners could not protect exposed hands, necks, and faces, the convicts' fair or ruddy complexions blistering and peeling. The dried grass teemed with poisonous snakes.

In his novel *Moondyne,* O'Reilly would render a vivid depiction of the rugged bush country and the grueling, soul-deadening labor in the highest heat of the day:

> Had there been any moisture in the bush, it would have steamed in the heavy heat. During the midday heat not a bird stirred among the mahogany and gum trees. On the flat tops of the low banksia the round heads of the white cockatoos could be seen in the thousands, motionless as the trees themselves. Not a parrot had the vim to scream. The chirping insects were silent. Not a snake had courage to rustle his hard skin against the hot and dead bush-grass. The bright-eyed iguanas were in their holes. The mahogany sawyers had left their logs and were sleeping in the cool sand of their pits. Even the traveling ants had halted on their wonderful roads, and sought the shade of a bramble.
>
> All free things were at rest; but the penetrating click of the axe, heard far through the bush, and now and again a harsh word of command, told that it was a land of bondmen.
>
> From daylight to dark, through the hot noon as steadily as in the cool evening, the convicts were at work on the roads—the weary work that has no wages, no promotion, no incitement, no variation for good or bad, except stripes [from a whip] for the laggard.

Martin Hogan had the misfortune of working in a quarry near the Swan River, digging out, hauling, and blasting boulders and often chained day and night to thieves and killers. With the sun's glare off the limestone and granite walls, many men first suffered "moon-blindness," reportedly caused by the jarring effects of daylight hours in the quarries followed by no twilight and the sudden onset of darkness.

After toiling by day in the quarries or in the bush, the nights in convict camps furnished little relief of any sort for the Fenians. Some of the encampments had rude huts of sticks nailed together and capped by a roof made of rushes; other crews slept out in the open, their chains clanking every time one of the men tossed or shifted in fitful sleep. In a letter home to Dublin, George Connolly, a civilian Fenian who labored alongside Hogan, wrote: "To lie upon we have each got a hammock, but neither sheets, beds, or pillows, and at night our only visitors are fleas and mosquitoes. . . ."

All of the military Fenians lost weight in the quarries or in the bush, and all began to fret at the slow, certain ravages of toil, sun, and often meager rations. As the long months of 1868 stretched on, the nightmare of "penal servitude for life" ripped at the thoughts of the ex-soldiers, especially at night amid the cursing, snoring, and grunting of the genuinely depraved criminals. The emotional anguish of the military Fenians' life sentences added to their careworn expressions, and for O'Reilly and Hassett in particular, the mental strain edged toward desperation.

Shortly after O'Reilly reported to the Bunbury depot and Woodman's road gang, the warder not only recognized the Irishman's intelligence, but also developed a liking for him. Woodman soon excused O'Reilly from full-time labor with the bush crew and made him a clerk and a courier who carried weekly messages to the chief warder of the Bunbury region. Although O'Reilly had to deliver the letters within a set time or face punishment, his unescorted trips offered the closest thing to a whiff of freedom he had experienced since his arrest in Island Bridge Barracks. His captors did not worry that he might flee— there was nowhere for him to run to except into the bush or the shark-infested Indian Ocean.

Despite those brutal realities, O'Reilly continued to dream of escape and believed that the ocean offered his only chance. Unable and unwilling to concede that only a life in the penal gangs and a slow, certain death lay in front of him, he sought the help of Father Patrick McCabe, who was rumored to be a Fenian sympathizer. McCabe, a ruddy-cheeked, broad-shouldered man in his mid-thirties, was the parish priest of Bunbury, where a brick church was rising under his direction. To the sunburned scarecrows of the road gangs and the quarries, he served as "parish priest of the bush country," riding the vast distances from one penal camp to another.

On a night in May or June 1868, the priest rode into the Koagulup camp, where the men of Warder Woodman's road gang were slouched in coarse woolen blankets beneath sprawling mahogany trees. As Father McCabe settled in his own blankets, John Boyle O'Reilly walked over to him, sat, and asked if he might have a word or two with him in confidence. McCabe, bushy auburn sideburns covering the sides of his square jaw and brushing against his stiff white collar, was accustomed to convicts approaching him to confess crimes seemingly beyond any penance he could administer. His stern light-blue eyes fixed upon the prisoner, whom he recognized as Woodman's clerk and one of the famed military Fenians, and the priest gestured for O'Reilly to continue.

As O'Reilly confessed his determination to escape and described several desperate schemes he had devised, Father McCabe listened patiently. He had heard the same litany from other prisoners and knew firsthand that the bush, Aborigine trackers, the water police, or sharks would end any hopes of freedom for runaway convicts. McCabe allowed O'Reilly to finish. Then the priest declared, "It is an excellent way to commit suicide."

As he further examined the haggard, still handsome features, Father McCabe detected a desperation so deep in the man's eyes that he realized O'Reilly would welcome a suicidal dash for liberty rather than a life in the road gangs or Fremantle Gaol. Discomfited by the sight of a young man on the edge of madness, a man who the priest believed was a patriot, not a criminal, Father McCabe said something he had never offered to another prisoner: "Don't think of that again. Let me think out a plan for you. You'll hear from me before long."

O'Reilly returned to his blanket, his hopes swelling.

On March 12, 1868, the fallout of an event in Sydney made life even harsher for O'Reilly and the other Fenian prisoners. A self-styled Fenian named Henry O'Farrell stepped from a vast crowd at Clontarf, a park in Sydney Harbor, and fired a bullet into the back of the visiting Prince Albert, Queen Victoria's youngest son. As the police seized O'Farrell, he shouted: "I'm a Fenian—God save Ireland!"

The prince would recover, but the backlash against anyone in Australia with suspected Fenian sympathies lasted months, police and officials questioning and harassing Irish immigrants and especially former Fremantle Irish whose sentences had been reduced. In Fremantle Gaol and in the penal work crews, warders incensed by the assassination attempt took their rage out upon the known Fenians.

In April 1868, Martin Hogan was toiling in a quarry near Perth when Warder Munday stormed through the work site, threatening the Irish convicts, denouncing the Fenians, and hurling every bit of invective he could muster against Ireland and the Irish in general. Hogan, his chain taken off for the day's work, strode up to Munday, glowered at him, and launched into a tirade against the startled warder. Then the ex-dragoon, his face tight, the saber's scar standing out jagged and white on his sun-reddened face, reportedly threatened to pummel Munday if he uttered another epithet against Ireland. Hogan turned his back on the warder, climbed from the rock pit, and walked away from the camp. He did not get far. Within an hour or two, police officers converged on him and hauled him to a courtroom in Perth, where a judge was waiting for him. The dragoon was sentenced to six months of hard labor by day and solitary confinement by night at Fremantle Gaol. For six months, he would not be allowed to talk to anyone, would subsist on rations of bread and water, and would be allowed neither bedding nor clothing in his cell.

From June to December 1868, as Hogan began his latest ordeal, O'Reilly, still awaiting word from Father McCabe, continued to carry Woodman's correspondence back and forth from Bunbury. He, too, incurred the anger of an official rankled by the assassination attempt against Prince Albert, when the chief warder of Bunbury accused O'Reilly of tarrying in delivery of the mail. The official ordered that O'Reilly be denied letters from home for six months, though still allowed to carry other convicts' letters back and forth from camp. In June 1868, the chief warder waved a letter with black edges in the ex-Hussar's face and snapped, "You will receive it in six months."

Among the messages that O'Reilly carried to Bunbury each week were notes from Warder Woodman to his wife and his attractive daughter Jessie. According to O'Reilly biographer A. G. Evans, a romance that would remain historically enigmatic may well have sprouted between "the warder's daughter" and the handsome Irishman. Tantalizing clues have emerged from a small volume of bound vellum, the booklet signed, "By John Boyle O'Reilly, 13 March sixty eight, in the bush near Bunbury." The pages are filled not only with some twenty poems by O'Reilly, but also notes in a coded shorthand that defied translation until Perth historian Gillian O'Mara cracked some, though not all, of the keys.

"I wish she [Jessie] were not so fond of kissing [following words still untranslated]," one of O'Reilly's notations relates. Another asserts: "I am in love up to my ears . . . it would take a saint to give her up."

If, as seems likely, a deep love developed between the couple, the longer it went on, the more hopeless it would have become. Warder Woodman might have liked O'Reilly, but the notion that the official would ever have condoned a relationship between the Fenian and Jessie is absurd. That the two met clandestinely in secret spots outside Bunbury also appears probable, and local rumor would allege that Jessie became pregnant by O'Reilly. No concrete evidence supports the allegation. However, scholars poring over O'Reilly's state of mind in the twenty poems found in 1989 believe that the devoutly Catholic Fenian was grappling with guilt about a sexual relationship, despair over the hopeless-ness of that union and perhaps a change in Jessie's affections, along with visions of ignominious death in the bush country. Thoughts of escape nearly consumed him, adding to the torment his likely love for Jessie was causing him. The most revealing glimpses of O'Reilly's emotions by late 1868 are two poems under the single title "Night Thoughts":

> Have I no future left me?
> Is there no struggling ray
> From the sun of my life outshining
> Down on my darksome way?
> Will there no gleam of sunshine
> Cast o'er my path its light?
> Will there be no star of hope rise
> Out of this gloom of night?
>
> Have I 'gainst heaven's warnings

Sinfully, madly rushed?
Else why thus were my heart strings severed?
Why was my love-light crushed?

Oh! I have hopes and yearnings —
Hopes that I know are vain
And knowledge robs life of pleasure —
And Death of its only pain.

A. G. Evans speculates that in O'Reilly's novel *Moondyne*, the Irishman agonized over "deflowering" the warder's daughter:

> The moment of communion was reached at last, when her girlish life plunged with delicious expectation into the deep—and in one hideous instant she knew that for ever she had parted from the pure and beautiful, and was buried in an ocean of corruption and disappointment, rolled over by waves of unimaginable suffering and wrong.
>
> From the first deep plunge, stifled, agonized, appalled, she rose to the surface, only to behold the land receding from her view—the sweet fields of her innocent joyous girlhood fading in the distance.
>
> She raised her eyes, and saw heaven calm and beautiful above her . . . and she cried.

The second part of "Night Thoughts" hints that in the latter part of 1868, Jessie had either jilted or pulled away from O'Reilly because she had chosen a local farmer and suitor named George Pickersgill. O'Reilly's verse brims with distress and melancholia:

Oh! no! I would not love again

E'en had I still the power given;
I would not risk its pain and fears
E'en though its joys were taste of heaven.
A breath may blight the heart we prize;
A whisper weave deceit around it:
And then our heart's most tender chord
Is wounded by the chain that bound it.

'Tis hard to see death's chilling hand
The life-strings of our treasure sever:
But harder still when loving hearts
Are rudely rent apart for ever.
But ah! Such griefs are naught to those
That fill the heart where passion burned
Till falsehood burst the mask and showed
That love by heartless scorn returned.

Detractors of the theory that O'Reilly was suffering from the proverbial "broken heart" offer that he may well have fallen in love with Jessie, but that anything more than an unrequited love proved out of the question, as her mother would never have allowed her to slip off to meet a convict.

Few could doubt O'Reilly's plunging emotions by December 1868, and, with nothing but a lost or hopeless love and a life sentence facing him, a third and crushing emotional blow assailed him. The chief warder in Bunbury handed O'Reilly the correspondence he had been denied for the past six months. Among the letters, O'Reilly encountered the black-rimmed envelope that the official had waved in the prisoner's face earlier in 1868. John Boyle O'Reilly now learned that his mother, to whom he was devoted, had died.

Two days after Christmas 1868, O'Reilly carried letters to Bunbury and started back for the bush camp. A. G. Evans surmises that the Irishman might have stopped to see Jessie and left the visit crestfallen. O'Reilly wandered out into the bush to take his own life. A journal entry by Bunbury Police Sub-Inspector William Timperley recorded: "Started for the Vasse at 4 P.M. Overtook Dr. Lovegrove as far as Woodman's camp where the probationary constable [the title of convict letter-carriers] Riley [*sic*] one of the late head centres of Fenianism had attempted suicide by cutting the veins of his left arm and being accidentally discovered by another prisoner when in a faint from loss of blood . . . was saved."

Physically, O'Reilly soon recovered from his near-suicide, and Father McCabe, fully aware of the desperation destroying the young Fenian, was about to risk imprisonment himself to make good on his promise to help O'Reilly escape. The cleric would risk even more than prison time: the Catholic Church in Ireland had condemned Fenianism again and again and could request the excommunication of a Fenian priest.

A Path to the Sea

Early in January 1869, John Boyle O'Reilly tramped across the Bunbury horse-racing course on his rounds for Warder Woodman. His left wrist was still bandaged, the self-inflicted wounds there still raw.

He had heard rumors that in Britain, the new prime minister, William Gladstone, was determined to bring peace to Ireland and willing to remit the sentences of civilian Fenians imprisoned in Britain and Western Australia. In the *Fremantle Herald* and other Western Australian newspapers, letters and various news accounts from Britain speculated about the growing movement to release the civilian Fenians. But O'Reilly, Cranston, Darragh, Harrington, Hassett, Hogan, Wilson, and the other military Fenians understood that for them, neither release nor even a reduction of their life sentences was likely. The Duke of Cumberland, commander of the Royal Army, who had urged the Queen to hang all of the military Fenians eventually transported to Australia, would fight to keep O'Reilly and the other Fenian soldiers in servitude at least.

O'Reilly stopped at the sound of a "coo-ee" rising from the scrub. A brawny man stepped from a stand of trees with an ax slung over his shoulder.

"I'm a friend of Father Mac's," he said as he handed O'Reilly a card. O'Reilly read it and recognized the priest's handwriting.

The man introduced himself as Irish immigrant James Maguire, a local justice of the peace and chairman of a regional roads board. The thirty-four-year-old Maguire said that several American whaling ships would dock at Bunbury in February 1869 and that he and Father McCabe would pay one of the captains to let O'Reilly stow away on his vessel. Of course, if the water police were to search the ship, as was likely as soon as O'Reilly or any other prisoner "went missing" around Bunbury, and found him aboard, O'Reilly must vow not to reveal the names of any who had helped him.

Several weeks dragged on without a word from Father McCabe or Maguire. The sun during O'Reilly's second Australian summer was blistering, and his frustration mounted. Then, in February 1869, a local woodcutter strolling in from the bush passed O'Reilly, standing near the edge of the Koagulup camp, and murmured that a trio of American whaling barks had anchored off Bunbury and that O'Reilly should be ready. The woodcutter strode away, leaving O'Reilly wide-eyed, shaking, and smiling all at once.

While O'Reilly had worried that Maguire might be all talk and Father McCabe had thought better of his promise, the priest and his friend had placed their own futures in jeopardy by striking a deal with Captain Anthony Baker, master of the 215-ton American whaler *Vigilant.* McCabe paid the passage for O'Reilly, the priest having dipped into his own meager savings and raised the rest from closed-mouthed Irish parishioners sympathetic to the Fenians. Baker, accepting the cash, promised to pick up O'Reilly in international waters north of Bunbury, which meant that the Fenian had to find a way to meet the whaler twelve miles from the coast. Father McCabe told the shipmaster to leave that up to the plotters. All Baker needed to do was cruise off the coast for three days. If O'Reilly failed to show, Baker was to sail off with the money.

On or near February 13, 1869, as O'Reilly was walking to Bunbury with a satchel of letters, the unmistakable "coo-ee" of James Maguire stopped the Frenian again. Maguire stepped from the brush and asked, "Are you ready?"

"Yes!" O'Reilly exclaimed.

As O'Reilly's heart raced, Maguire explained that he was to sneak from camp on Wednesday evening of February 17, 1869, and head northeast—away from the water to temporarily throw pursuers off his track. Then O'Reilly was to meet Maguire, who would be waiting with horses, under an ancient gum tree on the Bunbury–Dardanup road.

Warder Woodman summoned O'Reilly on the morning of February 17 and handed him dispatches to carry to the Bunbury Depot. Startled because it was not one of his usual delivery days, O'Reilly feared that Woodman's business might keep the Irishman in town too late to return to camp and force him to report for the evening to the Bunbury jail. If he failed to show up at his rendezvous near the Bunbury–Dardanup, his only chance for escape—remote as that chance already was— would vanish. O'Reilly alternately ran and walked in the swelling heat and reached the depot by late morning to discover that the police cutter *Wild Wave* had recently docked with seven Fenian prisoners aboard. As he delivered the letters to the chief warder, he also learned that his comrades were languishing in the lockup, just a flight of stairs away from the official's office. The men had put up a fight when told they would be assigned to separate road gangs and would be shipped out to the bush the next day.

Perhaps wanting a last word with his old friends, O'Reilly saluted the warder, left the office, and marched toward the cells.

Several guards blocked his way and "ordered [him] off very smartly."

O'Reilly reported back to camp in the late afternoon and lay in the hammock of his ramshackle hut, pondering the likely fatal action he was about to take. Between 6 and 7 P.M., he penned his father a letter that outlined his escape plan. If he failed to turn up in America, O'Reilly wrote, his family could assume he had perished from the lash, the noose, or the elements of bush or sea. In all likelihood he planned to hand it to Maguire to mail; some would speculate that either Jessie Woodman or Father McCabe posted the letter.

A figure in the hut's open doorway pulled O'Reilly from his letter. Warder Woodman, on his 7 P.M. rounds to take a head count of his road gang, nodded at him. As the warder left the hut, he reminded O'Reilly that it was the Irishman's shift as "night constable," whose duty it was to prevent "absconders" from slipping out of camp. Woodman had hardly departed when another visitor, a fellow convict, appeared in O'Reilly's hut and asked him for a measure of tobacco. When the man stayed to chat, O'Reilly began to fidget, knowing that every wasted minute could make him late for his rendezvous. Finally, near 8 P.M., his visitor said good night to O'Reilly.

Eyeing the doorway, pulling off his convict boots, and shedding his uniform, with its hideous convict arrows, O'Reilly donned the civilian clothes that Maguire or perhaps Jessie had provided and he had hidden in the hut. He put on a pair of "freeman's boots," a crucial element of his impending flight; prisoners' boots were immediately recognizable to any tracker because of the unique pattern their spikes left.

O'Reilly looked around the hovel, extinguished the small lamp, slipped out the doorway, and walked quickly into the forest on the northeast rim of the camp. Praying that no one had spotted him in his civilian garb, he covered several hundred yards. Then, from behind him came the crunch of footsteps on dried brush. O'Reilly stiffened, turned, and waited.

Through a gap in the trees, a single figure materialized and walked straight up to O'Reilly. The man was no tracker or policeman—he wore a workman's jacket, trousers, and bush hat. As the man came closer and stopped a few feet away, O'Reilly recognized him as a mahogany sawyer named Tom Kelly, a ticket-of-leave Irishman, which meant he was a convict allowed to live freely outside Fremantle Gaol or the camps, but banned from leaving Western Australia until his five-year ticket had ended.

Kelly whispered: "Are you off?"

O'Reilly said nothing, his clothing an answer to the question.

When Kelly realized he would get no reply, he said, "I saw you talking to Maguire a month ago, and I knew it all."

Terror flooded O'Reilly's thoughts. If Kelly turned him in, a handsome "capture fee" awaited.

Kelly extended his hand. "God speed you," he said. "I'll put them on the wrong scent tomorrow if I can."

In the dark clearing, the two shook hands, and Kelly vanished into the woods as quickly as he had appeared.

O'Reilly turned quickly and headed to the northeast. He picked his way through brush and trees for more than three hours, the night sky above the bush country clear and awash in the glow of countless stars. Every step of the route, he listened for the snap of a twig or the cries of trackers' voices. Around midnight, he halted. A massive gumwood tree soared directly ahead, and just beyond, stretched the arid dirt track of the Bunbury–Dardanup Road. O'Reilly lay down near the thick base of the ancient tree trunk and waited. On the other side of the road stood the sagging wooden walls and collapsed rush roofs of an abandoned penal camp. As O'Reilly knew, no convict from that old road-gang station or any other such camp in Western Australia had ever made a successful escape. Brooding, he listened for Maguire's signal—not the "coo-ee" this time, but the whistled opening bars of the song "Patrick's Day."

He heard the notes a half-hour later, scrambled to his feet, and walked to the tree-shrouded edge of the road. Maguire and two other men, his cousin and a rescuer O'Reilly would later refer to only as "M," rode up, leading another horse for the ex-Hussar O'Reilly. Within seconds O'Reilly climbed into the saddle with the easy grace of a born cavalryman, and the four riders galloped northeast for the Collie River and their second rendezvous point, the Leschenault Estuary. O'Reilly reveled in the rhythm of the ride, the effect an almost intoxicating taste of action after the soul-deadening months of hard labor.

A few hours later, they reached the estuary, which was shielded by a long, low spit of land. Beyond it the Indian Ocean gleamed in the starlight. Three of Maguire's friends waited on horseback on the spit. Two of them, Irishmen Mickie Mackie, a Bunbury shoemaker, and Mark Lyons, held Fenian leanings so strong that they were putting their lives in jeopardy for a former soldier and centre they had never met. The third man, convicted burglar and ticket-of-leave man Joseph Buswell, was an Englishman who owned a fishing boat and whom Maguire and his friends trusted to keep his mouth closed for a fee.

O'Reilly's excitement escalated as he spotted the boat, a low-hulled craft equipped with oars and a sail, on the landward side of the spit.

The men all dismounted, scampered to the vessel, and lugged it across the spit to the waterline. As they slid the craft into the lagoon, climbed aboard, and fitted the oars to the oarlocks, "M" balked. When Maguire yelled at him to hurry, the man replied that he had promised his wife not to get on the boat. Maguire's cousin chided, "All right, go home to your wife!" Then the makeshift crew bent their backs and rowed into the lagoon.

With several hours before dawn, they pulled past Bunbury, O'Reilly crouching as low as he could. As the first glow of sunrise lit the horizon, the boat slid into the open waters of the Indian Ocean, only the faint white outlines of sand dunes marking the Australian coast. O'Reilly and the others kept rowing and watched for the first hint of a whaler sailing north.

By early afternoon, the sun was scorching and the *Vigilant* nowhere in sight. Hungry, thirsty, and concerned that a police cutter on its routine rounds might appear at any moment, Maguire decided to run the boat back to shore and try again the following morning. He assured the crestfallen O'Reilly that there was a three-day window for the whaler's departure and she would surely sail tomorrow.

Battling a high and quick surf, they rode the waves onto a broad expanse of beach and hauled the fishing boat onto a sandy shelf. Maguire and the others hid O'Reilly amid a stand of trees and told him to be patient as Maguire headed to Bunbury to find out what time the *Vigilant* would haul anchor and depart from Bunbury the next day. O'Reilly spent a long night listening for trackers and police. He killed a possum and ate it raw and, with a soldier's resourcefulness, covered himself in the sand with peppermint tree branches, which repelled snakes.

To his relief, his allies appeared early the following morning, February 19, 1869, with the news that the *Vigilant* had put out from Bunbury and was sailing northeast along the coast. One of the men climbed a sand dune and trained a telescope on the horizon.

The lookout dashed back to the others near 1 P.M.—he had spotted the *Vigilant*. The men raced to the fishing boat, pushed it down the shelf and into the surf, and rowed in a near-frenzy into open water. Maguire tied a white shirt to an oar and waved it again and again as the *Vigilant* came into sight, but a haze was rising to the east and swirling about the whaler. O'Reilly and the others shouted over and over, but the ship did not come about. They gaped helplessly as the whaler slowly turned west and sailed away, disappearing into the haze.

As they rowed back to shore, barely a word was said. Once the men beached the boat, O'Reilly, shaking his head again and again, followed Maguire and Lyons deep into a swamp where Lyons's brother-in-law, a man named Jackson, and Jackson's wife lived in a small hut and tended a herd of water buffalo. Apprised by Father McCabe of O'Reilly's suicide attempt and still volatile state of mind, Maguire did not want to leave O'Reilly alone in the dunes a second straight night.

Before Maguire left for Bunbury, he buoyed O'Reilly's sinking hopes by assuring him that Father McCabe would make arrangements to stow him aboard one of the other whalers—the *Classic* or the *Gazelle*—set to depart from Australia within the next week. As Maguire and the other rescuers left the hut, he urged O'Reilly to be patient for at least a week. Maguire did not tell O'Reilly that the police and trackers were likely searching for O'Reilly already from Koagulup to the dunes north of Bunbury. They were.

On February 19, 1869, Sub-Inspector Timperley of the Bunbury Police received a dispatch from Woodman: ". . . No. 9843 John O'Reilly has absconded from the Vasse road party." Woodman's report included, "I may also state that this same prisoner attempted suicide on the 27th of December last by cutting the veins in his arm."

Maguire, back in Bunbury, quickly discovered why the *Vigilant* had departed a day late. On the same night of O'Reilly's escape from the camp, a convict named Thompson had fled from his work detail, and the police had boarded and searched the whaler for him. He was not aboard, but the *Vigilant* was forced to sail the next morning, a day late for O'Reilly. Now, however, Timperley believed that O'Reilly had been concealed all along aboard that same departing whaler, but the police had not known it—had not yet received the report of his escape—as they vainly combed the vessel for Thompson.

On the day that O'Reilly and his would-be rescuers had vainly attempted to flag down the *Vigilant*, Timperley had interrogated Warder Woodman about his prisoner's disappearance. In either an outright lie or a mistake, Woodman contended he had seen O'Reilly at his convict constable post at 10:30 P.M. The father of O'Reilly's alleged paramour, Jessie, went a step further by stating that he had warned O'Reilly at that time to keep watch on a bush fire edging close to the camp. Perhaps hoping to buy time for O'Reilly, whom he apparently liked, or figuring that his daughter would be better off if O'Reilly slipped out of Australia or, more likely, died in the attempt, Woodman misled his fellow police in their search for the Fenian. The difference of at least two hours between O'Reilly's actual exit and one based on Woodman's statements led Timperley to calculate that O'Reilly could not have reached the *Vigilant* before she left on the morning tide at Bunbury on February 19. Now the question was whether the prisoner had slipped into the bush or was hidden in the dunes.

On February 20, police officers and Aborigine trackers scoured the dunes and inlets north of Bunbury, searching futilely for any of the distinctive spike marks of the convict boot. Timperley also boarded the *Classic* and the *Gazelle* in Bunbury Harbor, but his men found no sign of O'Reilly as they prodded heaps of spare sails with steel poles and bayonets and searched the bilges and the vessel's nooks from bow to stern. They peered at the faces of the crewmen, but found only the typical New England whaling contingent: a handful of Yankee officers and the rest of the faces Malay, Portuguese, or Cape Verdean, with the occasional Indian in the mix. Before the police marched back down the gangplanks, they offered five pounds sterling to anyone who turned in O'Reilly. They had posted the same offer onshore in Bunbury.

However, Timperley held no great hopes that anyone would turn in O'Reilly: "I am . . . certain that many would assist a Fenian who would not stir a hand or foot for an ordinary prisoner of the Crown." In Western Australia, many did not view the Fenians as criminals, but as political prisoners; O'Reilly was finding that out not only from transplanted Irishmen such as Maguire, Mackie, and Lynch, but also from the Jacksons and even a bonafide English criminal such as Buswell.

In the provincial capital of Perth, Police Superintendent Hare, as an Orangeman, a staunch Protestant, and one who loathed Irish Catholics in general and Fenians in particular, erupted at news of O'Reilly's escape and the Bunbury police force's floundering search for the Irishman. When Timperley reported that he was convinced that O'Reilly had somehow gotten aboard the *Vigilant,* Hare retorted, "Is any horse missing in the neighborhood, for O'Reilly was a cavalry soldier?"

Timperley offered: "That O'Reilly has friends, I can have no doubt, having had constant and frequent opportunity for communicating with different persons while traveling about as a constable [convict courier] . . ."

None of the police thought to ask Father Patrick McCabe about O'Reilly's whereabouts. He was well-liked, respected, and immersed in building his new church in Bunbury. Or so the authorities assumed. As squads of officers and trackers combed the dunes and the bush, the priest, who had just paid the large sum of twenty-six pounds to a local carpenter to construct the church's floor and carve altar rails, struck a different sort of deal.

Father McCabe met with Captain David R. Gifford in Bunbury and negotiated a new opportunity for O'Reilly, paying Gifford ten pounds to pick up the wanted man in international waters northeast of the port.

In the Jacksons' hut, O'Reilly brooded about the *Vigilant* and agonized that the whaler was still searching for him. He worried that with the police hunting for him, Father McCabe would not find another American captain willing to take the Fenian aboard. When the Jacksons' son Matthew told O'Reilly of a discarded dory (a flat-bottomed craft) abandoned in the sand six or seven miles north, O'Reilly decided to act on his own, defying Maguire's instructions to stay put.

O'Reilly sneaked out of the hut early on February 22, 1869, and trudged some seven miles along the deserted shoreline at risk of running into trackers every step of the route. If caught he knew what awaited: he would be dragged off in chains to Fremantle to await a hundred lashes and solitary confinement or the noose dangling from the steel crossbeam of the prison's scaffold. Still, he wandered northward, searching for the dory. He found it on a desolate, scrub-choked patch of shore. As he stooped to brush off the sand, gaps in the craft's seams appeared. The oars, however, seemed in decent shape. For the next few hours, he gathered strips of paper-bark from several trees beyond the dunes and stuffed them into the open seams as makeshift caulking. The job stretched into the late afternoon, so O'Reilly decided to trek back to the hut for some rest and come back to the dory at dusk the following day. After heaping sand atop the boat in case trackers happened upon it, he backtracked to the Jacksons' home.

Near dusk of February 23, 1869, he returned to the dory, carrying a satchel of possum meat and a length of rope with which he tied the satchel to the stern to keep the meat cool. He dragged the dory to the water, pushed it into the surf, climbed into it, and rowed out to sea. Not a sailor, O'Reilly pulled straight out from shore but wisely kept the coastline just in sight, reckoning that he must be at least ten miles out—enough for the *Vigilant* to spot him if she was still in the vicinity. The hours dragged on, his arms deadening, the waves sloshing over the shallow craft. Sometime that night several sharp thumps jarred the boat. Sharks had found the satchel of meat dangling at the stern, and their fins sliced the water inches from O'Reilly.

At sunrise, O'Reilly rubbed his bleary eyes, encrusted with salt spray, and peered at the horizon. Only the spreading light across the turquoise waters greeted him. The sun climbed higher, and the heat enveloped him. The dory drifted.

Near noon, something in the distance caught O'Reilly's eye. A sail slowly took shape, then another. As a dark hull materialized and grew larger with each moment, O'Reilly shook with relief and elation. The *Vigilant* loomed closer, drawing so near that he heard the shouts of officers and crew, cries that must mean he had been spotted. Then slowly, with a creak of rigging and the sudden crack of canvas billowing with a breeze, the whaler began to turn away from O'Reilly and head straight west. He rowed furiously, but the distance lengthened, and by nightfall he could no longer make out the sails on the horizon. His mind numb, he brought his dory about and began the long pull for shore, his muscles protesting, his throat raw and parched. Somehow, he rowed back to the beach where he had found the dory, dragged it back to its original resting place, covered it with sand again, and staggered off into the dunes. He collapsed in a sandy stretch shaded by pepperbark trees, shrubs, and sand hills. "After that," he would say, "I left the sand-valley no more." Drained in every way, he spent the next five days there sleeping and regaining his strength.

Maguire and two other men found O'Reilly there and escorted him back to Jackson's hut. Huddling around a storm lantern casting its pale light across O'Reilly's haggard face, Maguire broke the news that Father McCabe had arranged a rendezvous with the *Gazelle*. O'Reilly was delighted, and Maguire handed him a letter from the priest, who had asked the military Fenian to "remember me in your prayers." Tomorrow, Maguire told O'Reilly, they would row out to the New Bedford whaler.

Within moments O'Reilly's mood darkened as Maguire introduced him to one of the other men. Thomas Henderson, a convict who also went by the name Martin Bowman, was neither a friend of Maguire's nor McCabe's, but had somehow found out about the plan to free O'Reilly (some have suggested he overheard one of the plotters in Bunbury). Henderson had a reputation as a thief, attempted murderer, and perennial troublemaker at Millbank and had been transported to Fremantle aboard the *Runnymede* in the late 1850s. Loathed by warders and fellow prisoners, described as an "incorrigible scoundrel" by Comptroller-General Wakeford, Bowman was denied a conditional pardon, but wrangled a ticket-of-leave to live and work outside Fremantle, although not outside of the Bunbury area. He had approached Maguire and threatened to turn the rescuers in unless they took him to the *Gazelle*.

Maguire and his friends might well have killed Bowman but would not risk implicating Father McCabe in murder. Stuck with the blackmailer, Maguire and now O'Reilly worried that Captain Gifford would take one look at the unexpected passenger—a common criminal—and refuse to take anyone aboard. Still, the Fenian and his helpers had no choice.

Throughout the long night of March 2, 1869, O'Reilly and his friends found little sleep. O'Reilly later noted the hours passed with "someone always keeping an eye on Bowman." O'Reilly would write: "He [Bowman] was all evil, envious, and cruel; detested by the basest, yet self-contained, full of jibe and derision, satisfied with his own depravity, and convinced that everyone was just as vile as he." In short, Bowman was just the sort whom O'Reilly craved escape from—even at the risk of death.

As the sun of March 3, 1869, began to rise and break across the dunes, O'Reilly embraced the Jacksons. Little he said could convey his thanks to the family, and Jackson and his son Matthew accompanied the military Fenian, Maguire, his friend James Milligan, and Bowman to the beach, where they helped shove the fishing boat into the lagoon. Then, as the Jacksons, standing in the surf, waved farewell, the other four men rowed northeast. By noon, the craft bobbed some three miles from the coast, and through a telescope borrowed from Buswell they could glimpse Bunbury—and two ships under full sail gliding on a northerly course from the port. The carved figurehead of a gazelle beneath the bowsprit of one vessel confirmed its identity. The rowers pulled frantically for open waters and the rendezvous, O'Reilly praying that the *Gazelle* would stop for him. In hiding for nearly two weeks, he could not endure much more of life on the run.

They had reached the general rendezvous area by dusk and could still make out a sail on the western horizon. All they could do was to wait, as they could never catch up to the distant whaler, and hope that the ship was the *Gazelle*.

At nightfall, the "wide-away" ship turned and sailed straight toward the fishing boat. A cheer burst from O'Reilly and Maguire, and as the trim black-and-red hull of the whaler loomed larger, a shout came from its deck: "O'Reilly!"

O'Reilly called back. The *Gazelle* pulled close, but not so close as to swamp the smaller craft, and the rowers eased the fishing boat alongside the whaler. For the first time in his life, a broad Yankee accent filled O'Reilly's ears: "Come aboard!"

A rope ladder cascaded over the *Gazelle*'s gunwales and into the fishing boat. O'Reilly clambered up the ladder onto a shelf packed with tied-down barrels of sperm oil and was hauled aboard by a grinning, broad-shouldered New Bedford salt named Henry C. Hathaway. A lifelong friendship between Hathaway, who was the vessel's third mate, and O'Reilly was beginning now in the waters off Australia and would lead back there several years later.

Captain Gifford, convinced by McCabe that O'Reilly was a patriot and political prisoner, clasped the Irishman's hand and promised him safe passage. As Bowman hopped aboard, however, the Yankee shipmaster glared at him. Father McCabe had explained to Gifford that the blackmailer could ruin everyone— including the captain—in the plot; Gifford ordered crewmen to escort the convict to the ship's forecastle and watch him until the ship put in at the first safe port and dump him there.

Standing with Gifford and Hathaway at the gunwales, O'Reilly turned around to bid his friends good-bye. Maguire, beaming, tears streaming, stood up in the boat, cupped his hands to his mouth, and cried: "God bless you! Don't forget us, and don't mention our names until it is all over!"

Tears poured down O'Reilly's face too as he waved, so choked that he could not say a word in reply. As the *Gazelle* turned west and toward freedom for the Fenian, he prayed for his comrades: Hogan, languishing in solitary at Fremantle; Cranston, Darragh, Harrington, Hassett, and Wilson, all of them weakening more in body and spirit each day in the road gangs and in the quarries. O'Reilly vowed that in America, he would not forget them. They must be saved.

Part 2
A Voice from the Tomb

We Must Not Despair

The news that John Boyle O'Reilly had escaped and not been found sent shock waves through Western Australia. His fellow Fenians in Fremantle Gaol and scattered in the colony's quarries and construction gangs were elated, but they worried as months passed without a word from "Boyle," as they called him. Penal officials were enraged that a convict who did not even have a ticket-of-leave had beaten The Establishment for the first time.

In the summer of 1870, Father McCabe received a letter from O'Reilly, who used another name, and quietly spread the news that the ex-Hussar had reached Boston, Massachusetts, cheating the sharks, the elements, and the warders of Western Australia. McCabe's letter back to O'Reilly informed him that his comrades were ecstatic that he had pulled it off and that Jessie Woodman's father had incurred nothing more than a stiff reprimand for O'Reilly's escape, a fact that soothed O'Reilly, as the warder had taken a genuine liking to him and may well have bought him the time he needed to elude his pursuers in those first days amid the dunes of Western Australia. O'Reilly soon took a job as a reporter with the *Boston Pilot* and began to carve a stellar career as a journalist, poet, and novelist. Thoughts of his comrades still wasting away in the penal colony, however, tore at him. He could not and would not forget them, and was resolved to help them somehow.

In mid-1870, a series of stunning directives from the British government of Prime Minister William E. Gladstone were sent to the superintendents of prisons from Millbrook to Fremantle. Honoring Gladstone's commitment to assuage tensions in Ireland, the Crown and Parliament granted conditional pardons to the civilian Fenians in the jails. The stipulation was that they could not return to Ireland or to any part of Britain. Many of the released Fenians chose to start a life in Australia. Others, including John Devoy, gaunt but still defiant after his years of hard labor at Millbank, opted for America.

Devoy arrived in New York City with five other Fenian notables aboard the steamship *Cuba* in late January 1871 and received a heroes' welcome from the Irish community in the United States. To the surprise of the British government, even American newspapers with little sympathy for the Irish acclaimed the *"Cuba* Five" and other Fenians making their way to America as political prisoners, not criminals, as the Crown still maintained.

Almost immediately, Devoy immersed himself in America's Irish Republican Brotherhood, whose membership was swelling and seething with plans to reignite revolt in Ireland. Now known as Clan na Gael, the organization quickly appointed Devoy as one of its officers. Meanwhile, like O'Reilly, Devoy turned to journalism, eventually landing a slot as a reporter for the pro-Irish *New York Herald* and worked his way up to night-desk editor. Also like O'Reilly, Devoy could not forget the military Fenians still languishing in Western Australia. He would soon be starkly reminded of their ongoing plight.

Although the Crown had acceded to the release of civilian

Fenians, it would not budge in its view of the military Fenians, who were adjudged "traitor[s] pure and simple." The chief obstacle to any hopes that O'Reilly's former brothers-in-arms could gain probation or conditional pardon was the Duke of Cambridge, commander-in-chief of the Royal Army. Devoy sardonically wrote:

> The Duke of Cambridge . . . interposed an objection against the military prisoners, and his word was law with his august cousin Queen Victoria. Releasing these Fenian soldiers, he said, would be subversive of discipline in the army, and as the duke was a great soldier, as soldiers go near the top of the army in England, that settled it. He had won distinction in the Crimea by promptly falling from his horse . . . and had to nurse a dislocated shoulder at home in England during the balance of the war. But Cambridge knew all about discipline and red tape, and he was quite sure it would have a bad effect on the army to let those Fenian fellows free.

In early 1870 in Boston, O'Reilly received several letters including one from his old friend Denis Cashman, released from The Establishment and newly landed in San Francisco. O'Reilly immediately wired him train fare to Boston and a job on the *Pilot*. Cashman was soon on his way.

Another of those letters anguished O'Reilly, reminding him that his fellow Fenian soldiers were dying a little more each day in the bush and the rock pits. Thomas Hassett, his letter smuggled out to Father McCabe and mailed by the priest, related: "It is my birthday as I write this, and I know I am turning it to the best account by writing to such a dear old friend. Who knows?

Perhaps I may be able to spend the next one with you. If not, then we will hope for the following one. At all events, we must not despair."

The Duke of Cambridge's determination that the military Fenians in Western Australia would serve every day of their life sentences filled Cranston, Darragh, Harrington, Hassett, Hogan, Wilson, and their comrades with despair. Caught up by the very desperation that he had warned against in his letter to O'Reilly, twenty-four-year-old Thomas Hassett hatched an escape plan in the Australian winter of 1870, shortly after the first news that only civilian Fenians would receive conditional pardons.

In June 1870, Hassett decided he could not withstand another day on a road gang and turned his plan to action. The soldier who had walked from his sentry post at Kilmainham and straight to Curran's slipped away from his work party's encampment in the bush, "with his eyes on the doom and danger" of his flight. Since O'Reilly's escape, the water police routinely searched all foreign ships in Bunbury's waters, but Hassett was determined that he, too, would follow O'Reilly's "path to the sea." He worked his way to the port, finding refuge and a little money from Fenian sympathizers along the route. Outside Bunbury, an Irish family hid him for months as he tried to make arrangements through Father McCabe and other locals for passage aboard an American ship. When an American whaling captain agreed to take him aboard for the hefty sum of thirty pounds, Hassett tried to raise the money from pardoned Fenians in the region, his friends conveying his verbal pleas as he hid from the police, who, even though ten months had passed, suspected that he was concealed somewhere near the port. The funds never arrived, and the whaler weighed anchor without him.

Risking all, Hassett stole down to the Bunbury docks in May 1871, sneaked aboard the American vessel *Southern Belle,* and hid under some tarpaulins. As the crew made ready to depart the harbor, the water police marched aboard and searched the ship. Hassett climbed out of his hiding place seconds before the police could slam their long steel probes into him.

The police chained him and dragged him to the Bunbury lockup. Not long afterward, he was shipped back to The Establishment, where he was sentenced to six-months' solitary confinement and three years in a Swan River work gang known as one of the most brutal in the colony. Hassett had "grasped the flower [of freedom] but to clutch the sting." In many ways, both physically and emotionally, the tough, daring Hassett would never recover from the effects of his punishment.

In the summer of 1871, Peter Curran, who had turned up in New York after his conditional pardon, walked up to Devoy's desk at the *New York Herald* and handed him a letter from one of Hassett's comrades. The envelope bore a Bunbury postmark and the name of Father Patrick McCabe.

As Devoy opened the letter and began to read, he was jolted by memories of those meetings at Curran's public house over six years ago. A newspaper article chronicling the jubilant reception in New York for the *Cuba* Five and including Curran's new address, had been smuggled into The Establishment, probably by Father McCabe. The words of Martin Hogan riveted Devoy:

Perth, Western Australia, May 20th, 1871

My Dear Friend,
In order that you may recollect who it is that addresses you, you will remember on the night of January 17th, 1866, some of the Fifth Dragoon Guards being in the old house in Clare Lane with John Devoy and Captain McCafferty. I am one of that unfortunate band and am

now under sentence of life penal servitude in one of the darkest corners of the earth, and as far as we can learn from any small news that chances to reach us, we appear to be forgotten, with no prospects before us but to be left in hopeless slavery to the tender mercies of the Norman wolf.

But, my dear friend, it is not my hard fate that I deplore, for I willingly bear it for the sake of dear old Ireland, but I must feel sad at the thought of being forgotten, and neglected by those more fortunate companions in enterprise who have succeeded in eluding the grasp of the oppressor. If I had the means, I could get away . . . . I therefore address you in the hope that you will endeavor to procure and send me pecuniary help for that purpose and I will soon be with you.

Give my love and regards to all old friends . . . Devoy . . . McCafferty and others, not forgetting yourself and Mrs., and believe me that, even though it should be my fate to perish in this villainous dungeon of the world, the last pulse of my heart shall beat "God Save Ireland."

Direct your letter to Rev. Father McCabe, Fremantle. Do not put my name on the outside of the letter.

Yours truly,
Martin J. Hogan

Shaken by the letter, Devoy knew that he was obligated to these men whom he had known and who still suffered. Believing himself personally responsible for their flight because at their court-martials later, they had been convicted in large part due to their connection to him, Devoy wrote, "I felt that I, more than any man then living, ought to do my utmost for these Fenian soldiers."

Through letters that Father McCabe smuggled into Fremantle Gaol, Devoy told Hogan and Wilson that he, Devoy, was working on a plan for their rescue. He did not reveal that his initial attempts to persuade Clan na Gael's board members that they all had a moral obligation to save the military Fenians' lives met with little enthusiasm. The organization's leaders responded with protests that a rescue attempt would be too dangerous and therefore a waste of funds needed to ignite another revolt in Ireland.

John Bull Has Not Succeeded in Reforming Us

John Devoy kept up his one-man campaign for the Fenian soldiers, but as 1871 and 1872 passed without any real promise of a rescue, the months took their increasing physical and emotional toll on the military prisoners in The Establishment and in the bush. Other letters for Devoy soon arrived from both Hogan and James Wilson, who was wasted with fever and dysentery and "nearly worked to death." From Devoy, frustrated and unwilling to write a letter that would further dash the flagging hopes of the ex-soldiers, Hogan and Wilson received no correspondence for much of 1873.

John Boyle O'Reilly, tormented by nightmares of his imprisonment, feeling guilty at times that he was now free while the agony of Hogan, Wilson, and his other Establishment comrades stretched on, had urged Devoy and Clan na Gael to act on their behalf as early as February 1871. "Remember your military compatriots," he exhorted, "who carried your principles into the ranks of the British Army, and who now suffer for it, [so that they] may soon be permitted to rejoin you here."

On September 4, 1873, Wilson wrote to Devoy: "Month after month we were waiting with eager eyes and beating hearts the arrival of the mail, expecting to hear from you what we were sure would be glad tidings; but we were doomed to disappointment . . ."

Wilson described beatings, solitary confinement in which prisoners were left naked in dank, dark cells for months at a time, poor food that had turned the military Fenians into skeltons, and emotional tortures inflicted by the warders "of so base a nature that it would be wrong to hide them." He wrote of the despair that the former soldiers felt each time they thought of the pardoned civilian Fenians who had said good-bye with assurances that they would work for the release of their comrades left behind in The Establishment.

Relating news that would distress John Boyle O'Reilly, Wilson wrote that Patrick Keating, formerly of the Fifth Guards, was dying, wracked by malnourishment and heart woes and lying in a prison hospital bed for more than a year. To Devoy, Wilson appealed:

> Let me tell you that Martin [Hogan] and I expect you to do something for us. We look upon you as our leader and chief, and as such we expect that you will not forget your humble followers but that you will try to get us out of this mare's nest that we have got into. I must tell you that we are much altered in appearance, from young men we have become old ones, that our hair is now of a nice grey colour. . . . It is now seven years last month since we were tried, a pretty good apprenticeship in the trade of a lag [convict], and yet you know that John Bull has not succeeded in reforming us. I am afraid he never will. . . . Now I hope that on receipt of this you will write in return and let us know what we have to expect.

In that same letter, Wilson proposed an escape modeled on that of O'Reilly: "There are some good ports where whalers are in the habit of calling. . . . And if we had the means of purchasing horses [we] could make it through the bush to the coast where the vessel might be and so clear out. . . . "

Devoy did not have the heart to reply that, for the moment, the prisoners could expect little from his fellow Clan na Gael members.

As Wilson continued to appeal to Devoy in his letters, Hogan did likewise and also sent letters to his father, who lived on Barrington Street in Limerick City, Ireland. The elder Hogan passed his son's pleas for help to local IRB men who had eluded arrest in the 1860s and, while diminished, were still plotting against Britain.

Neither Martin Hogan nor James Wilson received a letter from Devoy for nearly nine months. Despondent over his declining health and by the death of Keating, who had succumbed from "aneurism of the main artery . . . brought on by the rigors of imprisonment," Wilson composed one last appeal to Devoy in the Australian summer of 1874 and got it into Father McCabe's hands.

When the long letter reached Devoy at the *Herald* in June 1874, shame, guilt, and a renewed determination to somehow rescue the military Fenians engulfed him. Wilson wrote:

> Dear Friend,
> I think it my duty to make this appeal to you; my duty to my comrades as well as to myself because no man should surrender himself to death and despair without making some effort to save himself. . . .
>
> Dear Friend, remember this is a voice from the tomb.

For is not this a living tomb? In the tomb it is only a man's body that is good for worms, but in the living tomb the canker worm of care enters the very soul. Think that we have been nearly nine years in this living tomb since our first arrest and that it is impossible for mind or body to withstand the continual strain that is upon them. One or the other must give way. It is in this sad strait that I now, in the name of my comrades and myself, ask you to aid us in the manner pointed out. . . . We ask you to aid us with your tongue and pen, with your brain and intellect, with your ability and influence, and God will bless your efforts, and we will repay you with all the gratitude of our natures . . . our faith in you is unbounded. We think if you forsake us, then we are friendless indeed."

Wilson's closing lines echoed the Fenian oath and further prodded Devoy: "In the hour of trial we flinched not . . . the greenest spot in our memory is connected with you, and . . . we never forget that we are still soldiers of liberty."

No longer would Devoy defer in any way to the hesitation of Clan na Gael. Determining not to rest until a plan to wrest the military Fenians from "the jaws of the British lion," he began again his search for "money, a ship, and a strong wind." He also knew he would need to talk with the only military Fenian who had found his path to the sea from Western Australia, John Boyle O'Reilly.

With the 1874 Clan na Gael national convention slated for July 15–22 in Baltimore, Devoy frantically devised a rescue plan to pitch to the board members at the gathering. He met somewhere in upstate New York or Connecticut with conditionally pardoned Fenian Thomas McCarthy Fennell to get the "lay of the land" around Fremantle and Bunbury and to ask him if he thought a seaborne rescue of all the remaining military prisoners was feasible. Fennell not only urged Devoy to take action, but also suggested that "a vessel be purchased, laden with some legitimate cargo, sailed to Australia and under some ruse free the prisoners."

Devoy boarded a train for Baltimore in the second week of July 1874. In his pocket were two letters, one from Hogan and one from Wilson.

On July 15, 1874, Devoy and sixty other Clan na Gael delegates, representing eighty-six branches throughout the United States, convened, and from the opening moments, the journalist took the arms of each man and implored them to consider the straits of the Fenians of Fremantle. At a private conference of the organization's five-member board, presided over by Fenian stalwart Jeremiah Kavanagh of Louisville, Kentucky, Devoy delivered an impassioned speech on the prisoners' behalf. He showed them his letters, and Wilson's missive stunned them, some of them questioning whether his grim and desperate words were genuine. Devoy convinced them of their authenticity by showing them the envelope's Australian postmark and Father McCabe's name. Then he described a potential rescue effort that was a more belligerent variation of Fennell's proposal: "My idea was that we should send from twelve to fifteen carefully selected men, fully armed, on a ship calling at an Australian port, get them ashore in some unobserved way after a man sent by a steamer had perfected his plan of rescue, and take the prisoners off, by main force if necessary."

Devoy wrote: "I proposed the resolution with a full sense of the risk involved in entrusting the knowledge to such a gathering and the necessity of later making it known in a more guarded way to the whole membership"—over 6,300 and swelling each week—of the organization."

Devoy cleared his first barrier when the committee agreed to cautiously endorse the proposal and put it to the entire body of delegates. As Devoy stood at a podium and presented his rescue plan to the rest of the delegates, many gaped at him; others interrupted with skeptical questions. Devoy pressed on, his speech passionate and incisive, jabbing the consciences of the men— especially those who had served time in British prisons. Then Devoy held up Martin Hogan's letter and began to read. In an instant only Devoy's voice filled the hall. He omitted Father McCabe's name, unwilling to risk any "loose lips" that could implicate the priest for his Fenian sympathies.

Following the speech, Devoy's proposal was put to a vote. The delegates decided unanimously in favor of a rescue. In short order they selected a committee of ten men, with Devoy as chairman, to plan the attempt. Devoy would shoulder most of the work with four others—John W. Goff, of New York; James Reynolds, of New Haven, Connecticut; John C. Talbot, of San Francisco; and Patrick Mahon, of Rochester, New York.

Entitled the Australian Prisoners Rescue Committee, the body's first task was to raise funds. Clan na Gael had amassed a war chest of forty-two thousand dollars over the past seven years, but the organization's charter banned the use of that money for anything other than an insurrection in Ireland. To finance the potential rescue, Devoy and his friends took a huge gamble: they printed not only Hogan's letter, but also Wilson's "voice from the tomb" letter, and sent copies with a rough outline of the rescue scheme to each Clan na Gael branch, praying that an informer would not tip off British officials. Donations came in from laundresses and ditchdiggers as well as from bankers, attorneys, physicians, and Irish men and women all over the United States moved by the anguish of Wilson and Hogan.

The committee reported:

The subscriptions came in slowly and the project met with opposition in many branches, but finally, when it was ascertained that from six to seven thousand dollars had been raised, a meeting of the committee was called and the matter laid before it. Seeing that there was not money enough to purchase and fit out a ship, it was thought that a bargain might be made with a whaler to call at a port agreed on in Western Australia and take the men on board when agents sent by steamer before-hand should have effected a rescue. The difficulties in the way were clearly seen, and the danger of failing to connect with a ship which could be more profitably employed in whaling than in waiting for the chance of a successful rescue was a source of anxiety, but for want of funds no other plan seemed then feasible.

On Friday, January 29, 1875, Devoy took a train to Boston to meet with O'Reilly to discuss the rescue plan. A letter he had received in mid-December 1874 from O'Reilly had fired his curiosity. O'Reilly suggested: "The only way to do your work clean, sure, and well *is by a New Bedford Whaler.* The more I think of it, the easier it does appear to me."

Now the editor of the *Boston Pilot* and a well-known figure in Brahmin Boston's literary and social circles, O'Reilly remained an Irish patriot who reviled informers, adding a warning to his letter: "Above all things you should keep your *means of proceeding* a secret. The crowd may know [what] you are doing; but they ought not to know—not half a dozen men should know—*how it was to be done.*"

Devoy took O'Reilly's warning to heart. Rumors of a plot to free the military Fenians did reach the British embassies in New York and Washington, but referred to a purported "Fenian raider" that would sail to Fremantle and storm the town and prison to rescue the Irish prisoners. Along the docks of America's eastern seaports, British spies and informers watched for any sign that Clan na Gael might be readying a warship, but found nothing. Several dispatches wired to the Foreign Office in London dismissed the "Fenian raider" scenario as a fiction.

On Monday, February 1, 1875, Devoy walked into the *Pilot* offices, in the heart of Boston's commercial district. The bustle of the newsroom brought a knowing grin to the dark-bearded night editor of the *Herald* as O'Reilly, his sleeves rolled up, came over to the visitor and clutched his hand. Then, O'Reilly, calling for Denis Cashman to join them, grabbed his coat and led Devoy across the traffic-choked street to Marliave's Café, the gathering place for Boston's journalists and authors.

Settling into the leather-cushioned booth where O'Reilly and Cashman sat five or six times a week, they discussed the rescue plans, constantly looking around to make sure that the wrong ears were not listening. O'Reilly convinced Devoy that Clan na Gael should buy a whaler and find a veteran Yankee skipper to sail it to Western Australia. Smoking a cigar and jabbing it in the air to emphasize his point, O'Reilly said that his friend Henry Hathaway, the man who had pulled O'Reilly aboard the *Gazelle*, could put Devoy in touch with the right people in New Bedford— men who would keep their mouths shut.

Devoy wrote, "[O'Reilly] offered to come with me and introduce me to Hathaway if I could wait till Tuesday, Monday being [O'Reilly's] busy day. Gladly consented, knowing his influence with Hathaway."

That evening, inside O'Reilly's trim brick town house on Winthrop Street in the Boston neighborhood of Charlestown, Devoy and O'Reilly sat in front of the fireplace in O'Reilly's study long after O'Reilly's wife, Mary (Murphy), had gone to bed. They talked of the old days at Curran's and Pilsworth's, of their ordeals in British prisons, and most of all, of their moral duty to save their comrades in Fremantle.

O'Reilly was up early the next morning, Tuesday, February 2, 1875, to rush off to the newspaper office. In midmorning, Devoy walked into the *Pilot* to find O'Reilly tied up with work. He handed Devoy a letter of introduction to Hathaway, assuring him that Hathaway would know exactly how to proceed, and Devoy walked several blocks to the train station and boarded the afternoon train to New Bedford.

When he stepped from the train and onto the platform at New Bedford, near the harbor, countless masts jutted into sight, and the mixed odors of fish, whale oil, and hemp assailed his nostrils. Gulls wheeled and darted all along the waterfront, adding their shrieks to the din of dockside wagons and carts that groaned beneath the weight of barrels loaded with sperm oil.

Devoy gazed at the address O'Reilly had inked on the envelope—New Bedford Police Station, Water Street.

Until This Thing Is Settled

John Devoy strode along the ice-slicked paving stones of Water Street and halted in front of a stark granite building with a pitched roof. His battered valise in one hand and O'Reilly's letter tucked in his coat pocket, the Irishman strode through the arched doorway and into the New Bedford Police Station. At the reception desk, he asked a blue-coated constable for Captain Henry Hathaway. The officer nodded, vanished down the hall for a few minutes and returned with the brawny, fortyish New Bedford Chief of Night Police, who glowered at this stranger Devoy.

The Irishman handed Hathaway O'Reilly's letter and waited. As soon as he saw the familiar handwriting, Hathaway's demeanor changed. Devoy recorded the meeting in his reporter's shorthand style:

> When I gave him O'Reilly's note, [I] saw a good effect produced at once. . . . [He] told me quietly to follow him. Went into courthouse [next door] and locked door.

Sat down and talked whole thing over. Entered warmly into project. Found he knew all about our men. Recommended strongly the buying of a vessel and gave solid reasons why any other course would not be safe. Showed how it could be made to pay expenses. Splendid physique; handsome, honest face; quite English-looking. Wears only side-whiskers; very reserved in manner; speaks low and slowly, but every word fits. Never without a cigar in his mouth. Eighteen years to sea, whaling all the time.

Devoy left the courthouse convinced that Hathaway measured up to everything that O'Reilly had said at Marliave's: "There was one man in all the world best fitted to give counsel and aide in such an enterprise [the rescue plan] . . . Captain Henry C. Hathaway. . . . He had retired from the perilous adventures of his youth . . . only his loyalty and courage had not changed with the years. He entered into the plan with zeal, bringing to the council the best attributes of an American sailor, a warm heart, and a cool head."

As Devoy had just discovered, Hathaway, who had shared his cabin on the *Gazelle* with O'Reilly, had heard firsthand of the horrors of The Establishment and had quickly compared the Fenians to the rebels who had fought for American freedom from Britain a century ago. Although Hathaway had no Irish forebears, his bond with O'Reilly extended to any Irishman, whether in New Bedford or in a penal road gang in the bush, for whom his friend vouched.

In his first night in a New Bedford waterfront boarding house, Devoy composed the first of many letters from the seaport, straining his eyes in the sputtering glow of a cheap whale-oil lamp, the dull thumps of hulls against the wharves with each swell of the tide like some maritime metronome. Devoy's thoughts raced as he scratched out his impressions of Hathaway to James Reynolds:

From John Devoy to James Reynolds.
NEW BEDFORD,
3 February, 1875

My Dear R.,

I only got here this evening, having met with considerable though unavoidable delay in Boston. I have seen the man [Hathaway] I expected to meet and found him to be up to my highest expectations.

A trustworthy man will be starting this spring, but he can't possibly get to *where we want him* till next January or February. That is a bad job, but there is only one way of bettering it. A ship could be bought and fitted out for $12,000, to go there direct—ostensibly on a whaling voyage—and bring them straight to San Francisco, where it should be sold for $4,000 or $5,000. By doing a little whaling or taking a cargo *all the other expenses could be cleared.* It would have to be kept a profound secret and should clear in the regular way. There is a very trustworthy man in the business here, an Irishman named McCulloch, who could be got to do the whole of that part of the work.

I have to wait some days here to look into the whole thing and I may be able to arrange for a meeting with you by Sunday. You must manage to come some time as it is necessary to have a witness to prevent misunderstandings hereafter.

I see no way of doing it in less than fifteen or sixteen

months except if we get a ship, and the money must be got some way—by loan or any other feasible method.

This would be far cheaper in the end as it would pay for itself, or nearly so and do the work quicker. We can't go back on this matter and I am decidedly in favour of borrowing what we are short from the other funds at once. I will write to all F.C. [Finance Committee], to same effect.

I may, between Boston and New York, be able to raise $2,000 more through private sources and perhaps more, but I may also fail entirely. Fifteen thousand would ensure complete success and leave us a fund after for such purposes.

Drop me a line, care of O'Reilly, *Pilot* Office, and I will get it.

I will stay around here till this thing is settled one way or the other. I shall have something more definite in a day or two and will let you know at once.

Yours,

J. D.

Having arranged a leave-of-absence from the night desk of the *Herald* and staying at the rooming house under an alias, Devoy met with Hathaway every morning in his home and again in the evening in the New Bedford courthouse for several weeks. The more they talked, the more impressed Devoy was by the man. Hathaway urged that Clan na Gael buy a whaler and elaborated an idea to hire a skilled captain not only to rescue the military Fenians, but also to turn a profit out of the venture. As Hathaway tallied the potential cash that even two large whales would generate, Devoy realized that the amount eclipsed any amount that the Rescue Committee could offer, especially after laying out the funds for a ship. At the moment, he had roughly seven thousand dollars in donations.

Devoy wrote to Reynolds again on February 10, 1875,

My Dear R.,

I ought to have written before, but I have been writing to the whole of them and my eyes were bad for some time, and it was painful to write. I did not ask to bring you on because nothing definite could be done, nor can it be for some days yet, and I will see you and talk it over first. I have written fully to all, will wait here for answers from all the near ones, and then return by New Haven, when we can talk with a better knowledge of what can be done. I can't get there till about Monday.

The more I see of this thing the more clear it appears to me that we can't do it *in our time,* not safely at any time, unless we buy a ship, and then no matter what happens, some of our money will return to us. Even if all failed in Australia the vessel could go whaling and clear all expenses. The money can be got easily by borrowing from a few D's [Clan na Gael delegates], if a majority of the F.C. [Finance Committee] consent, and I hope they will. We want $15,000 to start with, but can recover nearly all, and in fact all, if the ship whales enough. She could then either be kept and sent whaling again to raise a fund or sold off. I wish you had time to spend a couple of days in New Bedford as a little contact with practical seafaring men would soon convince you of the feasibility of this mode of working it.

Will you send me the address of the S.G. [head of a

Clan na Gael branch] in Fall River [Massachusetts]. I am going there next Thursday and may remain a day or two. Drop me a line anyhow and let me know how things go.

Remember me to all the boys and to your family, and don't forget to write soon. I will see you on Tuesday evg., at the farthest.

Yours,

J. Devoy

Hathaway had sold Devoy on the necessity for a whaling expedition to cover costs. To plan and outfit the voyage, Hathaway stated, they needed a savvy whaling agent who would underwrite some of the costs, outfit the vessel, file the ship's papers with the Custom House, act as financial trouble-shooter, and receive a sizable share of any profits. Hathaway recommended whaling agent John T. Richardson as a man of stellar business sense and integrity.

In mid-February 1875, Hathaway took Devoy to Richardson's ship-outfitting store on 18 Water Street, just a short walk from the police headquarters. A tall, dapper man in his sixties, with silver hair and probing eyes, Richardson, like Hathaway, knew about the Fenian movement, having chatted with a number of Irishmen who had settled over the years to work in New Bedford's textile mills that overlooked the harbor. Although Richardson had been born in Virginia, he had been raised in New Bedford and had risen to become one of the seaport's most prominent ship's agents.

A Quaker with a revulsion for injustice, Richardson also had a knack for sniffing out profitable whaling and mercantile voyages. Despite the dangers, the Clan na Gael proposal intrigued Richardson. According to a local source, "he sympathized fully and with sturdy Yankee spirit went into the enterprise, fully aware of the risks it involved."

Devoy and Clan na Gael now needed a captain. Hathaway and Richardson both had the same man in mind, one with whom the whaling agent had a close relationship. The captain for the job, Richardson and Hathaway asserted, was George Smith Anthony. Hathaway added that Anthony might well be the only New Bedford shipmaster who would honor his word, if given, to go through with the rescue attempt no matter what and would not abandon it even if the whaling proved unusually good.

Richardson vouched for the captain's character: George Anthony was married to the whaling agent's daughter.

Devoy asked them to set up a meeting. While he had already come to rely on Hathaway's advice, the Irishman would entrust no one with the details of the plot until he had sat down with him, stared straight into his eyes, and sized up his words and demeanor.

Just the Man
for the Job

In New Bedford, Massachusetts, on February 24, 1875, a stocky man in a dark-blue pea jacket and a whaling captain's visored cap picked his way along the icy paving stones of Second Street and slid onto Union Street. Directly below him, a half a mile away, an ice-caked forest of masts and spars glinted in the waxing moonlight. The riding lights of dozens of whaling ships, coastal schooners, and fishing boats swayed with each pull of the tide, the swinging lanterns creating blurry arcs of light along the wharfs. Rows of giant oil casks lined the docks, testifying to New Bedford's status as America's whaling capital.

As thirty-one-year-old George Smith Anthony turned onto Johnny Cake Hill, he pulled his coat tight against the freezing gusts that roared up the slope from the harbor, and trudged toward Water Street. He was headed to Richardson's ship-outfitting store, hurrying past seamen who staggered to or from the waterfront grogshops and stumbled to the brothels or up to the Seamen's Hotel on Johnny Cake Hill, or other boarding houses along the streets leading to the docks. Recognizing Anthony as a shipmaster, many of the men doffed their caps to him and stepped aside to let him pass.

Anthony's thoughts churned from the events of what had been

a perplexing day and promised to be a strange night. As always, he kissed his wife, chestnut-haired Emma—"Emmie"—Richardson Anthony and their infant, Sophie, good-bye that morning and walked to the Morse Twist Drill Works, near the bustling wharves. Married for a year now to the vivacious daughter of John T. Richardson, one of New Bedford's wealthiest shipping agents and owner of the lucrative ship-outfitting, or chandler's, store on Water Street, for over three years Anthony had not set foot on the deck of a whaler putting out to sea.

The memory of his last voyage lingered in his mind, and he yearned for another command. As captain of the whaling ship *Hope On,* owned by one of Richardson's competitors, Jonathan Bourne, Anthony's "lay," his take of the two-year voyage's profits, had allowed him to pursue and marry Emmie Richardson. The cash from whale oil and spermaceti also paid for the newlyweds' house on Second Street, with its fan-lighted doorway.

From the second floor, the home provided a panoramic view of New Bedford Harbor, a scene that greeted Anthony each morning before he left for the twist drill factory. Working as an engineer and mechanic, Anthony brought home a stable and comfortable income, but he chafed for one more voyage, one more chance to chase sperm whales in the hunting grounds of the Atlantic and the Pacific. Only one restraint stopped him from filing shipmaster papers at the New Bedford Customs House: before his marriage, he had vowed to Emma that he would "abandon the longboat forever" so that she would never become a whaling widow."

His promise reflected the depth of his love for Emma. George Smith Anthony, the son of Humphrey and Phoebe (Smith) Anthony, was born into modest means in New Bedford on August 23, 1843, and was educated in the city's public schools. For several generations of young men in New Bedford, the lure of sailing, fishing, and especially whaling took hold early in life, the chase and profits of the grisly business literally flowing through the commercial sinews of the seaport. George Anthony had heard the proverbial Siren's call of the sea as a boy, charging with his friends down to the docks to watch ships coming and going from the hunting grounds of the world's oceans, listening wide-eyed at old tars' thrilling stories of life and death at sea.

All roads in George Anthony's New Bedford literally led to the ocean. Although the 1857 discovery of petroleum in Pennsylvania, and elsewhere, forecasted the decline of the whaling industry as the source for fuel to light homes and towns, the hunt for the sperm whale remained profitable all the way through the 1870s. Refined petroleum began to replace whale oil, but sperm oil remained in demand for lubricating machinery.

Stretching eleven miles along the western bank of the Acushnet River, which flows into an inlet of Buzzard's Bay, New Bedford is surrounded by rolling slopes. White birch, elm, oak, maple, and pine trees once covered the hills, but by Anthony's boyhood, only isolated stands remained, most of the trees felled over the decades to build ships.

Along with whaling, the fishing industry ruled the region's commerce. While George Anthony had never craved to work in the fleets that hauled herring, cod, mackerel, shark, and squid from the waters off New Bedford, he was raised on the soups, stews, and famed New England chowders made from the fishermen's catch. Clams and oysters also appeared routinely on the Anthony family's table.

Anthony came of age during the golden era of whaling, which spanned from 1833 to 1863, when New Bedford's whalers and tonnage eclipsed that of all the rest of America's whaling ports combined. Two years after his birth, 736 whalers put to sea from New Bedford with over 10 thousand officers and crewmen, and returned to off-load 158 thousand barrels of sperm-whale oil, 272 thousand barrels of other whale oils, and 3 million pounds of whalebone on the city's docks.

As Anthony slipped down Johnny Cake Hill on that February night in 1875, the sights, sounds, and smells of the whaling industry permeated the air. Even at night, metallic rasps pealed from the sawmills cutting timber for new ships and repairs for the older ones. In the hemp factories stretched long, narrow "rope-walks," whose twisted fibers turned out piles of cordage. Showers of sparks darted from the open entrances of waterfront blacksmiths' forges as the smiths hammered lances and blubber hooks for the whalers.

Anthony passed the coopers' plants, where countless sperm-oil casks fitted with iron hoops would be hauled by horse carts to the waiting whale fleet. From bakeries came the aroma of hard biscuits that were a bland, sometimes tooth-cracking staple of the seaman's diet.

As Anthony neared Water Street, the Hastings and Company processing factory sprawled along three acres of the waterfront. The plant's wharves stretched four hundred feet, the air above the complex reeking of the two hundred barrels of whale oil boiled daily for the manufacture of heating, cooking, and lighting oil, paraffin, and soap.

Those sights, sounds, and smells of the whaling town were once a source of excitement for Anthony, hinting at voyages to come. In February 1875, however, they fueled his frustration, that of a man who had "pledged his life to the sea at the age of 15. . . . [He] had been "a successful whaleman, and his faithfulness had been demonstrated in a service of ten years in one ship [the *Hope On*], of which Jonathan Bourne was the agent." Though Anthony was deeply in love with Emma and doted on little Sophie, named for her maternal grandmother, he still longed to take the helm of a whaler one more time.

Emma and her husband's friends and associates realized that he was bored with his post at the Morse Twist Drill Works. One of Anthony's associates noted: "Mr. Bourne was inclined to make light of his [Anthony's] resolution to become a mechanic, and constantly dropped in upon him at the shop with tempting offers to return to his service, until the foreman suggested to Mr. Bourne that he should 'let Anthony alone.'"

Earlier in February 1875, Bourne, who considered Anthony almost a son and had handpicked him to command the *Hope On,* spotted him outside the drill works, hurried over to him, and slapped him on the back. "Well, Anthony," Bourne said, "I'll let you alone. But remember and let me know when you are ready to go whaling again."

Anthony shrugged, but later acknowledged to friends that he "felt out of place in a machine-shop." One of the friends would remark: "Anthony was growing restless."

Regarding that restlessness, Bourne evinced no doubt of the outcome: "I knew that he [Anthony] would come to my office, prepared to sign shipping papers." The shipowner and agent had it half right.

On February 23, 1875, the day before Anthony headed down Johnny Cake Hill to his father-in-law's store, he had encountered John T. Richardson walking along Water Street. Tall, nearly sixty, his face deeply bronzed and wrinkled from his own years at the helm of whalers, his well-tailored suit and coat emblems of his prosperous business, the whaling magnate greeted his son-in-law.

Speaking to Richardson as one whaling-ship captain to another, Anthony exclaimed, "I'm tired of this. Go down and see Mr. Bourne and ask him if he will let me have a ship."

Richardson knew seamen, and he knew that Anthony had attempted the "landlubber's life" too soon. As well-intentioned as

Anthony's promise to Emma was, her father wanted him to break it. Nodding, Richardson said, "Wait a few days; I have something better for you."

The wait lasted less than a day. Richardson, having already proposed his son-in-law as the perfect shipmaster for the rescue scheme, "carrying the secret about with him," was waiting outside the house on Second Street the next morning when Anthony came out the front door to walk to work.

"Come to the store this evening at 8 o'clock," Richardson said in a near-whisper to his surprised son-in-law. "There will be two or three men there whom I wish you to meet." Richardson strode away without another word.

Now, on February 24, 1875, Anthony turned right onto Water Street and slogged a hundred yards or so to Richardson's granite-walled, slope-roofed store, the glare of whale-oil lamps within reflecting off the windows. As he reached the front door with the brass number plate "18," the sonorous bell of the Seaman's Church on Johnny Cake Hill tolled eight times. Anthony opened the door and entered.

Richardson greeted him, brushed past him and outside to the street, shoved the ponderous iron shutters in front of the windows with a bang, stepped back inside and closed the thick oak door. Quickly he bolted it, opened the windows, locked the shutters, and closed the windows again. Then he snuffed all but one of the large brass whale-oil lamps and, even with that one, turned down the wick so that it cast only the palest glow. Anthony could barely make out the tables piled with neat rows of sailor's clothing, watch caps, boots and shoes, and everything from brass and leather telescopes to ship's clocks, sextants, and charts.

Richardson beckoned Anthony behind the main storeroom and into the ship agent's office. In a low voice, Richardson said, "There's someone in my office that wants to see you, George."

Anthony followed his father-in-law, who opened the office door and closed it as soon as Anthony had stepped into the familiar room. From the ceiling, a whale-oil lamp dangled from a chain, a pair of wicks gently glowing. Several chairs of finished pine encircled Richardson's walnut desk, and the walls were lined with shelves stacked with boxes of ships' papers, each box emblazoned with black letters of whaling ships' names—*Ocean Wave, Arethusa, Hope On, Mary Ann, Peru, Sarah B. Hale,* and others—whose voyages Richardson had financed himself or in partnership with other agents such as Bourne.

Sitting near the desk was a cast-iron safe sporting a thick brass padlock, and on the wall behind it stretched a tall barometer sheathed in a wooden case. One of the whaling agent's key tools, a long tryrod with a small glass vial at the end for tasting whale oil to judge its quality, stood near the barometer.

In the glow of the lamp and the pot-belly stove in the far corner of the office, Anthony was startled to find five other men in the room. He immediately recognized Henry Hathaway, who was leaning against the desk and who greeted Anthony with a square-jawed smile. This night, Hathaway was not wearing his blue Chief of Night Police uniform, but a plain suit. Hathaway's deeply bronzed features stood out in the light, evidence of his years on whalers; like Anthony, the policeman had shipped out for his first voyage as a teen.

Anthony glanced at two of the men seated near the desk, both of them appearing to be in their thirties or forties. Richardson introduced Anthony to twenty-eight-year-old John W. Goff, a County Wexford Irishman who had the square features and craggy nose of a brawler, in his case an ex-pugilist, but was dressed in a dapper suit with a gold watch-chain and looked every bit the up-and-coming New York lawyer. Then Anthony was introduced to the second stranger, James Reynolds, a genial forty-three-year-old brass foundry owner who had fled Ireland in 1847, "Black '47," during the height of the Great Potato Famine and eventually settled in New Haven, Connecticut. He shook Anthony's hand as if they had known one another for years.

Anthony suddenly "remembered that he had seen them about Richardson's place for several days, and had once been on the point of inquiring who they were."

It was the third stranger who commanded Anthony's attention. The man was seated in a chair, his back partially turned from the others, his face shadowed.

"Captain Anthony," Hathaway said, "I want to make you acquainted with John Devoy, of New York City and of the *New York Herald*. Mr. Devoy, sir, this is Captain George Anthony, of whom I have spoken."

Devoy rose from the chair, walked over to Anthony, and shook Anthony's rough, calloused hand. Devoy's grip felt equally rough to Anthony, the effect of years of hard labor in Millbank's rock piles.

For several moments, the two men appraised each other. Anthony saw "a short man with full black whiskers in his thirties," with deep, haunted, dark eyes that at first glance made him seem a scholar, but on second look were the fierce eyes of a man who could command and fight.

Devoy, in turn, assessed: "The man [Anthony] who stood in the lamplight for a minute before the flame was extinguished was of athletic build, with black hair and eyes which were so black, bright, and alert that they were the conspicuous feature of the face. The brilliant color in the captain's cheeks indicated vigorous good health.

To all of the others, Devoy, his voice deep, said, "It's just as well to sit in the dark."

Richardson instantly snuffed out the wick of the whale-oil

lamp. Anthony's heart beat a little faster. "When the lights were put out at once, it seemed a rather singular proceeding," he would say.

As a gust roared in from the harbor and rattled the store's shutters, they sat for several minutes in silence, the only light the reddish glow emitted by the pot-belly stove. What could this be about? Anthony wondered. Why such a furtive air?

Devoy broke the silence, and his words startled Anthony: For the past three days, he explained, the three Irishmen had taken turns tailing Anthony to judge for themselves his habits, his demeanor, and his standing in the town. The trio had judged him as a good family man with no pronounced vices. They had decided that "he would do," as his father-in-law and Hathaway had vouched.

"Do for what?" Anthony asked.

Devoy asked the others to sit while he remained on his feet, his eyes boring into Anthony's the entire time. Then the Irishman posed a question solely for Anthony: Could Devoy, Goff, and Reynolds trust the former shipmaster to never reveal—until it was safe to do so—what was about to be said? Would Anthony give his word, as had Richardson and Hathaway?

Anthony nodded.

Hathaway leaned forward and told Anthony that Devoy and his friends needed a fearless and skilled captain for a special voyage, a rescue expedition. The police chief added: "We knew that you were just the man."

Then Devoy spoke again, directly to Anthony. The Fenian and Clan na Gael man began by revealing his own past and the history of the Fenian movement. Anthony later said, "Mr. Devoy was a brilliant talker, and he knew his subject well. He hurried over the story of the [Fenian] revolution in which the men were engaged, making prominent the fact that his friends who had not been released from Australia were political prisoners and freedom fighters for their nation's freedom."

As Devoy rendered a vivid account of the suffering and persecution of the military Fenians in and around Fremantle, Anthony was riveted, appalled that the British government could treat patriots as baser criminals than murderers and rapists. Still, he had no notion why he was sitting in his father-in-law's office, listening to Devoy's impassioned speech. What did all this have to do with a Yankee and Quaker shipmaster?

Irish historian Sean O' Luing notes of Anthony: "He was not bound to Ireland by any ties of blood or kin." As Anthony listened, that thought held him.

He stiffened as Devoy launched into the reason why Richardson had summoned his son-in-law that night. The Fenian described the rescue plan to the wide-eyed Anthony: "His [Devoy's] friends would provide a whaleship, fitted for sea. Captain Anthony was to sail as soon as possible, and beyond keeping up a pretense of whaling, his part would merely be to show his vessel off the coast of Australia on a certain date. There he would be hailed by a company of men in a boat. He would take them aboard and sail for home. The shore end of the escape would be managed by others."

"Aghast," Anthony sat silently for several minutes. "In his [Devoy's] enthusiasm," Anthony recalled, "it probably seemed the easy task to Devoy which he represented it to be."

From his years at sea, Anthony knew better, as did his father-in-law and Hathaway from their voyages. Anthony had seen firsthand how warships flying the Union Jack prowled the shipping lanes and whaling grounds across the globe. What chance would a whaler stand against a sleek British steamer bristling with cannon and Royal Marines? The question barely merited an answer, but Devoy seemed oblivious to such considerations. To

Anthony, the Irishman also appeared oblivious to the fact that if the U.S. Navy were ever tipped off to such a plan that could be construed as an act of war against Britain, American warships might descend upon the would-be rescuers.

Still, the sheer audacity of the scheme intrigued Anthony. If he did decide to sign on and "pluck these men from the jaws of the British lion," he might well go down in the annals of New Bedford as one of its boldest shipmasters. Conversely, he might end up in a Fremantle cell or on the scaffold.

Goff detected a glimmer of interest in Anthony even as the man sat and said nothing. "He was a descendant of an old line of whalers," the Irishman surmised, "a typical hard-headed, hard-boned, hard-muscled New England skipper." Like Devoy, Goff and Reynolds, also scrutinizing Anthony, felt certain that George Smith Anthony was "just the man for the job"—if only he would accept it.

Devoy, already having dealt with the quintessential hard-nosed Yankee businessman in Richardson, assured his Yankee son-in-law that if he did undertake the rescue mission, he would not only receive three times the normal captain's "lay" from whales taken, but would also receive a hefty bonus from Clan na Gael.

As he later stated, Anthony knew that if he accepted this command, it would be his last voyage. He had already edged toward breaking his pledge to Emma the moment he had talked to her father about a ship. If he could pull off this wild scheme, the lay and bonus would provide more money than he could earn in ten or fifteen years at the Morse Twist Drill Works.

Something else compelled Anthony not to decline, at least not yet. Devoy's words about the sufferings of the Fenian soldiers left behind in Fremantle had affected him. According to a descendant, Anthony said, "I'm sure you will be generous. And I will not deny that a profit from a successful voyage would be welcome. I see merit in your venture. I think someone should undertake it. I think it is barely possible that your plan might succeed. Mind you, I'm not saying it will. But whether I am the man —to take the law into my own hands—which is what you ask—I don't know. . . . "

He asked for time to consider the proposition.

Heartened that the man had not refused outright, Devoy nodded and told him he had twenty-four hours to decide. As Anthony rose from his chair, Devoy reminded him of his pledge to secrecy and warned him not even to tell his wife. Anthony nodded back and strode out of the store, his mind racing.

When he walked into the house on Second Street, everything he would leave behind and risk forever if he accepted the proposal lay before him. Devoy waited. George Anthony lay awake next to Emma all that night, hearing virtually every tick of the bedroom clock as rain slapped against the windows, and counting the strokes of the town clock until the black sky grayed at dawn.

Early on February 25, 1875, Anthony walked down the paved slope to the drill works. He had made up his mind.

He looked over his shoulder on the way, but none of the three Irishmen or anyone else tailed him. For the rest of the day, he went about his routine, overseeing the production of the twist drills, taking measurements of the steel bits, and filing them when needed. He went immediately home for dinner, as always, at 5 P.M. and paced around the house until nearly 8 P.M., pondering the words he would say to his father-in-law and to Devoy.

Shortly before 8 o'clock, Anthony donned a seaman's simply cut woolen pea jacket, put on a watch cap, gave Emma a quick kiss, and waded through gusts and sleet to the ship-outfitter's store. Richardson and the three Irishmen were waiting for him in the office, where once again only the reddish glow of the stove lit the room. Their eyes probed Anthony's for any clue of his decision.

Anthony cleared his throat and spoke.

Tersely, Devoy would record, "He finally accepted."

Devoy, beaming, gave Anthony and Richardson full authority to find a suitable ship. Satisfied grins also appeared on Goff's and Reynolds's faces.

Now that the shipmaster had made his choice, excitement penetrated his normally unflappable demeanor. Of his new command, Anthony would say, "To go where I liked, stay as long as I pleased, and return home when I got ready. I was to be at Australia in the spring of 1876 to cooperate with Fenian agents for the release of six prisoners confined at Fremantle."

Still, as a man who could have taken the helm of any other New Bedford whaler on a legitimate voyage, Anthony chose to risk his freedom, his family, and his life for a cause in which he had no previous stake. His friend Zephania Pease wrote:

> I have always suspected that Devoy and his friends must have aroused the sympathy of Captain Anthony and awakened within him a personal interest in the men whose zeal for patriotism had placed them in an unfortunate position. A promise that he would be well-paid was certainly inadequate to the weary voyage, the risk, and the sacrifice he must make in leaving his family. Captain Anthony had been married but a year, and there was a baby daughter but a few months old. His mother was ill, and had not the spirit which dominated Devoy appealed to [Anthony] there can be no satisfactory explanation of his assumption of the trust.

Later, Anthony himself would expound on his motives. For the moment, he needed to find a ship.

Two versions of Emma Richardson Anthony's reaction to her

husband's decision would emerge over the years. The romantic account claims that she was a true "whaling wife" of New Bedford and urged her husband, bored and frustrated at the Morse Twist Drill Works, to make one more voyage—so long as it was his last such expedition.

According to family members, however, Emma Anthony's reaction was quite different. She was furious that her husband broke his pledge to "abandon the longboat forever" and terrified that he had hooked up with the Fenians and their risky scheme. She was equally enraged at her father for bringing her husband into the plot. In revealing the plan to Emma, George Anthony had also broken his oath to Devoy, but the shipmaster knew that she would never utter a word to anyone else about the voyage—except to upbraid her father from time to time. The daughter of a whaling man and a whaling town, Emma Richardson Anthony would accept, though not agree with, her husband's choice.

Years later, Anthony's great-grandson Jim Ryan would say: "My great-grandfather talked about why he said yes. It was never about money or even adventure. Simply put, he said, 'It was the right thing to do.'"

We Have Bought
a Vessel

From February 27 to March 8, 1875, Anthony, Richardson, and Hathaway scouted New Bedford's crowded moorings for a suitable ship, preferably an older whaler that needed refitting and could be bought at a bargain price. They walked up the gangplank of the *Jeanette,* a once-sturdy whaler whose hull revealed the wear and tear of hard voyages to the ice-choked hunting zones of the Antarctic. All three men found her decks and rigging in passable condition, but decided that resheathing the hull with new copper plating, as well as replacing rotting oak timbers just above the waterline, would cost more than Clan na Gael could afford.

Next, the trio examined the *Sea Gull,* a sleek Boston clipper built for speed, which appealed to Anthony as he envisoned likely pursuit by British or even American warships. Again, however, there was a problem, though not with the ship herself. No seaman worth his salt would watch a fast clipper be converted to a whaler ship and not be suspicious. Disappointed, Anthony and the others made further inquiries along the docks and at the New Bedford Customs House, where all whalers in port were required to register papers.

In the final week of February, Richardson, Hathaway, and

Anthony learned that the *Addison,* a rugged whaler that had been converted several years ago to a mail packet running from Boston and New Bedford to the Azores, was for sale. The idea of a whaler reconfigured for speed sent Anthony, his father-in-law, and Hathaway scrambling to the waterfront, where the *Addison* sat in dry dock, affording the trio a close look at her hull and keel. The vessel was in good shape, and as Hathaway raced off to send a wire to Devoy, who had returned to New York for a few days, Anthony and Richardson went off to find the ship's owner.

They were told that they would have to bid quickly—another firm offer had been made. When Hathaway reappeared and Richardson informed him that they needed six thousand immediately to buy the ex-whaler, Hathaway persuaded the vessel's owner to delay any sale for a few days. But time was slipping away fast. Devoy had only been able to hand Hathaway two thousand. Adding to Devoy's distress, Hathaway warned that as May approached, the price of any available ships soared, May being the departure month for many whalers.

Devoy caught a train with Goff and two other Clan na Gael men for New Bedford and arrived on March 1, 1875, only to find that they were a day late. The ship had been sold the previous day. On March 2, the frustrated Devoy wrote to Reynolds:

My Dear R.,

We got here yesterday morning—too late to secure the ship we expected to get, and we must wait a few days longer. It went for $6,300. Others, suitable enough, but not having so good an inventory, are to be got, but we must have the money in hand.

We have lodged up to today, $2,000 in the hands of

Hathaway, and an agent [Richardson] who is trustworthy, and our friends must hand up the remainder so
as to enable us to buy this week, as it will take us six
weeks to get her ready for sea.

Goff and two New York men, Miles O'Brien of D. 13
[Clan na Gael branch], and James Muldoon, S.G., of D.
150, who is a marine engineer . . . were the only men
that came, and all but myself have gone home. I will
stay here until a ship is bought.

D. No. 1 [Devoy's own Clan na Gael branch] voted
$1,500 dollars last night and $1,000 more if required.
How is that for spirit?

Yours, J. D.

Buried with work at the *Pilot*, O'Reilly stayed in contact with
Devoy and, in early March, offered his services in a hands-on
manner to the Rescue Committee:

The Pilot
23, 25 & 27, BOYLSTON STREET,
BOSTON,
4 March, 1875.

Dear John,

If you would like to have me go down [to New Bedford],
I'll try and go. I would like to see those people. I wish
Mr. McCullogh [a New Bedford associate of O'Reilly's]
knew all about it before you pay more money. My
knowledge of ships, men, and arrangements of shipping *your* men may be of use.

Keep the idea of *your* 7 or 8 men from the Captain [Devoy's initial plan to place armed Irishmen aboard the ship].

> Yours,
> O'Reilly

O'Reilly told Devoy that the docks in Boston also teemed with ships and offered to take a look along the city's waterfront. Meanwhile, as the search for a ship went on in New Bedford, Devoy worried about the money required to make a purchase. In a letter to Reynolds in early March 1875, Devoy reflected:

My Dear Boy,

You must excuse me for neglecting you so long. Work, St. Patrick, and being talked to death are the causes.

I think we may tell . . . how much we have got and how much the job will take. The amount subscribed and voted up to this that has passed through the hands of our treasurer and the trustees is seven thousand and some odd dollars: amount in hands of D's [Clan na Gael delegates] and District trustees is not accurately reported, but is about $2,000 more. As it is all called in, we can say in a few days what is the exact amount. What will probably be voted by D's yet we can't say, but it will certainly require $15,000 to do the work— about $7,000 of that being *certain* to be refunded. That is as much as we know ourselves yet . . .

I have not had a solitary minute to myself. This thing must be made a success at all hazards.

Excuse this scrawl.

Yours,

J. D.

In the first week of March 1875, news reached Richardson, Hathaway, and Anthony that a former New Bedford whaler named the *Catalpa* was for sale in Boston. Whether O'Reilly or Richardson first learned of the vessel's availability is unknown, but the whaling agent and his son-in-law boarded the first train they could get to inspect the ship on March 8 or 9, 1875.

Richardson knew the *Catalpa* firsthand, as he had brokered one of her whaling expeditions in the late 1860s and had realized a decent profit. Built in a Medford, Massachusetts, shipyard in 1844, the vessel had roamed all over the world in pursuit of sperm whales. If still seaworthy, both Richardson and Anthony knew that she would do.

They alighted from the train at the Boston depot at South and Kneeland Streets at 9:45 A.M., hired a horse-drawn cab, and clattered down the cobblestones of Atlantic Avenue to the waterfront, all around them the blackened shells of buildings testifying to the Great Boston Fire of 1873. New construction was rising everywhere, carts hauling stones, bricks, and cement clotting the streets, the rasps of saws and thuds of hammers against stone deafening.

At the crowded docks, the two men boarded a ferry for Orient Heights, the East Boston harbor where the *Catalpa* lay at anchor. As the ferry pulled up to the wharf, Richardson and Anthony spotted her, a three-masted bark. Once aboard, Richardson and Anthony went to work, inspecting every inch of the ship. The *Catalpa*—202 tons, ninety feet long, twenty-five feet wide, and just over twelve feet deep—had been converted into a merchant ship and had just returned with a cargo of logwood from the West Indies.

Richardson and Anthony judged the vessel large enough for the job, with a substantial main hold, and fore and aft cabins that could be easily reworked into officers' quarters. For whaling purposes, the space between the stern cabins and the forecastle bulkhead, in the bow, provided ample space for oil casks.

The two New Bedford men also liked the size of the forecastle, which was large enough for the berths that would have to be built for the military Fenians if the rescue came off successfully. They climbed back on deck and examined the planking and scrutinized the *Catalpa*'s rigging, bowsprit, and masts. Then the two walked back down the gangplank and paced slowly alongside the vessel's hull to check as much of her copper sheathing as showed above the waterline.

Throughout the inspection, Anthony and Richardson mulled all of the refitting and repairs that the *Catalpa* would need to be converted back to a whaler, but if the Irishmen could come up with the money, she would do regardless. Devoy asked Richardson to contact the ship's owner, F.W. Homan, a Gloucester, Massachusetts, mariner, at his waterfront office immediately and hastened off to get a message to Reynolds. Richardson negotiated a deal with Homan within hours, the savvy New Bedford agent arranging a price of $5,250, nearly two thousand dollars below what the ship might actually have fetched with open bidding.

While Richardson struck the deal, Devoy took the train back to New Bedford, then rushed off to find Hathaway and tell him about the *Catalpa*. The Irishman wrote to Reynolds as soon as Richardson apprised Devoy of the quick developments and of the urgency of the financial situation:

My Dear R.,

I have been kept waiting here ever since though the money not being sent on. I don't know what is the cause of the delay, but if it lasts much longer we shall be in an embarrassing position. We have bought a vessel and she must be paid for by Saturday. The amount is $5,250, and there are some fees, pilotage to this port, ballast, etc., to be paid besides, and some of the outfit and stores already bought. All we have on hand is $4,900. The $1,500 of D. 1, partly through sulk on the part of two of the trustees, partly, Goff says, through the S.G.'s neglect, has not come in yet, and no districts but A and F have yet sent anything. If we had the necessary funds now she could be ready for sea in three weeks. I could get $7,000 for her if I agreed to sell her, as she was not advertised for sale and is coveted by a man for the West India trade.

I will leave here at all hazards on Saturday morning and will stop in New Haven on Sunday.

Keep this matter quiet, as we must move with great caution now.

Yours,

J. D.

On March 13, 1875, the buyers were back in Boston to sign and finalize the agreement.

When O'Reilly had learned of the impending deal, he rushed a letter to Devoy on March 12 expressing caution before they signed the agreement:

The Pilot
23, 25 & 27 BOYLSTON STREET,
Boston
12 March, 1875.

Dear John,

A hundred unexpected things have prevented me from going to see you. My dear boy, I feel as if it were unkind; but can't help it. And if I had gone I could, probably, have not advised anything better than your own good sense will suggest. I will see about that ship at E. Boston. I will ask Lieut. Tobin, of the U.S. Navy, a friend of mine, to look at her, without letting him know why. *Don't* buy her without seeing her. It costs a good deal to copper a ship, and a whaler above all ships, needs copper, I *can't* go to you now before—oh, I *don't* know when. I have to go to Hartford on Wednesday. Why *don't* you take a run to Boston? Come, and see that ship with me and Tobin.

> Always,
> J. B. O'Reilly

Devoy agreed to meet with O'Reilly and Tobin, but could not do so before the sale. Unless the plotters handed Homan the cash or a bank draft for $5,250 sometime between Saturday March 13, 1875, and March 16, 1875, they risked losing the *Catalpa*. To seal the bargain, Richardson agreed to advance Devoy and Clan na Gael $4,000 but, ever the pragmatic businessman, made Devoy endorse a note in which he agreed that Clan na Gael would reimburse the whaling agent within thirty days.

Devoy rushed back to Boston to meet with O'Reilly and his friend. At O'Reilly's Charlestown town house, the ex-Hussar introduced Devoy to Lieutenant Tobin, a naval engineer of Irish American lineage. A tall, robust man, Tobin impressed Devoy immediately. The officer, however, knew nothing about the real purpose of the *Catalpa*'s intended mission. Devoy wrote: "He [Tobin] and I dined at O'Reilly's house in Charlestown under the shadow of Bunker Hill on the Sunday after the purchase of the *Catalpa*. O'Reilly had introduced me under my proper name, told him I had been in prison for Fenianism with him, that I represented a firm that was going to embark on the fruit trade and, as I knew nothing about shipping, he would be greatly obliged if he would come over and take a look at the vessel. Lieutenant Tobin entered into the examination with great zest, never for a moment suspecting our object."

On Monday morning, March 15, 1875, the three men boarded the *Catalpa*, Tobin wearing the blue and gold-braid tunic of a U.S. Navy officer and he sliced several slivers of the vessel's timbers with his jackknife and examined them. He slowly walked every inch of the ship from the main deck to the bilges belowdecks. Devoy looked on anxiously, praying that the ship was as seaworthy as Richardson and Anthony had deemed.

Tobin concluded his inspection and turned to Devoy. Relief washed over the Irishman as Tobin nodded. The *Catalpa*, the officer pronounced, was a bit old and weatherbeaten, but seaworthy enough to sail anywhere. If she had a drawback, he said, it was that she was slow and that little could be done to change that.

To Devoy's query about the vessel's worth, Tobin responded that she was worth up to ten thousand dollars on the market, and when Devoy told the officer how much had been paid, Tobin said that the Irishman had caught a real bargain. "A splendid fellow," mused the elated Devoy, and "hoped [Tobin] would yet be an admiral."

Also eager to inspect the whaler that Devoy had purchased was Henry Hathaway, who traveled to Boston shortly after Tobin's examination of the *Catalpa*. Hathaway, using a bit of code to describe the ship as a "race horse" and mask location, wrote:

To John Devoy Esq.

Dear Sir: You perhaps noticed my short stay in Boston in the presence of J. B. O'R. I could have stayed a short time longer, but for fear we might be overheard as he talked pretty loud.

I hope you had a look at the *Horse* [*Catalpa*] in Charleston [Boston] and was [*sic*] satisfied with it. I think it's a tip-top bargain. I liked the looks of him [the ship] first-rate and think he will bring more than we paid for him any day. We have already been offered $1,000 more than we paid for him, but think he will more than pay for himself this coming season on the track. We are going for him this week. The weather is now very favorable, and think we can get him here [New Bedford] by Thurs. or Fri. . . . We have commenced this morning in earnest and will pay for the *Horse* today [March 15, 1875].

Not yet aware that Richardson would front the money for Devoy, Hathaway warned: "I hope you will be punctual in sending us the fodder, as grain is on the rise here." Hathaway concluded his letter with a testimonial to Anthony's abilities:

"How do you like the looks of the man that we chose to take charge of the *Horse?* He is the right man for it."

With that assessment, Devoy had no argument.

To ensure that Richardson would not balk at his decision to put up four thousand dollars to cover the agreement, James Reynolds mortgaged his house as collateral for the New Bedford agent and wrote to him: "$4,000—Thirty days after date I promise to pay to the order of John T. Richardson, at the Mechanics National Bank, Four Thousand Dollars, Value Received." The New Haven Fenian would pay in installments from April 29 to May 24, 1875.

"It was he [Reynolds]," wrote an admirer, "who mortgaged his home, who placed a chattle [*sic*] upon his household goods, who beggared himself for the time, that the sinews might be forthcoming to inaugurate and sustain the expedition. . . . James Reynolds gave his all that the mission might be consummated."

By week's end, the *Catalpa* passed into the hands of the plotters, with the bill of sale recording that Richardson had purchased the bark for James Reynolds. In official legal terms, the *Catalpa* was transferred from F. W. Homan to Reynolds: "To have and to hold the said seven-eighths bark *Catalpa* and appurtenances thereunto belonging to him, the said James Reynolds, his executors, administrators and assigns, to the sole and only proper use, benefit and behoof of him the said James Reynolds, etc."

The men of Clan na Gael would dub Reynolds "*Catalpa* Jim."

At noon on March 19 or 20, 1875, George Anthony stood at the helm of the *Catalpa* in the waters off Orient Heights as a towline from a tug ahead stiffened and the bark lurched into motion. Richardson and Anthony had decided that the repairs would be undertaken in New Bedford, where they knew the repair crews and bosses and where prying eyes—British spies—were less likely to turn up than in Boston. As the tug pulled the *Catalpa* past Boston Light and into open waters, Anthony reveled in the pitch of the deck beneath his feet after so many long months in the drill works. The tug plowed slightly southwest into open waters, and by dusk, the *Catalpa* reached the hook of Cape Cod.

As darkness came on, the tugboat captain navigated the tricky waters off the Cape, following the bright arcs of the lighthouses at Nauset, Chatham, and Monomoy. Anthony, meanwhile, ached to prove to himself that the practiced ease he had once shown at the helms of whalers had not deserted him during his months on land. He knew he would have to wait several weeks for that opportunity. For the moment, he joyfully drank in the salt air of deep waters.

The tug hauled the bark on a course through Nantucket Sound, with Nantucket and Martha's Vineyard to the *Catalpa's* port rail, and as dawn broke, the tow captain laid a westerly course. Into Buzzard's Bay the tug pulled the *Catalpa* through the ferry channel between Woods Hole and Monamesset Island. The two vessels cast mooring lines at New Bedford's City Wharf in New Bedford late on the afternoon of March 20 or 21, 1875.

Anthony, Richardson, and Hathaway hired John W. Howland, New Bedford's finest shipwright, to handle the *Catalpa's* extensive repairs. Having quit the drill works, Anthony oversaw the refitting of the vessel each day at Howland's City Wharf shipyard, and Hathaway also checked the progress daily. Howland built quarters in the forecastle for the whaling crew, a half-deck where the crew would cut up whales and boil the blubber, pens to store pigs and chickens, and storage space for provisions and whale-oil casks. Workmen's saws and hammers knocked two rooms on the starboard stern into one large room for Anthony, an ample cabin for the first mate on the port side of the stern. Berths for the second and third mates sat in the forward cabin.

With Hathaway and Anthony keeping an eye on the repairs and preventing delays, they managed to cut these costs considerably, but the refitting bill mounted. They had to order new sails, an anchor, and a chronometer—the handheld brass instrument by which captains of the era fixed their ships' global positions. Provisions, water and oil casks, harpoons, lances, medicine, first-aid chests, and wine and rum—all had to be ordered in quantities to last two years at sea. Devoy had to present each bill to Clan na Gael and fight for new funds from grumbling members. One of the largest expenses, $1,600, was paid out to resheathe the ship's keel with fresh copper to prevent sea worms from eating the timbers.

Richardson had initially figured that the purchase price and the repairs would total around twelve thousand dollars, but an unexpected problem drove the bill much higher. Howland discovered that the "riding keelson," where the base of the mainmast rested, had rotted nearly all the way through. Anthony and Hathaway knew as well as Howland that a ship could not sail without the keelson, and that no one had attempted to build a new keelson around a sitting mainmast. Howland proved up to the task: "A new piece was put in with such skill that the rigging did not settle throughout the voyage."

For five days, Howland worked on a mechanical marvel. He made a new riding keelson for the oak mainmast and slackened the mast's ratlines, main chains, after-shrouds, mainstay, and preventer stays. With ponderous tackle, he and his crew lifted the heavy mast just enough to remove the rotted piece and slip in the new one. Howland's innovative feat, however, escalated the price tag of his services.

On April 16, 1875, Richardson wrote to Reynolds, who was raising funds for the rescue, as well as contributing his own savings:

Dear Friend and Partner,

I have this moment received your check for $4,344.30, for which I sent you this receipt. . . .

The ship is now all coppered and off the ways all ready for stowing and painting. It will take us but a few days to finish up everything. The ship will sail for a great deal more than what we first anticipated, but we have a ship that we can depend on and one that will bring a good price any day when we are ready to sell. I hope that won't be for some time for she is worth as much to us as anyone else. I am in hopes at the end of the voyage to show you that this is the business to invest money in, and furthermore I am confident that your wish will be granted in regards to those men in Western Australia.

I think the vessel will sail for over $17,000 and I will be ready to meet my share of the expenses at any day when the bills are all in. I hope you will be punctual in forwarding more money as soon as possible, and when I send for you to come to N.B. you will be prepared to settle all bills, as we have agreed with all who I have bought goods off to pay cash. I think now the 26th of this month will be the day for her sailing. Please answer immediately and let me know what your expectations are in regard to the full amount.

I don't want to keep the ship waiting a moment after she is ready for sea as her expenses will be heavy, for each day she is detained, as some of the crew live in other places far from here, and if the ship is not ready to sail when they come it will create dissatisfaction with them. Besides, it will cost a great deal to keep them waiting.

Yours truly,
J. T. Richardson

Richardson's estimate of the costs proved wrong. The bill came to $19,010.

With the new keelson set, the *Catalpa* required a crew. Anthony knew the man he wanted for the key post of first mate and took a ferry across Nantucket Sound to Edgartown, Martha's Vineyard, where Samuel P. Smith, one of the best in the whaling business, lived. Richardson, meanwhile, as ship's agent, went to work assembling a crew, with the stipulation that he hire "no Englishmen."

Anthony found Smith on the docks, working on his fishing skiff. A tough, sandy-haired sailor who had just returned from a two-year whaling voyage, Smith was the son of Scottish immigrants and had little love for anything English. When Anthony offered him the post as the *Catalpa's* first mate, Smith hesitated, as he had recently proposed to his fiancée. Anthony told him nothing about the whaler's true purpose, but did offer Smith double the usual pay for a first mate, and the lure proved too much for him to decline. He promised to report for the ship's scheduled departure in the final week of April 1875.

Richardson had signed up twenty-two crewmen by the third week of April 1875, the roster composed mainly of Portuguese from the Azores and Cape Verde Islands, Malays, and Kanakas from the Sandwich Islands (Hawaii). Only one of those men knew the ship's true destination. His was the last name on the crew roster filed with the *Catalpa's* shipping articles at the Customs House: Dennis Duggan, the very same Dennis Duggan who had helped spring Fenian leader James Stephens from prison in Dublin.

After much wrangling within the Clan na Gael Rescue Committee, they had decided to put one or two of their men aboard the *Catalpa,* heeding Hathaway's warning that a whaler loaded with Irishmen—not known as whaling men—would raise suspicions at the Customs House. Devoy personally selected the thirty-year-old Duggan, a capable, cool, man willing to kill for his cause. In the abortive 1867 rising, the Fenian had done just that at the gun battles of Stepaside and Glencullen in the Dublin Mountains, forcing him to escape to America. A coach builder and carpenter by trade, Dublin-born-and-raised Duggan could actually fulfill a working role on the whaler. Moreover, Devoy had known Duggan since their days in Dublin's public schools and trusted him.

John Goff was willing to accept Duggan, but only if Goff's man, Tom Brennan, also shipped out aboard the *Catalpa*. Devoy also knew Brennan, who had proven his courage during the fighting in the Dublin hills and, like Duggan, had eluded capture by the British. The night editor of the *New York Herald* considered Brennan impetuous and hot-tempered, however, and appealed to Reynolds as "owner-manager" of the ship to choose Duggan alone.

When Anthony, Hathaway, and Richardson sent Reynolds an urgent note that under no circumstances could they take more than one Irishman aboard without tipping off authorities that "something was up," Reynolds made a quick decision. The New Bedford men warned Reynolds that "customs officials were very persistent in their inquiries about the destination of the whaler." Richardson told them that due to his own status in whaling circles, "Captain Anthony is going where he has a mind to and will stay as long as he pleases." But even Richardson's stellar reputation in the seaport's whaling fraternity would not be enough to ward off questions about more than one Irishman aboard the *Catalpa*. Duggan was the man, said Reynolds, a choice that Anthony and Hathaway, who had met the Dubliner and sized him up as a steady, if lethal, man, accepted.

On April 22, 1875, Hathaway informed Reynolds that the

Catalpa's departure date was drawing close: "Mr. Richardson . . . says the vessel will go to sea next Tuesday morning, April 27th, without fail. . . . I hope you and Mr. Devoy will be here in time to see her go. . . . You have got a good ship.

Perhaps you had better telegraph to Mr. Devoy at once and be here by Sunday, or Monday sure, as there will be no delay in her sailing."

But Hathaway's assurance of no delay in the sailing turned sour. Anthony's mother fell gravely ill on April 25, and for two days he was at her side, his crew ready to leave but spending another night or two in their boarding houses, the grogshops, and in the brothels. When she rallied after two days, Anthony knew he could wait no longer to put to sea. The *Catalpa*, he informed the others, would set sail on the morning tide of April 29, 1875.

Devoy had arrived in New Bedford just as Anthony's mother was stricken, and agreed to wait until Anthony felt he was ready to leave. Now the Irishman delivered the captain his final instructions: "You will cruise until fall, about six months, in the North Atlantic. Then you are to put in at Fayal, ship home any oil you have taken, and sail at once for Australia, where we expect you to arrive early in the spring of 1876. You are to go to Bunbury, on the west coast, and there communications will be opened up with you from our Australian agent."

Devoy did not tell Anthony that possible trouble from Goff might jeopardize the mission. On the day Devoy had reached New Bedford, a telegram from Goff awaited the *Herald* editor and stated that Goff and Brennan planned to take a train to the seaport. Goff insisted that his man be placed onboard the *Catalpa*. If Anthony's mother had not taken sick, the whaler would have sailed away before Goff and Brennan arrived. As

Anthony walked home for what might well prove the last night he would ever spend with his wife and infant daughter, Devoy could only hope that Goff's imminent arrival would not unravel the rescue plot.

A Supreme Test
of Pluck

O n Thursday, April 29, 1875, rain splattered against the windows of every home in New Bedford. George Anthony lay awake next to Emma, as he had all evening. First Mate Sam Smith stirred in his portside cabin aboard the *Catalpa* as the whaler rocked at her mooring with the first gusts that drove the rain across the maindeck above him. Like Anthony, he listened for a moment to the wind and pelting sheets of water and relaxed slightly—it was only a passing squall. The *Catalpa* would leave with the tide.

As both captain and first mate had surmised, the rain ceased and dawn broke across New Bedford's sloped roofs and jutting spars in a splash of gathering sunlight and wispy clouds. From his hotel room on Johnny Cake Hill, John Devoy could spy the *Catalpa*'s masts and furled sails.

Not far from the Irishman's lodgings, George and Emma Anthony were up early, saying their good-byes, the seaman torn with doubts over his decision as he looked again and again at his lovely young wife and tiny daughter, Sophie. Emma planned to bring Sophie along to the dock to see Anthony off, but the more he gazed at them, the more he realized he could not endure that fairwell scene and that "he could not trust himself to bring his wife." Adding to his agony, April 29, 1875, marked the couple's first wedding anniversary, a year to the day that the Reverend O. A. Roberts had married them. Emma agreed not to come to the wharf.

A sleek carriage clattered up to the Anthony's house around 10 A.M. George Anthony stepped out his front door, carrying a brass telescope and his new chronometer, and climbed in the rig beside his in-laws, John T. and Sophie Wrisley Richardson. No one questioned that Anthony came alone.

With the clap of hooves against cobblestones, the carriage swung downhill to the waterfront, where a large party of Anthony's friends were gathered on the dock alongside the *Catalpa*, the smell of the ship's fresh paint and tar filling the breeze.

Devoy was seething dockside; as near him stood Goff and Brennan, with Hathaway looking to play peacemaker. According to Devoy, Goff had rushed to the waterfront "to argue it out on the dock as the vessel was about to sail."

Richardson's carriage pulled up on the dock, and Anthony emerged to find himself surrounded by well-wishers—and by Devoy, Goff, Brennan, and Hathaway. When Goff insisted that Anthony take Brennan aboard immediately, Anthony snapped that Duggan was the ship's carpenter and had been cleared by customs officials. Brennan had no papers, Anthony growled, and under no circumstances would he allow him onboard. Besides, Anthony said, any sudden change in the ship's roster by adding a man who was neither a sailor nor possessed any useful shipboard skill would bring a customs or U.S. Navy vessel down on the *Catalpa*. Watching the scene with no conception of what was at stake, Anthony's friends could only wonder what the furor was about.

Hathaway proposed a solution delivered with the harsh logic of a veteran whaler. Invariably, he pointed out, all whalers lost a man or two at sea or in foreign ports, so why not send Brennan to the Azores or Fayal aboard a passenger vessel, and then "Captain Anthony could take him onboard or not, according to his judgement or discretion."

Grudgingly, Anthony and Goff agreed. For the first time, Devoy glimpsed the steely, hardnosed *Captain* Anthony and was even more certain that the shipmaster was indeed the right man for this voyage.

Anthony turned and strode up the gangplank, and some of the gathering, including Goff and Brennan, followed him onto the varnished decks of the whaler. They would accompany him to Buzzard's Bay for a farewell dinner and return later that afternoon aboard a skiff that had trailed the whaler.

Near noon, a tugboat puffed alongside the *Catalpa*. Harbor Pilot Will Nickerson's crew fastened towlines to the whaler. Then, Anthony barked the order to cast off his ship's mooring lines. The *Catalpa*'s red-and-white flag perched atop the mainroyal mast and emblazoned with the bold black letters "JTR," Richardson's "house flag," snapped in the breeze. So too did the bark's "burgee" pennant, a large blue "C" for *Catalpa* on a field of white. The Stars and Stripes rippled from the spanker. Brightly hued signal flags danced on the lines between the masts.

Slowly, the *Catalpa*'s bow swung out from the dock to the cheers of those onboard and those who waved and shouted from the wharf. Cries of "Greasy Voyage!"—a tradition wishing a whaler blubber-soaked decks—echoed in the air.

The *Catalpa*'s crew unhooked the towlines as the bark slipped from the harbor and into the deep-blue, whitecapped-flecked waters of Buzzard's Bay. As the men of the tug called out their good-byes and turned back for port, the Reverend O. A. Roberts asked if he might see the ship's chronometer and learn how one would use its winding key to arrive at the ship's position. Anthony opened the instrument's case and discovered that he had left the key in his home. To his relief, an old friend and mechanic named Arnett had come along for the dinner and quickly filed an old clock key to wind the chronometer.

In midafternoon Anthony and his guests sat down to dinner in his cabin. Then they headed back on deck, and with handshakes and claps on shoulders, Devoy, Richardson, Hathaway, Goff, Brennan, and the rest climbed down into the skiff that had pulled alongside the whaler. As the skiff turned away from the *Catalpa* for the run back to shore, the full weight of the mission seized Anthony's thoughts as he watched his coconspirators sail away, back to safety, sheltered from any British warships or scaffolds.

Anthony would describe his plunging emotions to Zephaniah W. Pease: "During the remainder of that day Captain Anthony was in the depths of despondency. While in the companionship of Devoy and the conspirators, he had imbibed the enthusiasm and spirit of the affair. But now he was alone with the responsibility. There was not an officer with whom he could share his secret. With a hulk of a whaleship he was defying the mightiest naval power on earth."

As night descended and he set a westerly course, a sudden gale and heavy seas forced Anthony to set short sail, and the ship's dips and rises amid the frothing waves mirrored his mood. As he would relate to Pease, "the captain thought of his wife, his child, and his mother sick at home, and he thought of the task he had assumed to accomplish in the convict land of Australia. There was gloom within the little cabin that evening, as well as without."

Ashore in New Bedford, John Devoy would never have guessed at the doubts and fears assailing Captain Anthony. Devoy wrote to Reynolds on that storm-wracked night:

Goff, Brennan and I have just returned from seeing the ship 40 miles out to sea, eating our dinner of hard tack, salt beef and cheese aboard. She looked splendid with every sail set, a clear sky overhead and a calm sea beneath, and the scene at parting was one we shall not soon forget. About 30 men, all expecting our three being friends of agent, captain or officers, went out in a yacht, got on board and remained there till she was well out, giving three hearty cheers, with the usual "tiger," for the barque and her crew. Not a man but ourselves had the least suspicion of her mission, and she is well on her way now.

We have made arrangements for Brennan to go by steamer to St. Michael's in the Azores and there get on board and go the rest of the way.

It was too late when we came back and all were too tired to do any business, so we stay over till tomorrow, to get the exact items of expenditure, see bills, etc., and hope to go home by boat at 5:20 P.M.

Long before dawn of April 30, 1875, Captain Anthony, though wracked by images of his wife, daughter, and mothers, steeled himself for the mission ahead. His first task was to go whaling—and convince his crew that, for the moment, that was the only mission of the *Catalpa*. He could not afford to think yet about how he would handle a crew of tough whale men suddenly informed that they had signed on for a rescue mission that could land them in British irons or worse.

Anthony's laconic entry in the *Catalpa*'s logbook on April 29, 1875, reflected that he was in control of his ship and his emotions within scant hours of his dark reverie:

A military Fenian is stripped of his uniform.
(National Library, Dublin)

Outside the Fenian trials, soldiers and police kept watch over the
crowds. (Harper's Weekly)

A military Fenian on trial in Dublin for treason, 1866. (National Museum, Dublin)

Prison photo of John Devoy, 1866. (National Museum, Dublin)

Prison photo of John Boyle O'Reilly, February 1866. (National Museum, Dublin)

Kilmainham Gaol, where some of the Fenian prisoners were held in 1866. (National Museum, Dublin)

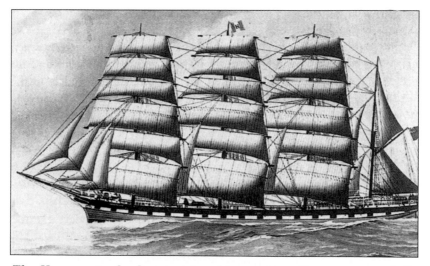

The Hougomont, *the last convict ship to Australia, transported the Fenian prisoners to Fremantle, Western Australia, October 1867-January 1868. (Battye Library, Perth, Australia)*

The convict-built jetty at Fremantle, Western Australia, where the Fenian prisoners were landed on January 10, 1868. (Battye Library, Perth, Australia)

A view of Fremantle Gaol, "The Establishment." (Photograph courtesy of Brendan Woods, Perth, Australia)

Father Patrick McCabe, the Irish priest who helped O'Reilly and, later, the Fremantle Six to escape from Fremantle Gaol. (National Museum, Dublin)

John J. Breslin, who, with Tom Desmond, was the land agent of the six military Fenians' rescue. (National Museum, Dublin)

Captain George Anthony, the man at the helm of the Catalpa, in later years. (Courtesy of Jim Ryan)

Captain Anthony and the prisoners (foreground) race for the Catalpa *as the water police cutter (left) and the gunboat* Georgette *bear down upon the whaler. (National Museum, Dublin)*

The American flag flown onboard the Catalpa. *(National Museum, Dublin)*

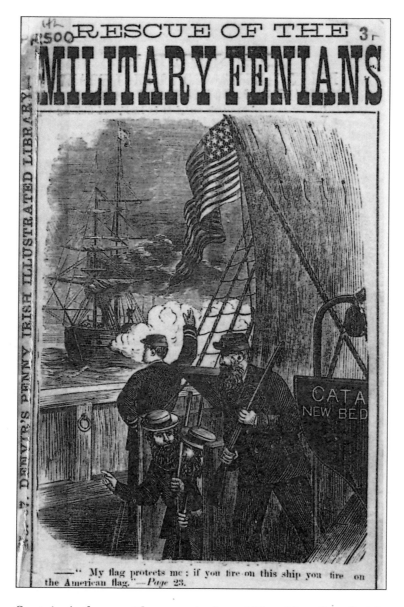

Captain Anthony, with arm raised, and First Mate Sam Smith, with musket, defy the Georgette *as she fires on the* Catalpa *on April 18, 1876. (National Museum, Dublin)*

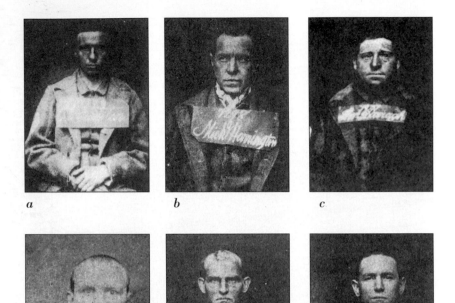

a   b   c

d   e   f

Prison photos of the six military Fenians who escaped from Fremantle Gaol. The condition of the photos is the result of corrosive 19th-century chemicals applied to the plates. (National Museum, Dublin):

a. Robert Cranston, of the 61st Foot, escaped Fremantle Gaol by persuading a warder to let him pass out of the prison's main gate.
b. Michael Harrington was a highly decorated combat veteran of the 61st Foot.
c. Sergeant Thomas Darragh, 2nd Queen's Regiment, was, like Harrington, a well-regarded veteran of the Royal Army until his arrest as a Fenian.
d. Martin Hogan, 5th Dragoon Guards, was one of the British cavalry's most vaunted swordsmen.
e. James Wilson, 5th Dragoon Guards, was the writer of the "Voice from the Tomb" letter.
f. Thomas Henry Hassett, 24th Foot, tried to escape from Western Australia in 1870, some five years before the Catalpa *rescue, but was recaptured.*

Remarks on Board Bark Catalpa, Captain Anthony,
Outward Bound, Thursday, Apr. 29th, 1875
This day commences with light breezes from the S.E.
and clear weather. At 9 A.M. took our anchors and stood
to sea. At 11:30 the captain came on board with officers. Crew all on board.

"[Anthony's] heart-heaviness did not last long," Pease would
write. "If Captain Anthony had not been a man of exceptional
pluck, he would not have been bound to Australia in the
Catalpa."

Throughout the evening of April 29, 1875, Devoy's thoughts
raced westward to Australia, where Cranston, Darragh,
Harrington, Hassett, Hogan, and Wilson wasted in The
Establishment. O'Reilly, who anguished always about his comrades trapped in "the tomb," prayed that their deliverance was at
that very moment on the seas.

Devoy had witnessed the beginning of the rescue's seaborne
phase, but unless Clan na Gael placed the right man or men on
the ground in Australia, Anthony would never have the chance to
extract the military Fenians from shore. Nerve, cunning, and a
pronounced knack for deception—all of those traits and more
must govern the agents devising "the land end of the conspiracy."
They would literally work in the shadow of The Establishment.

Devoy already had a man in mind.

Part 3
Bound for
The Establishment

The Other Members
of the Syndicate Are
Agreed

In the days shortly after the *Catalpa*'s departure, the Rescue Committee met in Manhattan to choose the man who would sail to Australia and arrive months in advance of the whaler to set up the Fenians' escape. John Devoy stood up early in the meeting to present his ideal candidate—himself. Goff immediately objected, the only initial dissenter, according to Devoy.

His zeal notwithstanding, Devoy remained too high-profile a rebel to suddenly appear in Fremantle without every warder, policeman, and detective in the region noticing. Even in New York, agents of the British consulate watched his movements, though none had tracked him vigilantly enough on his trips to Boston and New Bedford. Devoy acknowledged: "Conditions arose, owing to impatience and dissatisfaction on the part of men who had helped to raise the money, which made it absolutely necessary that I should remain in New York. In fact, my disappearance would have at once indicated that I had gone to Australia and the consequent loose talk would almost certainly have ruined

[the] chances of success. I gave up the idea very reluctantly, mainly at the request of Mahon and Reynolds."

Goff pointed out that Devoy "is to this day forbidden to set foot on British soil." If Devoy landed in Australia, chances were that the police would be waiting for him.

As the Rescue Committee mulled over candidates for their land agent in Western Australia, rumors of escape plans had already reached the British consulate, yet they had never considered the prospect that Clan na Gael would buy a whaler outright. Still, in Fremantle, Detective Thomas Rowe had been tracking the limited movements of the military Fenians for the past several years and had warned his superiors as early as 1870 that the ex-soldiers would eventually try to escape or die in the effort.

Rowe noted: "I reported by letter and a private interview to the then Comptroller-General (Wakeford) that from observation I had taken and information received arrangements were being made for a projected escape of the Military Fenian Prisoners."

Expounding his suspicions about O'Reilly's ex-comrades, Rowe continued: "About the 8th of July 1874 one if not more of the Fenian convicts applied to the Acting Comptroller-General, asking that they may be allowed the same privileges as other Convict Constables [messengers]. . . . "

The official, deciding that the military Fenians were no longer a real threat and confident that O'Reilly's run was an aberration, extended a bit of mercy toward the ex-soldiers sentenced to life in The Establishment. He ordered them to be treated as regular penal couriers able to carry official messages and dispatches.

To Rowe, the move constituted a grave mistake:

> Then commenced the origin of the plan of escape. Cranston, Darragh, and Keily [another ex-soldier] were

at that time [1876] employed in the Accountant of Stores [at Fremantle Gaol] every facility then being at hand for correspondence [by the Fenians] outside the prison. . . .

When Darragh was appointed Groom and School Monitor to the Protestant Chaplain [at the prison], he then had opportunities of going out of Prison three times a day for periods varying from one hour to three. Cranston was occasionally employed as Messenger into the Town [Fremantle] and elsewhere. Keily was employed about the beginning of 1876 as a servant to the Adjutant General. In correspondence of Cranston being employed as he was, Hassett wished to be with him and by some means got removed from the Carpenters' Shop to the Stores as a Laborer. . . .

Rowe did not mention the reason that some of the military Fenians were being granted duties outside the quarries and the road gangs. The prisoners, as they had written to Devoy, were literally wasting away, worn down from physical toil and the emotional duress of no relief from their life sentences.

Keily's next move was to quarrel with the Acting Comptroller-General's Servant Girl, and was then (for Punishment) sent to work in the Street Pipelaying Party. [James] Wilson refused to do indoor work at the house of the Clerk of Works and was sent to work at the Jetty [Fremantle Harbor] in Assistant Warder Booler's Party in which Party Harrington was already located.

Just previous to Hassett being sent to the Stores, Darragh went to spend an hour or so with Cranston, ostensibly assisting him in issuing Rations, etc.—

Darragh was also sent on Messenger outside the Prison.

Rowe's concerns that the prisoners were using their limited range of movement to establish contacts among local Fenian sympathizers went unheeded by prison officials, who were still convinced that O'Reilly's escape was a feat that could never be duplicated.

As Rowe was penning his entreaties that the military Fenians bore surveilance, Devoy offered the name of John J. Breslin for "Australian agent" in his stead back in New York. The proposal proved one of the rare occasions when no one in the Clan na Gael leadership leapt from his seat to protest.

In Irish nationalist circles, Breslin held the status of a bonafide Fenian hero. Breslin stood "5 feet 10 inches, splendidly built, with light brown hair and flowing beard, and blue-grey eyes of singular clearness and brightness"; and his intelligence and nerve made him an ideal choice for the mission.

Born in 1836 in Drogheda, County Meath, O'Reilly's birthplace, Breslin was a fine student in the national school, his reading and language skills winning him accolades from his teachers. Described as a man of "fine appearance, good manners, a natural courtesy, keen intelligence, and a prompt and decisive mind," he entered the British prison service with the idea of bringing reforms to the penal system. When he joined the Fenians in 1865, he held the post of Superintendent of the Richmond Prison Hospital in Dublin.

Breslin, familiar with every inch of the prison, had planned the breakout of Fenian leader James Stephens and opened the padlocked door of Stephens's high-security cell with a copy of the key. Among the rescuers with Breslin that night was the *Catalpa*'s future carpenter, Dennis Duggan.

In the furor following the escape, Breslin slipped out of Dublin and boarded a passenger ship for America. He worked for several years as a railway agent in Boston and came to New York City just a short time before the Rescue Committee was formed. Only Devoy and, to a far lesser degree, Goff personally knew Breslin was in the city, and he was not even a member yet of Clan na Gael, but of the UIB (United Irish Brotherhood), which had just two branches, Boston and New York, in the United States.

Devoy made his way from the *Herald* offices the evening after the meeting and walked through the crowds and carts and carriages of the Lower East Side, turning onto South Street. He walked to the waterfront and approached a tract of modest brick flats and knocked on one of the scarred doors. The door opened a crack, and a pair of light-blue eyes stared at Devoy. Then the door swung all the way open, a bearded, handsome man grinning at the editor.

That night, Devoy told John Breslin every detail of the rescue plan, stating bluntly that the shore agent in Australia would risk his life from the moment he set foot in Fremantle. Breslin listened, as he always did, earnestly and knew what was coming. When Devoy requested that Breslin consider the mission, he did not hesitate. "Yes" was his unequivocal answer.

Perhaps fearing that some British operative in New York might spy Devoy and the man who had rescued James Stephens and alert the consulate that something might be in the works, the Rescue Committee met with Breslin in April 1875 in Hoboken, New Jersey. Some of the men gaped at Breslin, for as a contemporary noted, "Mr. Breslin was already a famous hero, and his burning love of country, his chivalry and his bravery, were written in the hearts of Erin's sons and daughters. . . . His history reads like a chapter from the days of King Arthur. His name will, in time to come, start wonderful echoes among the thousand hills of Ireland."

Shouts of assent followed Breslin's declaration that he would sail to Australia. He hoped that the flowing beard he now wore would mask his face from any British police or soldiers who had seen the lithographic renderings of the clean-shaven man who had sprung Stephens from Richmond Prison and embarrassed the Crown years ago. Breslin now assured his fellow rebels that he would find a way to rescue the military Fenians from another prison deemed "escape-proof." Breslin's friend O'Reilly had shown the way.

Too smart not to consider all that could go wrong, Breslin knew that since O'Reilly's flight, the British had closely watched every American whaler that dropped anchor in Bunbury and Perth. He knew that the military Fenians remained under close supervision by their captors. Still, having seen Hogan's and Wilson's letters to Devoy, he believed them when they said that escape by sea could work—so long as they had help from the outside, from their "friends in America."

Breslin was the man—all in the house agreed. Then to Devoy's shock, one of the members contended that before Breslin was approved, he must take Clan na Gael's oath. Breslin stood up, glowering, ready to leave the task to "one of their own boys." Devoy grabbed Breslin and urged him to stay until the matter was resolved. Eventually, Breslin's own desire to rescue the prisoners and the entreaties of every man in that New Jersey meeting assuaged him. Although he loathed secret oaths and Masonic-style rituals, Breslin pledged himself and his life to Clan na Gael—out of his deep Irish nationalism and the chance to plan yet another daring escape, one that far eclipsed the one he had pulled off in Dublin in 1865.

With Breslin handpicked, the Rescue Committee turned to an impassioned plea from the California branch of Clan na Gael to place one of their men at Breslin's side in Australia. Since nearly half of the funds for the rescue had been raised in California, the committee agreed. John C. Talbot, who lived in Sacramento and was the chief money man for the organization on the West Coast, urged the committee to choose Thomas Desmond, a Civil War veteran and deputy sheriff in San Francisco.

Seconding the nomination of Desmond was Fenian stalwart John Kenealy, a Cork Fenian who had been sentenced to ten years' penal servitude and knew all of the military Fenians well from his transport aboard the *Hougoumont* and imprisonment in The Establishment. He had been conditionally pardoned in 1870, had departed Australia for San Francisco, and had settled in Los Angeles, where he had found success with a dry goods store and was one of the most prominent Clan na Gael men in the region. Believing that two men on the ground in Australia seemed a sound idea, the committee asked Kenealy for a dossier on Desmond and liked what it related.

Desmond was described as "a Nationalist from the time he could stand alone." Born in Cobh, County Cork, on December 22, 1838, Desmond had joined the Fenians as a young man and had proven himself under fire in the American Civil War in a Union Army regiment. The man endorsed by Talbot and Kenealy was "in the prime of his life, a fine type of physical manhood, cool, self-possessed, and resolute—just the man for such an enterprise."

In early July 1875, Devoy met Breslin in his Lower East Side flat to deliver orders for the mission and inform him that he would be traveling with another agent, Desmond. Breslin leveled his piercing blue stare at Devoy and responded that if Desmond did not measure up to Breslin's liking, the former Richmond warder would not take him along, and even if he did, it must be understood that Desmond was an assistant to Breslin. Realizing that Breslin would not back down, Devoy agreed. Later, he wrote to

Talbot about Breslin's conditions regarding Desmond, and Talbot, unruffled, assured Devoy of Desmond's suitability for the job. Talbot wrote, "I think you will like him."

On July 19, 1875, Breslin, dressed in a summer business suit, locked up his flat, shoved his way through the crowds to the docks, took the ferry to Jersey City, hopped off onto the pier, and strode to the train station. He boarded a train for Chicago with his valise, and with the Rescue Committee's orders embedded in his memory. As the train pulled from the station with a hiss of steam and the loud clack of the wheels against the rails began to measure the first leg of the long trip to California, Breslin had plenty of time to ponder his orders and the scope of the mission.

In brief, he was supposed to establish contact with Father McCabe and organize the rescue of Cranston, Darragh, Harrington, Hassett, Hogan, and Wilson from Fremantle in time for the *Catalpa*'s planned arrival off Western Australia in January 1876. Once the ship landed, he was to establish contact with Captain Anthony and bring the prisoners home. How all of that was to be accomplished—with British warships, the water police, the warders of The Establishment, and the pensioner guards patrolling the coast and the bush—was left entirely up to Breslin.

Breslin arrived in San Francisco on July 26, 1875, to discover that Talbot, whom the agent was supposed to meet there, was home in Sacramento. Not willing to waste time, Breslin caught a Sacramento River steamer and set foot in the town three days later.

He found Talbot's new house on a sleepy side street, and when a big, bluff Irishman opened the front door to Breslin's insistent knock, Breslin handed him a letter of introduction from Devoy. Moments later, Breslin was the house guest of the good-natured Talbot.

The host sent telegrams that same day to Kenealy and Desmond in Los Angeles that "B" had arrived. Desmond left immediately for Sacramento, and when he entered Talbot's home three days later, Breslin was waiting.

Breslin sized up the broad-shouldered, thirty-seven-year-old Cork man with his bristling mustache and calm expression. Behind the seemingly placid blue eyes, however, Breslin detected a formidable resolve. He liked the tall, muscular Desmond right away.

In Talbot's house, Breslin laid out the opening steps of his plan. Breslin, with his urbane polish, would travel to Australia as "James Collins," a wealthy American businessman and speculator looking for gold mining deals and other ventures in Western Australia. Rougher in speech and appearance and once a carriage maker, Desmond would pose as a man named "Tom Johnson" and find work in that trade once they landed. From the moment they boarded ship for Australia, they were to pretend that they had never met and were to have no more interaction than a passing nod.

To carry off the ruse, especially Breslin's expensive one, Clan na Gael was supposed to wire funds to Breslin in San Francisco, but budget squabbles tied up the Rescue Committee's release of the money for nearly a month. Out of his own pocket, Talbot handed Breslin one hundred dollars a week.

Growing more anxious with each passing day, worried that each day lost would hamstring his chances of crafting a plausible rescue plan before the *Catalpa* dropped anchor in Bunbury, Breslin decided to head to Los Angeles to talk with Kenealy, who could provide firsthand knowledge of The Establishment, the shore north and south of Fremantle, locals who had Fenian leanings, and anything else from his time there that would be useful.

Breslin, with Desmond, returned to San Francisco by

September 10, 1875, and was exhilarated to find a letter waiting at their hotel with the news that the funds, several thousand dollars, had been wired in Breslin's name to the telegraph office and that more would be sent to him in Australia. They raced to the telegraph office to collect the cash, but to Breslin's fury, the clerk refused to turn over the money because Breslin was not a local and had no one to vouch for him.

A quick telegram to Talbot soon solved the crisis. Within a day, Judge M. Cooney, a member of the California Supreme Court and a fervent official of Clan na Gael, strode into the telegraph office with Breslin. The clerk promptly released the funds.

From the telegraph office, Breslin scurried down to the docks and booked two passages on the *Cyphranes,* a speedy mail steamer bound for Sydney, Australia. He also walked into a nearby bank and converted his dollars into gold—wealthy speculators' "calling card."

Breslin and Desmond arrived separately at the dock on September 13, 1875. The man with a flowing but well-groomed reddish beard strode up the gangplank in an expensive suit, a dapper brimmed hat, and a gold pocket watch and chain and was followed by cabin boys lugging his costly wood-and-leather steamer trunk and leather valises to his first-class cabin in the stern. He carried nothing himself except two letters. The first, from Judge M. Cooney, "confirmed" that "Mr. James Collins" was a wealthy owner of vast tracts of land and silver mines in Nevada and other states. Adding to the ruse, the second letter was a fictitious bank draft signed by a "C. Coddington Yardley": "It is advised that as of this date, $100,000 has been deposited to your credit in the Hollanders Bank. . . . The other members of the syndicate are agreed that they will allow you to be sole judge, whether to invest the funds in Australian gold shares, timber, farm or grazing land."

Among the other passengers, a tall, brawny man in a plain suit shouldered his battered trunk. He disappeared down the second-class hatchway.

John Breslin and Tom Desmond were headed for Australia.

I Think We Have All the Crew We Need

As the *Cyphranes* steamed through the Pacific, carrying Breslin and Desmond ever closer to Sydney, another vessel pushed into the open Atlantic. Captain Anthony's thoughts never ventured far from his own course to Australia, but he had business at hand: to kill enough whales to turn a profit for everyone—from Clan na Gael, to Richardson, and to the crew—before the port of Bunbury materialized on the horizon.

Still, on that first night at sea, as the *Catalpa*'s bow plunged and rose in the churning waves, and frigid spray washed across the decks, Anthony thought of Emma and Sophie, and of his ailing mother. He stood on the quarterdeck and beneath the wooden canopy of the wheelhouse as he took the whaler out, No Man's Land and Martha's Vineyard vanishing behind the *Catalpa*.

Anthony decided to take the *Catalpa*'s bearings with the chronometer the following day, April 20, 1875. With one of the Malay steerers at the helm, Anthony took the gleaming brass instrument from its case, inserted Arnett's makeshift key into the device, wound it, and took the vessel's position. Anthony looked at the reading, shook his head, and wound the chronometer again. Once more, he peered in disbelief at the reading of the whaler's longitude.

Anthony kept winding and frowning. He related: "[A]fter taking a number of sights and making a computation by it, the result showed the vessel to be in the interior of New York State. The hammering and pounding which the instrument had undergone in the process of fitting the key had changed the rate."

Anthony and Smith both went to work resetting the chronometer with Addison's key, and the next set of readings indicated that the problem was fixed. For three days, Anthony relied on the instrument to set a southwesterly course for the hunting grounds of the South Atlantic.

As on any whaling voyage, Anthony took stock of his crew, which, with the exceptions of First Mate Smith and Dennis Duggan, had been assembled by Richardson.

The captain was pleased with Richardson's choices for boat steerers, the men who would handle the tillers of the whaleboats (chase boats) and whose expertise, or lack thereof, meant the difference between taking a whale or losing valuable gear—harpoons, lances, and tackle. Chief among the four men was Cape Verdean Islander Antone Ferris. Over fifty years old, the eldest of the crew, Ferris stood five feet, eight inches tall, with alert dark eyes and gray hair crowning a dark face blackened by the sun during his many whaling voyages.

Anthony knew he could rely on Ferris, but within a few days out of port, the captain suspected trouble could erupt from Third Mate George H. Bolles, a dark-eyed, sandy-haired twenty-four-year-old from New Bedford. Although the man had a reputation as a skilled man in a whaleboat, Anthony detected a surly, defiant glimmer in Bolles's eyes.

Anthony's misgivings about Bolles aside, the captain found the crew passable enough, as most had sailed on other whalers. Above all, he was relieved that he had Sam Smith aboard as first mate, for early in the voyage the sandy-haired, balding Smith had proven with a couple of well-placed blows to the chins of insubordinate crewmen that any breaches of discipline would not be tolerated. Anthony's reputation, too, as a fair, but hard-nosed, whaling officer had preceded him aboard the *Catalpa*.

The captain also liked the second mate, forty-three-year-old Antone Farnham, a sea-savvy Portuguese resident of New Bedford. Lean, standing five feet, eleven inches, his wiry frame and fierce dark eyes cowed the crew, which pleased Anthony, as no whaling shipmaster could enforce discipline without trustworthy officers to dole out punishment. Even the best of whaling crews were comprised of hard-fisted, stubborn men, a fact that Anthony especially worried about on this clandestine voyage. At some point, as he had warned Devoy, Anthony was going to have to tell Sam Smith the *Catalpa*'s true purpose, and the captain feared that not even he and Smith could hide the truth from the crew long enough to attempt a rescue of the military Fenians.

As Anthony navigated the *Catalpa* southeast toward the Western Hunting Grounds, several thousand miles off the coast of Africa, the weather cleared, so that the whaler cruised under "easy canvas." Smith, Farnham, and Bolles selected crews for the *Catalpa*'s four whaleboats, thirty feet long and six feet from beam to beam. Readying the craft for the chases to come in the hunting grounds, the men packed lantern kegs, sealed small barrels containing lanterns, matches, candles, and hardtack for chases that stretched into the night. The crewmen stored water kegs, bailing buckets, and a mast and "mutton sail" in each boat. The grisly instruments of the whaler's trade—keenly honed darts and lances—were carefully laid in each boat, along with waif (identification) flags to drive into the carcass of a slain whale when the crew might have to leave it for a time in rough weather or if they were pursuing other whales. Other whalers in the grounds would honor the waif flags and leave the carcass for the boat that had taken the whale.

Each boat was equipped with a twenty-three-foot-long steering oar that the boat steerer would use to sidle up to a whale so that the mate could stand up and ram home the lance. The weapon would slice the whale's huge jugular vein and kill it in an explosion of blood that would douse the whaleboat's crew.

To tow the whale back to the ship, each whaleboat was also equipped with hundreds of fathoms of two-and-a-quarter-circumference manila harpoon line fresh from the ropewalks at Plymouth, Massachusetts. The crew did not put the line into the whaleboats until the moment the shout of "Ah! Blows!" or "Thar' she blows!" echoed from the crow's nest high on the mainmast.

The daily rituals of life aboard a whaler began the first morning at sea with the shout of "All hands!" announcing breakfast at sunrise. The crew assembled at the galley for hot coffee and trenchers piled with hardtack, potatoes, a portion of salted meat, and a bit of fruit to ward off scurvy. Then, as the crew went about their appointed duties of clearing the bilges, checking the rigging and sails, and laying on the amount of canvas dictated by Anthony according to fluctuations in the wind, every man awaited with combined boredom and tension the cry that would set off a burst of action as they scrambled to lower the whaleboats.

On Saturday, May 1, 1875, Anthony spotted a German bark, signaled her and went aboard to chat with the captain about any whale sightings he may have made in nearby waters. To Anthony's shock, when he talked with his German counterpart about the ships' positions, the New Bedford captain learned that his chronometer's reading placed the *Catalpa* forty miles off her actual position. He would have to factor in that difference on every reading he took until the ship put into port and he had the chronometer repaired or bought a new one.

The *Catalpa* approached the hunting grounds on Tuesday, May 4, under two lower topsails and a headsail. Anthony sent lookouts scampering to perches aloft on the foremast and the mainmast.

The first cry of "Ah! Blows!" rang out. The whale was moving too fast and was too far away to lower boats, but the sighting set the crew on alert. Although they spotted several schools of whales that day, an oncoming storm and rising seas made any chase impossible.

The *Catalpa* chased a school of whales on May 5, 1875, battling a squall under two lower topsails, and continued the pursuit on the following day. On May 6, 1875, the ship took its first kill, a small whale that the crew raised to the deck of the *Catalpa*. The gruesome work of cutting and boiling the carcass began at 5:30 P.M. and went on until 8 P.M. They sliced giant pieces of blubber, dragged them over the tryworks above the main hatch, and sliced them into small chunks called "horse pieces." Then the crew boiled the blubber into hot oil that was poured into casks, sailors washing down the decks with water all the while to prevent the woodwork from catching fire.

The first kill netted only twenty barrels of oil, but the crew knew that there were many more whales in those waters. There were also other whalers, and on May 8, 1875, the *Catalpa* hailed a vessel headed to New Bedford, and Anthony sent letters home to Emma and Richardson. The letters reached them in the second week of June, and on June 15, Richardson showed his message to Hathaway and asked him to convey the details to Devoy, who was fretting in New York for any news from Captain Anthony.

Hathaway quickly wrote to the Irishman:

Dear Friend:

Mr. R. received a short letter from Capt. A. dated May 8th, nine days from home. Boiling a sperm whale. . . . A did not write how much oil the whale would probably yield as he wrote but a few lines in haste to send by passing ship. In all probability we will get letters from him in a few days. . . .

This [the killed whale] is a first rate commencement and I am glad to hear of it so early in the voyage, as it will keep the officers and crew in good spirits. Capt. A. writes that he is much pleased with the ship and crew. Well he might be, for we were very particular in shipping good men and having things as near right as possible on shipboard. I think this voyage will be a success for all concerned. I have great faith in Capt. A., he being a young man who is looking ahead.

Mr. R. received a letter from Reynolds last night dated June 14th, stating that he would send the balance of the money in a day or two. I am glad this part of the job is drawing to a close; it will take a big load from my mind.

On May 12, four days after Anthony dashed off the letters, the *Catalpa* took two whales, filling scores of casks with sperm oil, and hopes of a "greasy voyage" spread through the crew. Only Anthony and Duggan knew that when the *Catalpa* unloaded her barrels at Fayal in the Azores, the *Catalpa*'s whaling would end, and the real voyage begin.

Prowling the Western Hunting Grounds over the next eighteen days, the *Catalpa*'s lookouts stared for the spouts of a whale but saw nothing. Men began to grumble, the more superstitious wondering if they had signed aboard an unlucky ship.

A lookout's cry brought the crew to the rails on May 30, 1875, but not to scan the waters for a spout. Drifting ahead was a brig with one mast gone and the other flying distress flags. Anthony brought the *Catalpa* in close to the vessel, the British whaler *Florence,* and boarded her to find the crew's water and provisions exhausted and the men starving. The fallen mast, ripped from its keelson during a gale, had killed one seaman and injured three others.

Anthony ordered his crew to stock the brig with food and water enough to see her to her destination of Annapolis, Nova Scotia, and set his crew to rigging two sails for the vessel. If Anthony saw any irony in assisting the British brig, given the mission he was embarked upon, he did not mention the thought. All he saw was a fellow ship in distress.

As the *Florence* limped off, eventually to reach Nova Scotia, distress descended upon the crew of the *Catalpa.* Nearly two weeks dragged on with no whales sighted. Then, in the late afternoon of June 13, 1875, the cry of "Ah! Blows!" sent the whaleboats' crews racing to their craft and lowering them into the water.

The whale sounded—broke the surface ahead—with a huge rush of water driven airborne by the slaps of the massive tail. In one of the whaleboats, Sam Smith urged his crew to row with all they had, and the craft shot toward the creature. Still the whale sped away. Relentlessly, calloused hands gripping the oar handles, the boat began to gain on the whale. Smith fired the harpoon, and it streaked across the waves and slammed deep into the creature, who gasped sounding nearly human. Pain now coursing through its every fiber, the whale thrashed and surged forward. The harpoon line stiffened and began to smoke as it passed through the eyehole in the front of the boat. Crewmen poured buckets of water on the hissing line. Then the boat nearly leaped from the water as the whale's mad burst pulled the craft on a "Nantucket sleigh ride" for a mile or more.

A subtle slackening of the line announced that the creature was tiring, and the whaleboat pulled close to the stricken mammal. Smith clutched a lance, poised for the death blow. The whale, as if in pain-wracked resignation, lay nearly motionless on the surface, waiting.

Standing in the boat inches from the whale, Smith drove the lance into the jugular. The whale thrashed its tail in one final spasm and struck Smith in the head. The impact knocked him overboard and several yards from the boat.

As blood burst from the whale's severed jugular, sharks swarmed from every direction. The crew rowed frantically to the unconscious Smith, who bobbed in the scarlet water. From the deck of the *Catalpa*, Anthony peered at the scene through his telescope, his stomach roiling for both Smith's plight and his own—he did not believe he could take the crew to Australia without Smith's firm hand.

Smith's chase crew hauled him from the sea seconds before the gray fins closed in on him, and rowed back to the *Catalpa*, blood streaming from deep gashes on his neck and head. Astern, the sharks were already tearing at the whale's carcass. The *Catalpa* plowed toward the boat, and by the time they lifted Smith over the bark's gunwales, his breathing came in shallow gasps. They carried him to his cabin.

That night, Anthony kept vigil with his first mate as the crew pulled the *Catalpa* alongside the whale, hauled him aboard, and left him on the tryworks for the rest of the night. Smith, weak from blood loss and undoubtedly suffering a concussion, rose from his berth the next morning, staggered to his feet, and insisted that he would direct the "cutting-in" of the whale as a first mate should. Anthony nodded.

Anthony would tell an acquaintance that "this little incident indicated . . . that he had made no mistake in selecting Mr. Smith, and he [Anthony] felt sure that when the supreme test came he would have at least one man behind him upon whom he could rely to the uttermost."

For the moment, the whaling went on, but each day brought Anthony closer to the supreme test.

John T. Richardson received a letter from Anthony in mid-August and relayed the captain's news to Reynolds and Devoy:

> Friend Reynolds:
>
> I have just received a letter from Capt. Anthony, dated June the 29th. He has taken 110 lbs. of sperm oil. He likes his ship first mate, and his crew. He thinks he will get a big catch this season. I should have sent you a letter before this time, but I had no news.

Henry Hathaway's calm assertion that Anthony would lose a man or two before the ship reached Fayal or Tenerife and possibly open a spot for Thomas Brennan proved accurate. Robert Kanaka, a Sandwich Islands boat steerer, died of a fever and was buried at sea, with Anthony presiding over the service.

As the *Catalpa* sighted the island of Flores on October 14, 1875, Anthony grimaced at the chronometer's reading—"120 miles out of his reckoning." The *Catalpa* moored off Flores for several days, taking on supplies of fresh water and fruit. On October 20, Anthony set course for Fayal to unload the voyage's take, 210 barrels of sperm oil, and to hire a merchantman to convey the casks to New Bedford. Although the cargo's value of twelve thousand dollars was disappointing, that amount coupled with the *Catalpa*'s open-market value could translate into a nice profit for everyone involved—as long as Anthony proved able to bring her home.

In the final week of October 1875, the *Catalpa* slid into the harbor of Fayal, where a massive cliff-top Portuguese fortress commanded the port, teeming with whalers, warships, and merchantmen. Anthony's crew, eager for their impending shore leave amid the grogshops and brothels of the port, unloaded the oil quickly and lugged casks of fruit, salted meat, and water for the second leg of the voyage.

Anthony was elated to find letters from Emma, Richardson, Hathaway, and other friends waiting. His thoughts clouded, however, as he stared at a photograph of Sophie, and all the fears that he might never see her or Emma again hit him.

Again, Anthony forced himself to focus on his mission. Spying the New Bedford whaler *Osprey* at anchor, he rowed over to her and met with Captain Crapo, who happened to have three chronometers aboard. He sold one to Anthony for a pricey $110, but Anthony "experienced much satisfaction in the belief that he now had an instrument which he could trust."

The money for the chronometer was part of $1,000 that Anthony charged to Reynolds's account at Fayal, the funds used to refit planks and fittings battered by nearly seven months at sea.

Anthony's instincts that he could not trust Third Mate Bolles came to pass in Fayal. As soon as Bolles and the crew went ashore, Bolles convinced a half-dozen of the men to desert with him, perhaps sensing that something did not seem quite right about the voyage. Anthony, in a desperate bind because he had already dismissed three of the crew due to illness, turned to a "runner" for help. In doing so, Anthony was breaking the law, thus risking his opportunity to sail for Australia, for runners were agents who rounded up sailors shanghaied or stranded without passports and, for steep fees, smuggled them aboard ships desperate for bodies. Anthony had no choice.

The *Catalpa*'s whaleboats were lowered from the ship on a moonless night in early November 1875, and the oars, muffled with cloth wrapped around the tips, dipped into the black waters and pulled the vessels to a rendezvous point directly beneath the massive walls and huge cannon of the fortress. They rowed to a sheltered scrap of shore, where the agent was waiting with half a dozen sailors desperate to escape Fayal.

The sailors scrambled into the boats, and once again the oars broke the harbor water.

Suddenly, Anthony, Smith, Duggan, and the rest froze—a Portuguese guard boat sliced the waves just ahead of the whaleboats. From the guard boat, a voice hailed the little flotilla but let them pass, the guards perhaps thinking that the whaleboats were picking up their men from shore leave.

If Anthony needed another reason to sail from Fayal as soon as possible, the impetus came from a letter that Dennis Duggan handed to him in the first week of November. Anthony winced as he read that Thomas Brennan was at nearby St. Michael's Island and about to board a steamer for Fayal. In showing Anthony the letter, Duggan, onboard in large part to make sure that Anthony's nerve would not ebb, indicated how much trust he now placed in the captain. As Anthony told a friend, "He [Anthony] and Duggan had agreed never to converse on the subject, lest the suspicions of the officers might be excited; but the carpenter promptly carried the letter to the captain."

If Duggan had not shown Anthony the letter, the sudden appearance of Brennan and his blustering demands that he be allowed onboard would have alerted the crew that something was wrong with the upcoming voyage. Duggan knew that Anthony had been given full discretion by Devoy to take Brennan or not, and also knew that Anthony did not want the man. Neither, it appeared, did Duggan.

Anthony said to Duggan, "I think we have all the crew we need at present. Mr. Brennan may get left."

Immediately Anthony ordered Smith to get the ship ready to sail, dashed to the Customs House, obtained clearance from Portuguese officials to head to Tenerife, in the Canary Islands, and rushed back to the *Catalpa*. At 5:30 in the evening of November 6, 1875, Anthony took the helm and steered the whaler out of the harbor as drizzle blanketed her shrouds and rigging and a southwest breeze began to blow.

Next morning, Anthony, with Duggan close by, spotted a steamer coming from the direction of St. Michael's and heading toward Fayal. The captain turned to Duggan and "bestowed a grim smile." They both believed they were done with the truculent Brennan.

On the deck of the steamer, however, a blocky, square-jawed man glowered as he watched the whaler slipping away in the direction of the Canary Islands. Tom Brennan pondered his next move and decided to wire Goff for funds as soon as the steamer reached Fayal and book passage on another steamer, but not one bound for America. "With remarkable tenacity," wrote an associate of Anthony, "[Brennan] decided that he must have a part in the rescue." As the whaler laid on additional sail for the run to Tenerife, Brennan was calculating the cost of passage to Australia.

As only Anthony and Duggan knew, Tenerife would be the *Catalpa*'s final stop until Western Australia. For Anthony, a critical juncture of the mission loomed as the whaler sailed for the Canary Islands. Anthony "knew that the deception could not be kept much longer from his chief mate, Mr. Smith, and had planned for many months to make a confidante of him on the voyage from Fayal to Tenerife. . . . The officer must be admitted into the secret before Tenerife was reached."

Anthony agonized about the meeting to come. Without a strong first mate, the rescue plot could unravel by the time the crags of Tenerife loomed in the distance.

If She Goes to Hell . . .

Several days out of Fayal, as the sun began to dip in the late afternoon, Anthony asked Smith to come to the captain's cabin to discuss some "ship's business." Anthony led his first mate into the two-room berth and gestured for him to take a seat. Pacing for a few minutes as Smith waited, a querulous expression on the first mate's ruddy features, Anthony searched for the right words.

Smith knew only as much as the rest of the crew about the *Catalpa*'s current course. Anthony had addressed the crew, assembled on the main deck shortly after passing St. Michael's. According to an interview with Zephaniah Pease: "[Anthony] had explained as a reason for going to Tenerife that he contemplated whaling about the River Platte [whaling waters in the South Atlantic off the eastern coast of South America], and proposed to stop there [Tenerife] for water."

To a veteran whaler such as Smith, Anthony's logic did make sense. As Anthony had noted, "the water at Fayal was taken from wells near the shore and was brackish, while that at Tenerife is much sought after by whalers."

Anthony thought: "So far there was nothing to arouse a question upon the part of the chief officer. But after Tenerife there was to be the long and dreary voyage around the Cape of Good Hope and across the Indian Ocean, with no pretense of whaling."

Now that the moment for revealing everything to Smith was at hand, Anthony worried about the man's reaction. "If he refused to assist the enterprise, he must be landed there [Tenerife]," Anthony decided. "[Smith] might be properly indignant at being inveigled into such a voyage and give away the plan."

From the moment that Anthony had convinced Smith to ship out on the *Catalpa*, the captain had believed wholeheartedly in him: "Of all men Smith the first mate was an officer among a thousand for such work. He was bold and adventure-loving."

Still, Smith's boldness troubled Anthony. He would tell a New Bedford historian: "[Smith's] very impetuosity was dreaded . . . in the interview to come; for whereas he might accept a part in the program with enthusiasm, he was perhaps as likely to be enraged at the deception practiced upon him."

Anthony had duped Smith into signing onto a secret and dangerous voyage. Now the captain could only hope that Smith would understand and, like Anthony, would be so outraged by the plight of the military Fenians that the first mate would pledge to help them. Anthony counted on the fact that Smith's Scottish heritage left him with scant love for Great Britain.

With the creaks of the *Catalpa*'s rigging and planks as a backdrop, Anthony stood still, met the first mate's gray-eyed stare squarely, and in a volume just a shade above a whisper, delivered the words that he had shaped in his thoughts for just this moment:

> Mr. Smith, you shipped to go whaling. I want to tell you now, before we get to Tenerife, that the *Catalpa* has done about all the whaling she will do this fall. We're bound to the western coast of Australia to try and liberate six Fenian prisoners who are serving a life sentence in Great Britain's penal colony. This ship was

bought for that purpose and fitted for that purpose, and you have been utterly deceived in the object of this voyage. You have a right to be indignant and leave the vessel at Tenerife. You will have the opportunity when we arrive there, and if you go, I can't blame you.

But this ship is going to Australia if I live, and I hope you will stay by me and go with me. God knows I need you, and I give you my word I will stand by you as never one man stood by another, if you will say you will remain in the ship and assist me in carrying out my plans.

Smith's mouth hung open beneath his sandy, walruslike mustache. Speechless, he simply stared at Anthony.

Before the first mate said anything, Anthony launched into a description of who the prisoners were, the torments they endured in the name of freedom, and the "bold, patriotic" Irishmen in America who had conceived the audacious plan to strike a blow against "British tyranny."

Smith listened, gaping but making no move to storm out of the cabin.

He still said nothing as Anthony assured Smith "that if any trouble came he would exonerate him completely from the conspiracy and would proclaim that he shipped to go whaling."

Anthony paused. He had said all he could and now could only wait.

Smith sat in silence for several minutes, his face tight. Then he stood, walked over to Anthony, and gripped the captain's hand.

"Captain Anthony," the first mate growled, "I'll stick by you on this ship if she goes to Hell and burns off her jibboom."

Both men sat at the captain's table and in low voices discussed the longshot mission to come. As they talked, Smith revealed that he had been curious about certain aspects of the voyage from even before the *Catalpa*'s departure.

Anthony would note: "Smith had wondered at the interest of the strange men, Devoy and Reynolds, who had visited the ship during her fitting, and he never had been able to understand how it was expected the vessel could go to the River Platte and return in eighteen months; but otherwise his curiosity had never led him to suspect that he was not in the entire confidence of the captain."

That night, Anthony slept well, relieved that Smith had embraced the secret mission and would be onboard to help keep the crew in line when Anthony sailed around the tip of Africa at the Cape of Good Hope. As Anthony and Smith both realized, the crew would quickly question the captain's course as he took the whaler east into the Indian Ocean rather than straight south for the Antarctic hunting grounds. Then, Anthony knew, trouble could erupt.

The cry of "Land, ho!" broke from a lookout's throat on November 19, 1875. The first outline of Tenerife's 12,182-foot-high peak appeared to the southeast. Anthony, who knew the distance to the shore from this position from previous voyages to the Canaries, took out his new chronometer, wound the key, and read—ninety miles away. Anger washed over him, for the number was twenty miles off. Anthony noted, "The new chronometer was no longer to be implicitly trusted."

He ordered that the *Catalpa* be "hauled sharp by the wind," and on the evening of November 20, 1875, the whaler entered the harbor, but as with all arriving ships, could not moor at a dock until inspection by port officials.

Almost immediately after she dropped anchor in the channel, Portuguese customs officials swarmed aboard the *Catalpa* and demanded to see the ship's "papers of health," signed and stamped documents from Fayal officials who testified that none of the crew carried disease.

One of the officials asked if Anthony had twenty-five men onboard, as the papers specified. Straining to control his sudden fear, Anthony said nothing for a moment as he considered how to explain that his crew was only twenty-two hands because of the desertions. Even worse, the men taken onboard illegally at Fayal had no passports to show officials.

When the officials ordered Anthony to muster the crew for a head count, he had no choice but to comply. An official counted, turned to Anthony, and asked where the three "missing" men were.

Anthony had no answer, for if he told the truth, the ship would be seized and he would be tossed in jail to await a formal hearing.

The officials—aware that many shipmasters routinely beat, whipped, keelhauled, or hanged crewmen in the course of a voyage—put a chilling question to Anthony: "He was asked if he had not made away with them."

"No!" Anthony protested.

The port officials responded with an order that Anthony produce his logbook, ship's papers, crew list, and certificates of discharges and desertions. Again, he had no choice but to hand the material over to the authorities. The Portuguese officers scrutinized the papers and told Anthony that they would detain the *Catalpa* until or unless he could account for the three missing men.

Anthony kept calm and, punctuating his appeals with profuse apologies, assured the officials that all was in order and that if permitted to speak with the Portuguese consul ashore, Anthony could explain the situation to everyone's satisfaction. For several long minutes, Anthony waited as the officials huddled and glanced over at him a few times. Deciding that he did not seem a murderer, they agreed to let the *Catalpa* dock on condition that Anthony report to the consul first thing in the morning; however, the captain understood their message—the whaler was detained.

Before Anthony left for the consulate on the morning of February 21, 1875, he told Smith to maintain a tight watch on the crew to prevent anyone from jumping ship. Smith, now aware of Duggan's identity and his abilities with pistol and blade, felt that he and the Irishman could dissuade any would-be deserters. Anthony hustled down the gangplank and off to the consulate, knowing that what he said in the interview would determine whether the *Catalpa* left port or he would languish in a prison cell, like the very men he hoped to pluck from The Establishment.

When Anthony, wearing a clean blue master's tunic and trousers, polished boots, and his visored cap, was escorted into the consul's office, the mariner had already decided to tell the truth about the desertions, but not about the replacements he had smuggled aboard the *Catalpa*. The consul, accustomed to the reality that crewmen regularly vanished from their ships on shore leave at Fayal and Tenerife, accepted the earnest American's explanation that he had docked at Fayal with twenty-five hands, but that a number had disappeared in the red-light environs of the port and he had been compelled to sign on three new men. He had time only to find three hands at Fayal, Anthony lied, but without a trace of deception in his steady gaze. Adroitly, he produced the passports of Bolles and other deserters to "identify" the men he had sneaked aboard who had no papers.

Satisfied by the captain's appeal and "forthright" manner of speech, the official made a suggestion that Anthony took advantage of immediately: "The consul advised him to ship the men taken aboard at Fayal regularly."

Anthony managed to show no surprise despite his true alarm at the official's next statement. He wanted Anthony to bring the three men to the consulate for inspection.

Calmly, Anthony suggested that the consul might agree to come aboard the *Catalpa* and see the men. The captain explained that he was on a restrictive schedule for the ship's owners and if any of the Fayal hands made a run for it once their feet touched the dock, the voyage would be ruined.

Again, the consul took the American at his word. Anthony would relate, "He [the consul] consented to go aboard the *Catalpa*."

A squad of soldiers in white jackets and black shakos accompanied the consul onboard, and the men they viewed may have appeared glum or surly, but on whaling ships, such expressions were common enough among tough crewmen. Well aware that without legal passports, they would be jailed in Tenerife with little prospect of release until they revealed their actual identities, the men hoped that the official would not ask any questions. In whaling ports, men who had no passports often had something to hide and were on the run from authorities somewhere. He scrutinized them, but did not interrogate any.

Satisfied that the Fayal "hires" had not been smuggled aboard, the consul and the soldiers left the ship. Anthony was free to stay or leave at will.

While Smith watched the crew, Anthony and Duggan spent three hundred dollars of Clan na Gael's money on lumber, boards, and joists at Tenerife, and when the goods were delivered to the *Catalpa*, Anthony told the crew that the giant spruce boards would be used for mending the whaleboats. He later would say, ". . . notwithstanding the absurdity, it was perfectly satisfactory to the men."

In reality, Duggan would apply his carpentry skill to the wood when the whaler reached Western Australia. The lumber was for a special job—"to build quarters for the guests whom the captain expected to take aboard."

Anthony guided the *Catalpa* out of Tenerife's harbor on November 25, 1875 and set sail for the "River La Platte and other places." Taking the ship on a slightly southwest course at first to create the impression that the ship was, in fact, bound for the southeastern Atlantic whaling grounds, Anthony decided that if they spotted any whales, they would take a run at them. He wanted to hide the true course as long as possible.

On November 16, 1875, as the *Catalpa* made for Tenerife and Anthony geared himself for the long journey to Bunbury, John Breslin and Tom Desmond walked down the gangplank of the Royal Navy steamer *Georgette* and onto the stone jetty of Fremantle, Western Australia. Onlookers on the bustling quay would never have guessed that the well-dressed "James Collins" and the man in the plain garb of a working man, "Tom Johnson," were anything more to each other than passing shipboard acquaintances. Breslin hailed a carriage and instructed the driver to take him to the Emerald Isle Hotel, Desmond walked up the road to the stage depot to board a coach for the dusty ride to Perth, where he was to find work at a carriage factory or a stable in order to line up horses for the escape attempt. As both men went their separate ways, they saw to the east the blinding white walls of The Establishment. Neither man could have missed the sunburned, bearded scarecrows wearing the Drogheda lines with their multicolored convict arrows, hauling and stacking timber on ships along the jetty. Warders carrying rifles or carbines chatted with each other and watched the sweating prisoners, whose careworn faces made them look decades older than they actually were.

Breslin and Desmond realized that Cranston, Darragh,

Harrington, Hassett, Hogan, and Wilson could have been any one of those gaunt figures, and if they made any mistake in the weeks to come, they too would wear those convict arrows.

Since the pair's arrival in Sydney on October 15, 1875, events had moved at a rapid and, at one point, alarming pace. Devoy had instructed them to look up Fenian stalwart John Edward—"Ned"—Kelly in Sydney, where he ran a small paper with another of the amnestied *Hougoumont* prisoners, John Flood. When Breslin and Desmond introduced themselves and their purpose to Kelly, they found a man whose sallow face, emaciated frame, and chronic cough testified to the effects of The Establishment and the road gangs. His pronounced limp, just one of the effects of the British bullets that had torn into his thigh and testicles at the Battle of Kilclooney Wood, in 1867, reminded the two visitors of how much he had suffered for Ireland's sake.

Despite his sagging health, Kelly remained a defiant foe of Britain. He was planning to join his friend O'Reilly in Boston, but had opted to stay in Australia long enough to help rescue his friends who were still imprisoned. By doing so, he risked another stay in The Establishment, one he knew would most likely be fatal. As he listened to Breslin and Desmond describe their plans, Kelly was shocked—he was immersed already in a separate plot to pry the military Fenians from the prison. Breslin and Desmond were equally stunned to learn that another plan existed.

Kelly quickly took the two new arrivals to meet John King, a prominent man among the IRB cells still operating clandestinely in and around Sydney. A Dublin Fenian who had fled to Australia after the 1867 debacle, King had worked as a grocer in Sydney and had later found modest success as a prospector in the gold fields of New Zealand and Western Australia. Back in Sydney by 1875, he hatched a scheme to rescue the military Fenians, secretly gathering funds from Irishmen throughout Eastern

Australia and New Zealand. Clan na Gael had no idea that this escape plan was in the works.

Shortly after Kelly met the Clan na Gael agents, he, Breslin, and Desmond climbed on a horse-drawn bus heading from Sydney to the town of Petersham, where King worked at a quarry. Breslin and Desmond risked being seen together on this occasion, as both wanted to make contact with King.

As the vehicle plodded out of Sydney, a bus returning to the city and carrying King drew near. King spotted Kelly sitting with a pair of strangers on the top of the outbound coach. Both carriages stopped.

King would write:

> There were strangers with him, and he signaled to us [King did not identify who was with him] to get down [from the coach].
>
> We all left the buses and sat down in the shade of a gum tree by the roadside. Then Kelly introduced me to the stranger and for the first time I had the pleasure of shaking John Breslin by the hand. He was traveling under the name of Collins. . . .
>
> We had a long talk there together and Breslin seemed very much surprised that we had been active and had a plan of escape under consideration. He showed us that his plan was the best and urged upon us strongly the necessity of absolute secrecy. Desmond was with him. He was known as Mr. Johnston [sic]. Breslin was supposed to be looking for an opening in the country to settle there. Outwardly they were utter strangers to each other.

When Breslin described his mission, and the involvement of Devoy and O'Reilly, the stunned Dublin Fenian shelved his own plan and pledged his own sizable rescue fund, between six and seven thousand dollars in gold—to Breslin. After all, Clan na Gael already had a ship en route to Western Australia, and even if King was disappointed that his long labors planning a rescue were now eclipsed by his counterparts in America, he placed the salvation of the military Fenians above his ego. Also, in Fenian circles the name of James Breslin, Stephens's rescuer, carried tremendous weight.

Of his own plan, King later stated:

> During all this time I was actively engaged in building up an organization among Irishmen with the idea of doing something for the release of the prisoners of Fremantle. This was the thought that was ever present in the hearts of Irishmen out there and they responded willingly to efforts on my part and contributed liberally toward a fund which was to be used for that purpose whenever the opportunity might arise. And we had a plan of rescue of our own out there. Our plan was to charter a steamer, man her with our own men, go to Fremantle, rescue the prisoners and take them to the French settlement at New Caledonia. . . . We had quite an amount of money at our command and all we were waiting for was the proper time to make the attempt at rescue.

Tom Desmond set out first for Melbourne, leaving Sydney by steamer on October 19, 1875, while Breslin remained behind to wait for King to make arrangements to put the gold at Breslin's disposal. King contacted several of his fellow New Zealand conspirators, most notably Michael Cody, who would deliver the money to King. King, in turn, promised to take the money to Fremantle once Breslin was settled in there.

On October 26, 1875, Breslin boarded a ship for Melbourne, where Desmond waited, and arrived on November 30. Breslin met with several of King's IRB comrades over the next few days, he and Desmond making a point to avoid each other in the port city, where Royal Navy officers who made the long trip from Melbourne to Fremantle once a month came to know and remember the faces they had seen in both places. Breslin booked passage—first class for Collins, second for Johnson—aboard the H.M.S. *Georgette,* a Royal Navy steamship that conveyed passengers on its trip from Melbourne to Fremantle and back each month.

Breslin opened his account of the plot with the following words: "I started from New York on the 19th July 1875 and arrived in Fremantle on the 16th November [1875]. Rode to Perth the following day, and finding Freemantle the best base for operations, determined to make it my headquarters. Engaged a room at the Emerald Isle Hotel. Patrick Maloney, proprietor, and Desmond went on to Perth and found immediate employment in a carriage factory."

With Desmond only twelve miles away in Perth, Breslin's first task lay in convincing the locals—especially the prison authorities—that he was wealthy American investor and speculator James Collins. He left his letters from Judge Cooney and the fictitious banker C. Coddington Yardley in visible but not obvious spots in his room, the best one in the Emerald Isle Hotel. He left a third message that also would catch anyone's attention:

> Mr. J. Collins, Esq.
> Plains-on-Hudson, N.Y.
>
> Esteemed Sir,
> Please be advised that the sum of one hundred thousand dollars has been placed to your credit in this

bank. You may draw on it through our home office or by
draft on any of our numerous agents.

Most respectfully yours,

> J. Carl Hartman,
> President,
> Hollanders Bank of New York

Breslin had the endorsement of yet another nonexistent
banker. Within hours of his registering at the hotel, word that a
Yankee tycoon was looking to invest a fortune in Western
Australia had spread throughout the town and reached the officers of The Establishment. In his natty clothes, with his cultivated demeanor, and now with letters "proving" he was a man of
means, Breslin had quickly begun convincing locals that he was
"James Collins," an American entrepreneur.

It did not take long for the news to reach the new governor, Sir
William Cleaver Robinson, in Perth's Government House. Eager
to bring outside investment into Western Australia, Sir William
decided he would meet this American.

In Fremantle, Collins spent his first few days striding about
town in his finely cut clothes and charming virtually everyone he
met. "His dignity and grace of manner enabled him to carry out
the role with success," wrote an admirer, "and it was not long
before he became a universal favorite."

He discovered on his walks to the jetty that civilians were not
allowed to talk with prisoners working in the gangs. Anyone who
tried met with a curt warning from one of the guards, which meant
that even if one of the military Fenians stood just steps away,
Breslin could not safely speak to him. He would have to find
another means of communication.

Surmising that the hotelier, Maloney, knew everyone in the

colony who mattered and may well have been the one who "happened upon" the letters of Mr. James Collins, Breslin cultivated a friendship with the former Dublin constable.

Someone else in the Emerald Isle Hotel also caught Breslin's notice. The daughter of a French immigrant with a winery in Perth, Mary Tondut was a pretty, dark-haired maid at the hotel. She did not discourage the almost shy smiles of the courtly "American." Although Breslin was a man of great self-control and high morals, he was drawn to the young woman. He could not afford to risk his freshly established reputation in town for a mere dalliance, but the more he saw of Mary, the more he sought occasion to speak with her.

As Breslin tried to quell any thoughts of romance, he went about his true business in Fremantle. The man he needed to see, he determined, was Father Patrick McCabe. He could hardly have been closer: Father McCabe said Mass every Sunday at Fremantle's Catholic church.

Breslin knew that the priest had long smuggled letters written by and for the military Fenians of The Establishment. What Breslin did not know was that Father McCabe had been removed from his post as pastor to the work camps because of his Fenian sympathies.

On a Sunday shortly after Breslin's arrival in the town, the "Wealthy Yankee trader" decided to go to Mass.

The Door of the Tomb Is Ajar

Father McCabe strode onto the altar of his church for Sunday Mass. The church, which could hold three hundred worshippers, was about half-full, cool and comfortable despite the dust and sultry midmorning sun. From the altar, McCabe scanned the congregation, tradesmen, artisans, farmers, and their wives and children in their Sunday best. A few "black fellows and women"—Aborigines—sat in the pews farthest to the rear.

As always during the start of Mass, the priest's gaze lingered longest on the front pews to the altar's left, where Martin Hogan, Michael Harrington, Thomas Hassett, Robert Cranston, and James Wilson sat in "scrubbed prison garb under the eyes of two guards." Just before he intoned the opening prayers, McCabe spied a newcomer to Fremantle, a full-bearded man with dark hair, bright blue eyes, and clad in the well-cut suit of a man of means. His bearing erect and redolent of authority, the man met McCabe's gaze, held it, and nodded.

The priest assumed that the natty stranger must be the "rich American trader" his housekeeper had told him was staying at the Emerald Isle Hotel. Something about the man unnerved McCabe for a moment, some suspicion, perhaps, he could not identify.

Father McCabe wheeled around in front of the altar, his back to the pews, raised his arms, and blessed himself. Fighting back tears, his face flushed, he whispered: "Judge me, O God, and distinguish my cause from the nation, Britain, that the nation is not holy. . . ."

Then, composed, he turned and began the Mass.

The stranger, John J. Breslin, alias "James Collins," experienced a "spiritual uplift . . . this simple bush pastor, in his quiet little church, touched me more than would any cardinal in his cathedral."

As Breslin was about to learn, the words "a simple bush pastor" hardly described the tough, nationalistic Irishman in the frayed and worn vestments who spoke to the congregation.

At the end of Mass, Father McCabe did not seek out the "American," nor did Breslin do more than tip his expensive derby hat at the priest before strutting down Water Street to the Emerald Isle Hotel.

Likely on the last Sunday of November 1875, Father McCabe watched Breslin take a seat in one of the front pews, on the right side, opposite the Fenian prisoners. The priest, clearing his throat, began to make his simple weekly parish announcements. Then, grinning wryly, he held up a sheaf of blue notepaper and said: "I have here a communication that has touched me deeply. It is from one who has been a stranger in our congregation, but who, from now on, must be reckoned as one to whom all our heart will go out."

McCabe gestured at Breslin. "Mr. Collins, as we know," the priest said, "is here on business from America." McCabe bowed slightly in Breslin's direction.

In turn, Breslin stood and bowed at the cleric as the congregation, including five prisoners in their yellow "Sunday" garb, strained for a look at the newcomer in the dim light cast by the church's tapers. Breslin settled back into the pew.

A grin creased McCabe's ruddy features. "Now, I did not realize that my vestments were so threadbare that it was noticeable to you people out there. I did know, of course, that our altar cloths were worn." Chuckling, he held up a thin corner of one of the cloths and let it drop.

"Now," McCabe went on, the lilt of his native Connemara in every syllable, "I am happy to say that these particulars were quickly noted by the keen eyes of our visitor from the United States, and he has sent me a note that he wishes to present a set of new vestments and new altar cloths to the church."

Pointing at his vestments, McCabe added: "If Mr. Collins would tarry awhile after Mass, I shall be most happy indeed to speak with him."

As the parishioners streamed out of the church an hour later, Father McCabe greeted them on the limestone steps of the main entrance, people blinking as they emerged from the semidarkness of the church and into the sunlight. He made a point to shake the hands of Martin Hogan and the other prisoners, holding Hogan's palm for a longer moment than usual. The Fenian noticed the prolongment, but said nothing with his guards standing so close.

When the crowd thinned, McCabe headed to the sacristy and began to remove his vestments. Someone knocked on the door, and McCabe opened it to find Breslin, a gold pocket watch and chain glistening against his costly light-wool suit and his derby in his hands in deference to the priest.

McCabe took Breslin by one of his brawny arms and led him to a chair.

"I don't know quite how to thank you, Mr. Collins," the priest said as both men sat.

"Thanks are not needed, Father."

McCabe instantly recognized the speech of a Dubliner.

Breslin leaned forward and clasped his hands atop a battered eucalyptus table separating the men. "Father, I have a confession to make."

McCabe folded his arms and waited, scrutinizing the bearded man whose pale blue eyes now narrowed. Something in Breslin's face looked familiar to the priest, yet he knew that they had never met.

"This confession is for your ears alone, Father—but not as a man of God." The businessman pulled a silk handkerchief from his vest pocket, mopped his brow, and laid the handkerchief on the table.

"My name is not Collins, Father."

McCabe nodded, and said, "There are many in this land who use names other than their own, my son. That is no particular sin hereabouts."

Breslin's eyes bored into McCabe, who did not turn away—he routinely dealt with "hard men": convicts, soldiers, seamen, and the like.

"First," Breslin continued, "let me tell you that we have mutual friends—John Devoy and John Boyle O'Reilly."

McCabe gaped, stiffening in his chair. Then he shot to his feet, nearly knocking the chair over. "You are the one. . . ."

"I am, Father. I am John Breslin."

McCabe pondered the name for a moment as he stroked his chin. "Breslin? Where have I heard of you?"

Breslin smiled wryly. "Would it help if I reminded you of James Stephens?"

McCabe grasped Breslin's hands. "John Breslin," the priest

whispered. "The man who broke James Stephens out of that British jail. I might have known that O'Reilly and Devoy would send the best here."

McCabe's eyes welled up. "Our poor men have waited so long. They've always prayed our friends in America would help them."

Now Breslin outlined the entire plot to the priest, who was stunned that Clan na Gael had actually bought a whaler for the task. "What are we going to do before the ship arrives?" McCabe asked.

Breslin replied that Devoy felt James Wilson was the prisoner to initally contact about the escape plans.

Breslin reached into a pocket, removed a small sheet of expensive blue notepaper, unfolded it, and handed it to McCabe.

McCabe read: "To James Wilson and all the rest, Greetings. Those who have not forgotten are close by. Destroy this for the sake of Old Erin. The door of the Tomb is ajar."

McCabe promised he would smuggle the letter into The Establishment.

Very Secure and
Well-Guarded

At dawn of a late November day in 1875, warders rousted James Wilson and the other prisoners from their cells, as they did each day except Sundays. The prisoners stumbled out of The Establishment and assembled on the parade ground, where the morning sun's reflection off the whitewashed walls was nearly blinding.

After the soldiers counted off the convicts, Wilson and the others shuffled to the prison mess hall and choked down a pint of wan oatmeal and potato gruel, and a half-pint of unsweetened cocoa. Then the guards assigned the prisoners to work parties. Hogan was dispatched to a painting detail inside the prison, and Wilson to the warden's stables, duty that the ex-cavalryman preferred to brutal roadwork parties.

At the end of spring 1874, the military Fenians, the health of all having deteriorated, had been sent in from the road gangs and assigned jobs in and around The Establishment. Darragh was working as a clerk and aide to the prison's Church of England chaplain; Cranston served in the prison storehouse. In the superintendent's garden, Hassett could be found tending the plants, produce, and shrubs. On the docks, forty-eight-year-old Harrington, the oldest of the ex-soldiers, still hauled and stacked timber. That Breslin and Desmond had still seen him as another nameless convict face among the lumber gangs on November 16, 1875, was a distinct possibility.

As Harrington trudged off to the jetty, Wilson walked to the prison stables and picked up a pitchfork to spread fresh straw across the horses' stalls. After the task was completed, he planned to groom the warden's horses in preparation for an upcoming visit by Governor Robinson. Several non–Fenian prisoners, were working nearby.

Wilson heard fellow military Fenian Will Foley greet the guards on his way to the inspector general's office. If not for the fact that the six-foot Foley, a Waterford native lauded by Devoy as "one of our best and most faithful Fenian men in the English Army," was suffering from congestive heart disease, Wilson and the other former soldiers might have envied him. Sentenced to life, his waning health, the result of poor diet and several fevers contracted in the road gangs, had compelled prison officials to grant him a ticket-of-leave. He could come and go from The Establishment as he pleased; the authorities believed that he no longer posed a threat to the Crown. Still, he could not leave Fremantle until his ticket-of-leave expired in early 1876.

None of the guards gave more than a glance toward Foley, in civilian clothes, shed of the loathsome convict arrows, as he walked over to the stables. Most of the warders had come to like Foley, a wry, witty man.

He ambled up to Wilson, who waited in his manure-stained boots. Without so much as a backward look at the guards, Foley stepped close to his friend and slipped a folded piece of paper into Wilson's hand. Casually, Foley walked away from the stables just as he had arrived.

Wilson worked his way to the stalls in the rear and found himself alone for a few minutes in the stables, where he fully expected to labor until the day when he toppled to the ground and was carried off to die in the prison infirmary. He opened his palm, unfolded the paper, and read the words that John Breslin had shown to Father McCabe. He stood stunned, but memorized each line. Then, he crumpled the tiny sheet, popped it into his mouth, chewed it to a pulp, and swallowed. Father McCabe had established contact in The Establishment for Breslin. Foley was the conduit.

Over the ensuing hours, Wilson sidled up to Cranston, Darragh, Harrington, Hassett, and Hogan with the news. As shocked at first as Wilson, they awaited the next message from Foley, fighting to keep their hopes, which had been crushed for so many years, in check. They decided unanimously not to tell two other ex-soldiers, James Keilley (or Keily) and Thomas Delaney, like Hogan an ex-Dragoon. A fractious alcoholic, Delaney might unwittingly blurt out the news within earshot of a guard. Keilley had been branded as an informer. The other military Fenians suspected that he was spying on them for the superintendent in exchange for increased privileges. It was a charge that Keilley would deny his entire unhappy life.

Realizing that the slightest change in demeanor or behavior could tip off the guards and warders, the six former soldiers reported to work as usual each day. They bantered as normal with the friendlier guards and kept their mouths shut around the warders, who were always looking to send a man to solitary or back to the road gangs or quarries. Meanwhile, they awaited the next message from Foley.

Breslin wrote, "I made use of him [Foley] to convey to James Wilson notice of my arrival and arrange our method of communication."

Down the road from The Establishment, Breslin, "Mr. Collins," was invited to dinners, parties, and meetings with Fremantle's most prominent citizens, including the new superintendent of Fremantle Gaol, Joseph Doonan, a friend of Patrick Maloney, the owner of the Emerald Isle Hotel. A gloomy, troubled middle-aged man, Doonan was charmed by Breslin, as was virtually everyone else in town. After several convivial meetings over brandy and cigars with Doonan, Breslin asked in passing what it was like to run such a famed prison. Doonan responded by asking the "rich Yankee" if he might fancy a look around The Establishment.

"About the middle of December," Breslin recorded, "I visited the prison, or, as they call it in the Colony, 'The Establishment,' and, in company with two other gentlemen, was shown through the interior by the Superintendent Mr. Doonan, visiting all the corridors, both chapels, punishment cells, hospital, cookhouse, workshop, and store room."

Breslin never showed a flicker of emotion as he viewed the triangle where brother Fenians had been flogged, the ink-dark, clammy cells for solitary confinement, and the steel scaffold with its dangling noose. He betrayed no hint of anger as he saw the stark infirmary where brave Patrick Keating had wasted away and died of heart problems ignored by his road-gang warders.

By the time he departed through the portcullis-style gate and left the twin octagonal towers behind, he had concluded that any attempt to break the prisoner out of the prison itself was doomed from the start. He wrote: "I found it to be very secure and well-guarded." He would have to find a way to launch the escape when each of the military Fenians was outside the walls, a tough proposition since all except Harrington worked inside the prison much of the time now.

An invitation arrived for Collins in mid-December 1875 to attend a Christmas party at Governor Robinson's mansion in

Perth. Amid the gowned and jeweled women, the government officials and "fellow businessmen" in their formal wear, Breslin worked his characteristic charm upon the revelers as he experienced his first and only Christmas season in the Australian summer. Governor Sir William Robinson, a member of the Anglo-Irish Ascendancy of County Westmeath, Ireland, and a career colonial official, showed an immediate affinity for the polished "American financier," hoping to convince Mr. Collins to invest a sizable sum in Western Australia.

Another "American" in Perth that night was not invited to the holiday gala at Government House. Nicknamed "Yankee" by his associates at a local carriage works, Tom Johnson did not seem the sort of man who would even know of the elegant Mr. Collins, but the likable carriage maker had ingratiated himself with several local stable owners who would have no qualms or questions if he ever asked to hire a horse and rig.

For the moment, the two "Yankees" were strangers. That was the way both men wanted matters, but only for the moment.

As New Year's Day of 1876 approached, and with it the prospect of the *Catalpa*'s scheduled arrival late in the month, Breslin had no way to know that the whaler was delayed west of the Cape of Good Hope by storms and unfavorable winds. He set about arranging face-to-face meetings with Wilson and, hopefully, the other prisoners in some way that would appear innocent, or else occur out of anybody's eyeshot. Breslin turned once again to Father McCabe.

The priest had taken again to rattling around in a horse-drawn trap to the convict camps and quarries throughout the region to administer to the Catholic prisoners. In early January 1876, he convinced Doonan to assign him a driver from The Establishment who knew his way around horses. That man was ex-5th Dragoon Guard James Wilson.

Four miles south of Fremantle, Father McCabe and Wilson drove into a dense stretch of coastal bush that concealed them from passersby. The sun bore down on the pair as they stepped down from the rig and approached a solitary figure waiting for them. John Breslin clutched the calloused hand of the haggard prisoner, whose once-ruddy features were a dark, wrinkled brown.

Breslin told him that an American whaler would soon arrive to pick up all six of the military Fenians as the *Gazelle* had rescued O'Reilly seven years before from the waters off Bunbury. Now, Breslin said, he and Wilson had to figure out a way to have all of the men outside the prison walls at a prearranged time.

Wilson, to whom O'Reilly's escape seemed a lifetime ago, incredulously asked how Breslin and his friends had convinced a Yankee shipmaster to smuggle six Fenians aboard and wondered if that captain would keep his end of the bargain. Obviously, the memories of the *Vigilant*'s sailing away from the shouting O'Reilly lingered among him and his comrades. Wilson was amazed when Breslin said that Clan na Gael had bought the ship and that the captain was utterly trustworthy.

Before the three men left the cover of the roadside brush, Breslin implored Wilson to make certain that none of the military Fenians stepped out of line for the next few weeks. Any of the men drawing increased scrutiny from guards would have to be left behind. If possible, Breslin urged, each of the six should try to wrangle a work detail outside the prison walls before the appointed date, which Breslin promised to give to Wilson in person or through Foley.

Back in Fremantle, Breslin met again with Foley. The Clan na Gael agent had promised to book Foley aboard a ship to Ireland, where the dying man wanted to see his family one last time. Breslin, however, insisted upon one condition: Foley must remain in his capacity as Breslin's courier in and out of the prison until no longer needed. Ever the loyal soldier and loyal friend to his comrades still locked in the cells of The Establishment, Foley agreed without protest. Now, in early January 1876, Breslin told Foley that his work was over. His passage paid, money from Breslin in the ex-soldier's pocket, Will Foley would depart for home in mid-month.

Foley walked into The Establishment two days before his ship was to depart, and went up to his friend Wilson. Neither man could say much, having shared the bond of soldiers and political prisoners together for so long since those exciting and ultimately disastrous days in Dublin more than a decade ago. Wilson said, "Don't write to us anymore. I am confident we shall all follow you soon."

They were the last words he would ever say to his friend. As Wilson watched the bony frame of his once-robust comrade pass through the main gate and fade down the road to town, he glimpsed Will Foley for the last time.

Wan and wracked by his chronic cough, Foley had quietly defied his captors to the moment he walked up the gangplank and gazed at The Establishment and the jetty of Fremantle for the final time. He could only hope that his friends would also see the white limestone walls vanish behind them for good.

Breslin met several more times with Wilson outside of Fremantle, urging the prisoner to remain patient. As Foley wrote, however, patience came hard to men who had suffered so much and now clutched at a glint of hope—one they believed was their last hope: "The ability of the agents was tested to the utmost, and the patience of the expectant prisoners was sorely tried."

Breslin continued to display a pronounced ability for subterfuge. Sensing that people in Fremantle might wonder why a man seeking investment opportunities throughout Western

Australia spent so much time in the prison community, Breslin set out on a "business trip" through the interior in the latter part of January. He met with "money men" in Perth, Guildford, York, Northam, Newcastle, and other towns and settlements throughout the colony. Again, no one questioned that he was anyone other than James Collins, an entrepreneur with a fortune to invest.

In late January 1876, Breslin returned to the Emerald Isle Hotel. He checked at the telegraph office for posted notices of ships just arrived in Bunbury, but found no mention of the *Catalpa.*

He did not worry yet. A stormy passage or even an unusually successful take from whaling grounds could easily delay the bark's appearance at Bunbury by a week or two. In his secret meetings with Wilson, Breslin emphasized that point.

Breslin had a personal reason not to mind another few weeks in Fremantle. He had fallen in love with Mary Tondut and the pair had become lovers, planning to marry. Already, he was making arrangements to bring her to America once he and the military Fenians had arrived safely—if they arrived safely.

Still, despite his ardor for Mary, Breslin was tormented that what he referred to as his "failing" would jeopardize the rescue. Whether Breslin ever confided his true identity or his mission to Mary would remain a mystery.

If Breslin and the other conspirators had known of another development in late January 1876, shock or even panic may have hit them. Governor Robinson received a dispatch from Lord Carnarvon of the Colonial Office in London. The communiqué warned that a plot to rescue the military Fenians was underway: "Money has been collected in this country [England] and Ireland and a scheme set on foot for the purpose of assisting the escape from Western Australia of certain Fenians (I believe Military) now in the colony. [The men] charged with carrying out this attempt have either lately sailed for Western Australia or may do so by the mail steamer which brings this dispatch."

Perhaps not wanting to tip off any conspirators in Australia until the agents from Ireland or England arrived, Lord Carnarvon ordered Robinson to apprise only a few trusted officials— Superintendent of Police Smith and Acting Comptroller-General William Fauntleroy—of the plot and not to tell any administrators or warders at Fremantle Gaol. Robinson wrote back to Carnarvon: "The eight [military Fenians, including Delaney and Keilly] who are in prison will be carefully watched by the Comptroller-General and I think I may assure your Lordship that any scheme of the nature referred to which may possibly be set on foot, will end in total failure."

Fauntleroy decided to keep the military Fenians in separate work parties rather than lock them up and alert the purported rescuers that the government had discovered the plot.

As January 1876 ended, the plotters already in Fremantle and still unknown to the Colonial authorities waited for word of the *Catalpa*.

The Very Chart

A t the end of November 1875, while Breslin made contact with the military Fenians, the *Catalpa* sailed on a southeasterly track, Anthony angling her for a run around the Cape of Good Hope and into the Indian Ocean. Several weeks of light breezes, however, stalled the vessel's progress.

The monotony of the cruise dissipated with the killing of three small whales on December 19, 1875, around the same time that Breslin dined at Governor Robinson's mansion. Although the crew's best efforts at the blazing tryworks boiled only forty barrels of oil, the catch allowed Anthony and Smith to maintain for a while longer the fiction that the ship was headed for the River Platte grounds.

On Christmas Eve 1875, Anthony took the *Catalpa* across the equator and held to his southeasterly course, far from the waters off South America. Day after tedious day, the whaler plowed along that course, the lookouts spying no hint of a telltale spout in the distance. The days bled into weeks.

Anthony took a chronometer reading on Friday, February 11, 1876, of latitude 41 degrees 11 minutes, longitude 17 degrees 58 minutes, placing the *Catalpa* still southwest of Africa. He waited to catch the Roaring Forties, the west and southwesterly winds sought by ships rounding the Cape of Good Hope to propel them past the storm-wracked waters off Africa's tip and into the Indian Ocean.

That night, the *Catalpa* did not catch the Roaring Forties, but a monstrous gale that burst upon the whaler. The wind ripped into the ship's rigging with a high-pitched shriek and drove giant waves against the ship's hull and across her deck, the rush of seawater spilling into the main hold.

Anthony cited the storm as one of the fiercest he had ever encountered, and for a time, all thoughts of reaching Australia vanished. Keeping his lurching spinning bark afloat was all that Anthony could think of as the sky turned so black and the rain so heavy that he could barely see past the helm. He would describe the storm thus: "The combers, coming in opposite directions, came together with reports like a clap of thunder, and the danger of a sea striking the deck was looked upon with no little apprehension. As the gale and sea increased the *Catalpa* hove to under the two lower topsails and mizzen staysail."

As a deafening sound of canvas ripping apart burst from the foremast, Anthony's head jerked upward. The lower fore-topsail hung in shreds that flapped wildly with each wailing gust.

Because the storm had exploded with such little warning for even a veteran shipmaster like Anthony, he had not had time to lay on enough canvas. For a flat-bottomed, shallow vessel such as the *Catalpa,* too little sail in a storm could prove fatal.

Anthony felt the whaler rolling to the windward side. He shouted to Smith, "Now look out for trouble!"

To the captain's relief, the vessel rolled but quickly righted herself before capsizing. He would relate, "The *Catalpa* came up into the wind and sea and lay like a duck, rising and settling in the surges with graceful, buoyant swell."

Anthony and Smith now knew that the bark would ride out the

gale, but the battle against the wind and waves went on throughout the following day. At 3 P.M., February 12, 1876, Anthony spotted another ship pitching in the storm "with nothing set but the main spencer and foretopmast staysail." As she rolled with a monstrous wave, her keel rode up, and Anthony caught a flash of her hull's copper sheathing. It was a whaler and probably one out of New Bedford, he realized instantly, and concern immediately clutched him. Once the storm abated, the other vessel's captain would likely want to "gam," pull alongside the *Catalpa* so that the crews could mingle on both ships' decks and the officers could chat.

Already running late for Western Australia, Anthony did not want to stop for a chat with the other captain. He also did not want to answer any questions about the *Catalpa*'s current course.

Anthony revealed that he wished the other ship would take a course in the opposite direction. To Zephaniah Pease, the captain said that "his presence in this locality would be difficult to explain to a whaling captain who knew that he [Anthony] had sailed ostensibly on a short voyage in the Atlantic, and he . . . determined to forego his inclination to hear the latest news from home." The high shine of the other whaler's coppered keel relayed to Anthony that the ship had left the New England port only recently.

When the other bark turned about and tacked on a similar course to the *Catalpa*, Anthony winced. Soon, however, the other ship faded in the distance to the *Catalpa*'s stern. Relieved, Anthony turned his full attention back to the helm.

Near midnight, the seas remained high, but the wind and rain died down. Anthony, peering at the horizon, believed that the dawn would bring clear skies on February 13, 1876. As his log-book records, he was right: "The weather was genial, the sun glowing, and to all appearances there never blew a gale over so placid a sea." Then, to Anthony's renewed discomfort, the other whaler again sailed within sight. She was making for the *Catalpa*. With his crew lining the rail in anticipation of a gam, Anthony resigned himself to a visit with the other captain.

Matters grew worse for Anthony as the other bark drew closer and he recognized her, the *Platina*. Not only was she out of New Bedford, but she was also commanded by one of Anthony's closest friends, Captain Walter Howland, who was a relative of John Howland, the shipwright who had refitted the *Catalpa* in New Bedford. Before the *Catalpa*'s departure, Howland had spoken with Anthony and knew that her scheduled course, filed for anyone to see at the New Bedford Custom House, put her nowhere near the Cape of Good Hope. Anthony dreaded the coming conversation with his friend.

Turning the *Catalpa*, Anthony ordered one of the chase crews to ready a whaleboat so that he could board the *Platina*. He climbed into the craft with them and shouted, "Lower away!" As soon as the hull touched water, the rowers pulled toward the oncoming *Platina*, which hove to and waited.

When Anthony climbed up the *Platina*'s rope ladder, Howland greeted him with a grin and a question: "What under heavens are you doing here, Anthony? You're the last man I expected to see out here. I thought you intended to make a short voyage in the North Atlantic."

Anthony replied that since the *Catalpa*'s owners had given him a "roving charter," he had chosen to extend the expedition. Trying to shift the subject, Anthony asked Howland where the *Platina* was bound.

"For the Seychelles Islands and through the Mozambique Channel," answered Howland, still shooting quizzical looks at Anthony.

Anthony continued to keep the focus of conversation on

Howland's voyage and said he might like to take the *Catalpa* in that direction. Taking Anthony at his word—or so Anthony thought—Howland led him down to his cabin, in the stern, spread out his charts, and showed Anthony the course that the *Platina* would take. Anthony pulled a small notebook from his pocket and copied Howland's calculations, trying to avoid his eyes as much as possible. A friend since boyhood of the lean, sunburned Howland, Anthony feared that no matter what he said about his roving charter, Howland would see through the lie.

When Anthony could no longer stall by scribbling in his notebook, he asked Howland how long he had been out of New Bedford and if he had any news from home. Four months at sea, with forty barrels of sperm oil taken, he replied. They spoke awhile about family and mutual friends and acquaintances, as a gentle breeze wafted into the cabin, and Anthony hoped that there would be no more talk about the *Catalpa*'s unusual location.

Howland paused, stared at Anthony, and asked, "Say now, honest, what are you doing here?"

Again, Anthony used his charter as his answer.

"Where are you going to refit?" Howland prodded, with the same suspicious gaze.

Though his stomach churned, Anthony calmly replied that since he might now steer for the Seychelles, perhaps Howland could suggest some ports of call. Howland ticked off several possibilities that Anthony jotted down in his notebook.

As Anthony inwardly squirmed in the cabin, his whaleboat crew smoked and talked with the men of the *Platina* on the main deck. Second Mate Antone Farnham, who had been wondering about the *Catalpa*'s course, learned from the *Platina*'s officers that the two ships rested in waters much closer to the Cape of Good Hope than to the River Platte hunting grounds.

Farnham's voice, rich with a thick Portuguese accent, carried down to Howland's cabin. "I tot [*sic*] we long time getting that River Platte," he said. "I tink [*sic*] maybe old man go to New Zealand catch whales. I there once. I tink nice place."

If Farnham, a veteran whaler, would buy New Zealand as the *Catalpa*'s destination, Anthony realized, so would the rest of the crew. He would not have to worry about a mutiny in the Indian Ocean from his crew so long as they believed they were headed to the Pacific whaling grounds off New Zealand.

Anthony and Howland bid each other good-bye late in the afternoon, Anthony fighting to hold back his eagerness to leave the *Platina* behind as he climbed down to the whaleboat and his men rowed back to the *Catalpa*. The wind began to pick up, and Anthony ordered his men to set the maingallants. In minutes the sails snapped and billowed as they caught the wind. Anthony steered south by southeast—"for New Zealand."

Three days later, on February 16, 1876, beneath a brilliant blue morning sky, Anthony spotted another ship, a large, sleek merchant bark flying the Union Jack. Deciding that he had little to fear from a merchantman, he ran up a signal flag, and the other vessel responded with a flag of her own. As the ships approached each other, Anthony put out in a whaleboat again and soon boarded the English trader, the *Ocean Bounty*. The two vessels lay about a hundred miles south of Port Elizabeth, South Africa.

He hoped to get a peek at the other captain's charts, for British captains naturally possessed the most accurate maps of Australia's coastline. Not looking forward to navigating the often treacherous waters of Western Australia with outdated, inaccurate charts, Anthony prayed that the *Ocean Bounty*'s captain would allow the American to take notes from the British shipmaster's maps as a "captain-to-captain" courtesy.

Anthony climbed onto the main deck of the British ship to find a large, smiling Englishman of "middling to later years." He escorted Anthony to the spacious captain's cabin and poured a measure of brandy for both men. Not much of a drinker, Anthony may have sipped at his glass, not wanting to offend the man whose charts he wanted to study.

Anthony would state that they "spent a pleasant hour in his cabin," where the man said the *Ocean Bounty* was sailing to Liverpool. "Finally," Anthony would relate, "[I] asked him if he had made many voyages in this direction [east across the Indian Ocean]."

Grinning, the Englishman shifted his blocky frame in his chair, and leaned back. "Been making them all my life," he said. "Why, I was master of a convict ship, the *Hougoumont*, and carried a shipful of prisoners to Australia in 1868."

Anthony was sitting with Captain Cozens, the very man who had transported the military Fenians to The Establishment. For a moment, Anthony's eyes widened. To Pease, Anthony spoke later of how "unnerved [he was] for a moment and if the Englishman had been observant he might have suspected from [Anthony's] conduct that the mention of the name of the vessel created an unexpected sensation."

As Anthony composed himself, Cozens, oblivious to the American's momentarily startled expression, sipped his brandy and reminisced about the voyage of the *Hougoumont*. He asked Anthony if he knew the name "John Boyle O'Reilly." Before Anthony could muster a "no," Cozens went on, "You may have heard of him, for he escaped in one of your [American] whaleships."

Anthony stiffened—maybe Cozens had sensed something after all. Anthony relaxed as the Englishman began to talk about Australia.

Likely taking a nervous deep breath, Anthony asked if any Western Australian ports might offer refitting and fresh provisions for a whaler bound for New Zealand. Cozens replied by urging Anthony to dock in the area, as "it was a cheap place to refit a ship."

After listening to Cozens laud Bunbury and other Australian harbors as ideal whaling spots, Anthony took his gamble. With all the calm he could muster, he asked, "Have you a sheet chart of the coast you could spare me?"

Having taken a liking to the serious, deferential younger mariner, Cozens smiled and pointed to a pile of maps and charts on the table between the men.

"Lots of them," Cozens said. "Here's the roll I used when I was master of the *Hougoumont*. Help yourself. You're welcome to any you want."

Anthony combed through the thick rolls of maps. Finally, he settled on one that he would describe as "a chart of Western Australia on a large scale, showing the survey about Swan River, Fremantle, Bunbury, Rottnest Island, and lighthouse."

At that same moment, both captains sensed that a strong wind was gathering and wanted to take advantage of it. Anthony rose, and as they shook hands, Cozens said, "Godspeed."

Clutching the map all the way back to his cabin, Anthony told Smith to lay on full sail and then come down to his quarters. A short time later, Smith entered the cabin to find Anthony "chuckling in great glee."

Smith, his gray eyes puzzled, asked, "What happened?"

"Why," Anthony replied, "would you believe it? I've just been given the very chart which was used by the captain of the *Hougoumont* to land the prisoners we're after at Fremantle. The captain little thought it was to be used in taking a ship there to rescue the same men."

We Declined Their Money, But Took Their Revolvers

A s Anthony pored over the *Hougoumont*'s chart in mid-February 1876 and plotted his course for the roughly 4,700 miles to Bunbury across waters he had never sailed, Breslin was worried. He strode to the Fremantle telegraph office every day now, sometimes several times a day, to check the shipping bulletin board hanging on the veranda wall. He found no mention of the *Catalpa* the entire month.

For the first time since his arrival in Australia, he brooded that the whaler had gone down or lay damaged in some port of call. As March approached, he wrote Judge Cooney a letter expressing fears about the *Catalpa*'s fate. Cooney forwarded the letter to Devoy, and when the Irishman read it, his mind turned to darker thoughts about the whaler's tardiness: he speculated that perhaps Hathaway and Richardson had been wrong about Anthony. For the first time since he had met Anthony inside Richardson's darkened store, Devoy considered the possibility that Anthony had abandoned the mission. Then Devoy thought of Duggan, who would have held Anthony to the bargain—by any means necessary. Reason tugged at Devoy, who believed that Anthony was the man for the job and that the *Catalpa* would appear off Western Australia at any moment now. But doubts continued to muddy Devoy's thoughts.

Doubts of other kinds assailed Breslin by the first week of March 1876. The man who was posing as a wealthy Yankee speculator was running out of money. On one of his daily trips to the shipping bulletin board, he walked into the telegraph office and wired Kenealy a note alluding that the "California finances" had yet to reach Fremantle. To Devoy's and Reynolds's fury, the Rescue Committee, particularly John Goff, questioned every cent allocated to the mission and held up the funds earmarked for Breslin.

Breslin continued to meet in the bush with Wilson as the ex-cavalryman drove Father McCabe's trap throughout the region. The Clan na Gael agent grew distressed by Wilson's recurrent warnings that the rescue must come soon because the other military Fenians might soon be shifted to road gangs far from the prison. Left unsaid was both men's belief that another season or two in the bush would kill several of the frail ex-soldiers. Breslin preached patience, a commodity that the military Fenians had nearly exhausted. From his cell on St. Patrick's Day of 1876, Martin Hogan addressed a letter to his father, William, of 6 Barrington Street, Limerick City, Ireland, and had it smuggled out of The Establishment, likely by Wilson or Father McCabe. The words reflected that Martin Hogan's store of patience had dwindled down to its last reserves:

Fremantle Prison
Western Australia
17th March 1876

My Dearest Father,

I received your letter of November which gave me some comfort to hear from you and I am so happy that you enjoy your health. You say, dear father, write every mail if possible. I am not able to do that. I will do my best to write every two months. [Under his warders' wary eyes, Hogan had a hard enough time smuggling occasional letters into Father McCabe's hands.]

Months and days pass away from me in my long suffering that often I wish to Heaven that the day I received sentence of life that it was death. It would keep me out of long years of misery. . . .

Despite the despairing lines, Hogan closed his letter with several cryptic sentences hinting that he still hoped for the *Catalpa*'s arrival:

Dear Father, send me nothing, no matter what kind it may be. Anything my dear mother has left me keep it till I get it in my own hands. Keep good heart, dear father, I will write a long letter next time.

Your fond son,
Martin J. Hogan

Hogan's five comrades also prayed for the *Catalpa* to come— their final chance, they sensed, to follow O'Reilly's path to the sea and freedom.

Each time Breslin spoke with Wilson or caught a glimpse of Harrington sweating and stooped beneath loads of lumber, his agitation and frustration grew. The consummate actor, he maintained the smooth confidence of a financier with little to worry about, maintaining contact with businessmen throughout the region and cultivating new contacts for show. Inwardly, he seethed with anxiety and found increasing solace in the arms of Mary Tondut. Her announcement to him in March that she was carrying his child heaped yet another worry upon him.

Tormented that his "indiscretion" might ruin both Mary's reputation and his own and somehow hurt the rescue plans, Breslin nonetheless went about his clandestine business. On one of his trips along the coast, Breslin had driven a carriage to the isolated settlement of Rockingham along the "Fenian Road," a hard macadam track hacked out of the bush in large part by Fenian prisoners. He guided his team onto a sandy turn-off that stretched seven miles and ran into a narrower road that wound through "black boys"—trees. After a half-hour's drive through the bush flanking the sandy tack, he pulled up at the wood-framed, two-story Rockingham Hotel.

Breslin climbed from the rig, tethered the horses, which were covered with lather and dust from the trip, at one of the hotel's rails, and strolled down a beach of hard-packed sand, his boots crunching against the granules. He reckoned that he and Brennan could drive a pair of carriages right onto the beach, and the prisoners could dash across that hard sand to a waiting whale-boat without slipping or stumbling as they would in the deep white sands he had found on so many other beaches north and south of Fremantle. From Fremantle to Rockingham Beach, he had covered the twenty miles in two hours and twenty minutes. Breslin's scouting was over. If he pulled this rescue off, Cranston, Darragh, Harrington, Hassett, Hogan, and Wilson would leave their last footprints on the Australian beach where Breslin now stood, staring out at the long, low expanse of Garden Island. Beyond the island glittered the Indian Ocean.

Although Breslin had located the exit point, he lamented, "I had no sign of the vessel I waited for."

He did see on the shipping board at Fremantle that the New Bedford whaler *Canton* had docked at Bunbury in early March 1876. Breslin walked into the telegraph office and wired the vessel's captain to ask if he had any news of the *Catalpa*. No news, was the captain's reply.

On March 6, Breslin settled into a first-class seat on a mail coach for the dusty 120-mile trip to Bunbury even though his cash was nearly gone. He hoped that the *Catalpa* would arrive in the next few days and was determined to be there when she did.

The Royal Navy steamer *Georgette* churned into Fremantle Harbor on the day that Breslin left, and a man hopped onto the jetty, walked to the Emerald Isle Hotel, and in a Dublin accent asked to see "Mr. Collins." Told that Collins had just left for a few days, the stranger, wearing a sober business suit and carrying a heavy case, checked into the hotel. He signed the register as "George Jones." If Patrick Maloney, the ex-Dublin constable, suspected that the new guest was no more a "Jones" than Maloney himself, he said nothing. Jones said that he was a gold-mining investor carrying a personal letter to Collins from banking partners in Sydney. Again, it appeared that word spread fast of the Yankee investor with an eye on opportunity in Western Australia. Gold mining, wool, land, timber—all had apparently caught the notice of Mr. Collins.

Breslin spent several days walking along the Bunbury water-front, staring at the harbor entrance for an American whaling bark to show, the cries of the gulls and shouts of dock workers filling his ears. He struck up conversations with several captains, but none had seen nor heard of the *Catalpa* out of New Bedford. On Saturday, March 11, 1876, Breslin, now perilously low on cash, bought a ticket on the coastal packet *May* and turned up at the Emerald Isle Hotel the following day with no idea how he could continue to pay Maloney and maintain his ruse as Mr. Collins unless Clan na Gael wired funds immediately.

Shortly after Breslin came back to his room, someone knocked on the door. Breslin opened it, and John King—"George Jones"—stepped inside and told him to close it quickly. Then, King unbuttoned his shirt, untied a money belt, and handed eight hundred pounds sterling from the "New Zealand boys" to the stupefied Breslin.

In a low voice, King said that he had contacted John Kenealy several times by coded messages and both men felt that King should remain with him in Fremantle as a "business associate," help with the rescue, and escape with him and the others aboard the *Catalpa*. Breslin quickly shook hands on the offer.

Breslin revealed the details of his plan to King. The *Catalpa* would wait in waters outside the territorial limit and send a whaleboat to Rockingham Beach; meanwhile, Breslin, Desmond, and now King would be waiting with horses and carriages at a rendezvous point just outside Fremantle for the prisoners to slip away from their work details. To get to the carriages, the military Fenians would have to rely on their own wits and pray for luck. As soon as Wilson and company reached the rendezvous, they would all race for Rockingham, climb into the whaleboat, and row out to the *Catalpa*.

Breslin pointed out that the prisoners were resourceful soldiers, who would use whatever means necessary to reach the rendezvous at the appointed time. As outlined to King, Breslin's plan sounded so simple that little could go wrong. Both men, however, understood that anything—from one overheard conversation inside The Establishment by a prison informer, to Royal Navy warships prowling the waters off Rockingham Beach, and to any number of possible missteps or sheer bad luck—could land them all inside Fremantle Gaol or could result in their deaths at any juncture.

On March 6, 1876, the day that King had checked into the

Emerald Isle Hotel, just such a potential catastrophe for the plotters developed. Acting Comptroller-General Fauntleroy requested that Superintendent Doonan meet him alone at ten o'clock that evening on the road beneath the watchtowers of The Establishment. Fauntleroy came right to the point: "When you visit the prison of a night, I want you to examine the exterior doors of the division and be exact about it."

Doonan, suspicious, asked for an explanation, but Fauntleroy sputtered that the superintendent need not know the reason. He wanted to raise no alarm whatsoever to suggest authorities had suspicions of an escape. Doonan protested, and as the two officials' voices rose and threatened to carry to the guards perched on the white limestone parapets, Fauntleroy backed down and whispered the escape plot described in Lord Carnarvon's secret communiqué.

When Doonan asserted that all the military Fenians should be locked up until the agents could be seized in Fremantle or elsewhere in Australia, Fauntleroy shook his head. Doonan's next argument—that Thomas Darragh must be removed from his post as the prison chaplain's groom because "he has every opportunity of communicating with pensioners and their wives and other people," and be dispatched to a road gang—brought another firm "no" from the comptroller-general. If they suddenly tossed the Fenians into punishment cells or abruptly farmed them out to the work camps, the agents would be alerted to the suspicions and turn back before they could be seized.

The small circle of officials were working from knowledge of an escape plot hatched in Dublin. They did not realize that a second plan was awaiting only the arrival of a ship.

Detective Sergeant Thomas Rowe, the Scotland Yard man assigned to check out new arrivals in Western Australia, tailed two men in early March to the Port Hotel, a Fremantle lodging that was known as "Irish" but not nearly as comfortable as Patrick Maloney's Emerald Isle. When he scanned the register, Rowe took down the names of "Alfred Dixon" and "Henry Hopkins." Neither man, he decided, appeared suspicious.

Dixon was actually Dennis Florence McCarthy, of Cork, and Hopkins was John Walsh, of Durham, England. Both men were members of the Irish Republican Brotherhood, the nameless agents Carnarvon had described in his dispatch, which had warned of a Fenian escape plot in progress.

In the small coastal town, people noticed new faces, and Breslin was wary of the two men strolling out of the Port Hotel and paying what he thought was undue attention to the hilltop prison. He confided his qualms about the pair to King: "He (Breslin) said that he was afraid they were spies sent out by the English government, as he learned from the prisoners that two men were expected from England to take an active part in a plan of rescue which had been formulated by patriotic Irishmen over there."

King's revelation that the men inside The Establishment knew of a second plot and told Breslin of it indicated that Wilson, Hogan, and the other four awaiting the *Catalpa* had either contacted or been alerted by IRB operatives over the years, that they had implored Devoy for help. The desperate prisoners, who had gotten wind of the IRB plot even as they wrote their appeals to Devoy and Clan na Gael, would grasp at help from whichever group put men in Fremantle first. King wrote: "Breslin was suspicious that these were the two men in question, and he was afraid of them, because if the government had any inkling of what was going on that would be just what they would do in order to get hold of the ringleaders—send out a couple of spies in the guise of friends to assist in this escape."

Breslin and King deliberated for hours on how to flush out the men's identities, not a pleasant prospect as both strange men, though well-dressed and well-mannered enough by all accounts, looked like detectives, soldiers, or both. Neither Breslin nor King doubted that the pair carried revolvers and blades.

King offered to take a terrible risk by approaching the men, taking them into his confidence as fellow "IRB" men , and portraying himself as the leader of a rescue plan in the works. That way, King argued to Breslin, if the men were truly IRB agents, they could all work together. On the other hand, if Breslin's suspicions that they were spies turned out to be accurate, King would be tossed into The Establishment, but Breslin, still "Mr. Collins" to locals, might still prove able to rescue the military Fenians. Breslin finally agreed.

King recalled:

> With this object in view I started out in the evening [in mid-March 1876] to meet these men. Fremantle is a small city, nearly all of the inhabitants being convicts—ticket of leave men, as they call them. There are few free men there. These convicts all remain under prison discipline, and when the curfew bell rings at ten minutes to nine they are all obliged to be in their houses for the night. This leaves the streets comparatively deserted after this hour. I was strolling up the principal street when I met McCarthy. He was traveling under the name of Dixon.

King demanded to know what McCarthy was doing in Fremantle. Gaping and stumbling over an answer to the stranger, McCarthy blurted that he had come to help out an uncle on his sheep ranch. King did not move a muscle. He glared at the man. Then he growled that he knew who McCarthy was and what he was planning. Now it was McCarthy who feared that King must be a British detective or soldier.

King quickly laid out all the details that Breslin had given him about McCarthy and Walsh, but before McCarthy could reach for the knife that King knew was hidden somewhere on the man, Breslin's aide said that he wanted to help, but only if McCarthy could prove that he and his associate were IRB men. McCarthy replied that he would meet King on the beach in half an hour.

While King nodded, he wondered whether McCarthy and Walsh would turn up with a detachment of police or shove a blade between his ribs and leave him in the sand. He cautiously started for the beach.

With moonlight rippling across the Indian Ocean and illuminating the white walls of the prison, King braced himself for anything as one man walked from the direction of the town and up the beach toward him. Dennis McCarthy halted close to King and handed him a paper—orders for McCarthy and Walsh from the IRB. King nodded. For several minutes, McCarthy explained his rescue mission, which he acknowledged was to find a way to smuggle the prisoners on a ship or ships by using funds from a satchel of cash that he and Walsh were carting. King believed that McCarthy was "all right" (used as an IRB password).

Late that evening at the Emerald Isle, Breslin answered King's familiar knock and gawked as King led McCarthy and Walsh into the room and shut the door. Breslin had told King to trust his judgment about the newcomers and accepted his statement that the pair were IRB. The four men spoke in hushed voices for hours, as King recorded: "There [in the Emerald Isle Hotel] we talked matters over. McCarthy stated his plans, which were somewhat similar to ours, but when he found that we had all arrangements perfected he at once volunteered the services of himself and Walsh. They also insisted on turning over a large sum of money, about $5,000. . . . We declined their money but took their revolvers. Their offer of assistance was accepted and to them was given the task of cutting the telegraph wires on the day of escape."

Breslin had assigned the plot's two new recruits a key task. By slicing the telegraph lines north and south of Fremantle, McCarthy and Walsh could buy time for Breslin, Desmond, and King to deliver the military Fenians to Rockingham Beach hours before the lines could crackle with alerts to the Royal Navy and the water police.

"Every . . . contingency had been provided for," King wrote. All except one. As the final week of March 1876 came, Breslin fretted over one critical question—where was the *Catalpa*?

Our Friend Has Reached Port

A s Breslin checked the shipping list each day and the six men daily trudged from their cells in Fremantle Gaol to work details, the *Catalpa* lagged in storms and contrary winds in the Indian Ocean. The strain showed in Anthony's physical condition as he lost weight and developed deep black rings around his eyes. At night he found little rest, lying in his bunk with images of Emma and Sophie circling in his mind; he would find fretful sleep, only to awake sweating and groaning from nightmares of British ships and an Australian jail. Duggan watched him closely but believed that Anthony would not buckle under the stress.

Anthony noted, "For eleven days, from February 29 to March 10 [1876] the vessel lay to most of the time under lower top-sails and staysails, in a heavy and prolonged gale from the S.S.E. [south by southeast]." Anthony worried about his delay—the *Catalpa* lurched only 120 miles east in those eleven days.

Around March 12, the weather shifted. Anthony, relieved, recorded, "But at last strong, fair winds from the west set in and the *Catalpa* sailed like a racehorse."

Anthony drove the crew hard and drove himself even harder. He stood at the helm for back-breaking sessions from dawn to dusk, reeled into his cabin for a few hours of tossing atop his berth, and dragged himself back up to the wheelhouse late at night. As Smith watched the captain's once-stocky physique whittle away and the man's face grow gaunt, the first mate worried but stood by his captain. Throughout the breakneck pace Anthony was setting, the captain confided his fears to Smith about what awaited in Australia as the *Catalpa* drew ever closer to the colony's western coast.

On March 27, 1876, the cry of "Land!" echoed from the mainmast lookout. The crew scrambled to the rails for a look, their shouts of "New Zealand" filling the warm air. Anthony peered at "the high land of Cape Naturaliste," at the southwestern tip of Geographe Bay—*Australia*.

Anthony anchored in the sheltered bay that evening. At first light of March 28, 1876, he hauled anchor and sailed for Bunbury. The *Catalpa* slipped into the Leschenault Inlet, and with Anthony at the helm, she tacked into Bunbury's harbor near 10 P.M., the lights of the port town casting a soft glow on the harbor waters, ships from all over the globe rocking at anchor. From his long hours with Anthony, Pease later wrote:

> So after nearly a year at sea, a year of worry and hard work, the rendezvous was reached. It brought little exultation to Captain Anthony, for he knew that the crisis was at hand which would be the supreme test of his courage.
>
> During these closing days he had said but little to his only confidant, Mr. Smith, but [Anthony's] mind had been busy with disconcerting thoughts. Whom would he meet? Might not the conspirators have failed in carrying out the land end of the plot? Possibly the plan had been discovered and the authorities were

awaiting his arrival on shore to take him into custody and seize the vessel. The long delay had been a long torture for a man of Captain Anthony's activity, and he welcomed the developments which awaited him on shore.

John Breslin woke early on March 29, 1876, dressed, and opened the curtains to find a clear azure sky. He walked from the Emerald Isle Hotel to the telegraph office and checked his watch. It read 6:30 A.M. Scanning the bulletin board, he started, then stood staring. Amid the new arrivals in Bunbury was the name *Catalpa.* He read it over a number of times, dashed back to his hotel room, took out a code sheet that he and Devoy had devised in New York just for this moment, and composed a message. Then, at 9 A.M., Breslin raced back to the telegraph office. Any passersby must have figured that the flushed American had a choice bit of business in the works.

Anthony was rowed ashore early that same morning and ordered the crew to return to the ship and return at dusk to pick him up. He had left Smith behind on the *Catalpa* to make sure that no one jumped ship. The captain, hoping that one of the Irish land agents would be watching for the *Catalpa* and waiting for him to set foot in the town, combed the waterfront all day. To Pease, he would describe the ordeal of that first full day in Bunbury: "He [Anthony] was on the alert for recognition, and wandered about the old town all day, momentarily expecting and hoping that some fellow co-conspirator would reveal himself."

No one approached him. As dusk neared, the disappointed Anthony returned to the whaler for "a serious consultation" with Smith, and both "agreed that there was nothing to do but to wait."

Anthony spent another sleepless night on the ship and stepped ashore early on the morning of March 30, 1876, peering at the crowd of sailors and civilians for any hint that someone was waiting for him. A boy ran up to the mariner as he stepped onto the jetty and asked if he was Captain Anthony. Anthony nodded, and the boy handed him a yellow telegram and scampered away.

In coded lines that would have made no sense to anyone but Anthony, Breslin, and Devoy, the message read:

TO CAPTAIN ANTHONY:—

Have you any news from New Bedford? When can you come to Fremantle?

J. COLLINS

Anthony scurried to the telegraph office to wire a reply to "Collins":

No news from New Bedford. Shall not come to Freemantle [*sic*].

G. S. ANTHONY

In the first line, "no news from New Bedford," Anthony informed Breslin that no one suspected the *Catalpa*'s mission was anything but a whaling expedition. The second line, "shall not come to Fremantle," urged Breslin to rush to Bunbury.

Before Breslin left for Bunbury on the mail stage the next morning, either he or Father McCabe placed a note in James Wilson's worn hands: "Our friend has reached port with greetings from Old Erin. He wishes you all well, and hopes you are always amenable to your warders. He hopes to see you soon."

Wilson read the note, destroyed it, and informed his five military comrades that their deliverance or death was at hand. With the combined anticipation and fear of soldiers on the eve of battle, Cranston, Darragh, Harrington, Hassett, Hogan, and Wilson steeled themselves. Now, more than ever since their arrival in The Establishment, they grasped the necessity, as Breslin put it, to be "amenable" to the warders.

In Bunbury, Anthony booked rooms at a waterfront hotel and visited a local butcher shop to purchase fresh meat for the *Catalpa.* The owner was a man named David Hay, and when he heard Anthony's New Bedford accent, the shopkeeper told him that there was another American who visited Bunbury from time to time, "an American of great wealth who was prospecting in the locality."

Hay added that the American "was the finest man he had ever met."

"What is his name?" Anthony asked.

Hay answered, "Mr. Collins."

At 4 P.M. the next day, March 31, 1876, Anthony was at the butcher's making arrangements for Hay to load the order of meat onto the *Catalpa.* Both men turned to the window as a mail coach rattled past, and Hay recognized a man perched in a seat atop the stage.

"Why, there's the very man I was telling you about," said Hay, who added that he knew where Collins always stayed in Bunbury. "Come up to Spencer's Hotel, and I'll introduce you."

For Anthony, the butcher's offer was a good omen. No one would think it anything but natural that a local would want to introduce two Americans far from home to each other.

The butcher and the shipmaster strolled up to the Spencer Hotel, Bunbury's finest, and sent a bellhop with a message up to Collins's room. When the employee returned, he announced that Mr. Collins would come down to the lobby in a few minutes.

Hay rose from one of the lobby's plush chairs as a broad-shouldered, bearded man in an expensive light suit sauntered into the lobby. Anthony stood up and was introduced by the butcher to

Mr. James Collins. "He was a magnificent fellow," Anthony would later remark. When Hay left, Breslin and Anthony chatted leisurely and agreed to have dinner together that night, both men saying nothing for the moment about their true purpose. They wanted any onlookers to believe that the two Americans were nothing more than newly introduced compatriots.

Breslin and Anthony dined at the hotel restaurant, again conversing about everything except the prisoners and the rescue plot, Breslin nodding and smiling at well-heeled local patrons of the hotel. Then he ordered cigars from the waiter and suggested that Anthony might like to take a stroll.

The two men walked in a hazy, golden twilight down to the jetty, where Anthony pointed out his whaler, swaying at its anchor chains in the harbor, her riding lights glowing along the rigging. Breslin led the captain nearly to the end of the long, wood-piled wharf to a secluded spot. After turning around to make sure no one was within earshot, Breslin grasped Anthony's hands and heartily asked, "How are you?"

Anthony would tell Pease: "Then . . . he [Breslin] quickly outlined the plan. [Several] of the prisoners, he said, were working on the road under a strong guard all day, and were locked in prison cells at night. Plans were to be devised by which the men were to escape and reach the coast . . . at Rockingham."

Breslin wanted Anthony to come with him to Fremantle aboard the Royal Navy steamer *Georgette* the next day, April 1, 1876, so that "the captain might study the coast and see the spot where the men were to be embarked, if the plans worked well." Breslin had fixed April 6 as the date of the escape attempt.

On the morning of April 1, Anthony took Breslin aboard the *Catalpa* to meet Smith. Breslin and Duggan, forever bonded as the rescuers of James Stephens, did not acknowledge each other in front of the watchful crew.

A short time later, with Smith left in command of the ship for the time being, Anthony and Breslin walked down the jetty toward the *Georgette*. Anthony froze. Barreling down the planks and directly at the pair was a burly man in a derby. Tom Brennan had finally found Anthony.

Breslin winced as Brennan blustered up to Anthony and demanded to be allowed aboard the *Catalpa*. In a huge understatement, Pease would write: "It must be admitted that neither Breslin nor Anthony were overjoyed at the meeting." Anthony would add, "Brennan was here, and there was nothing to do but take him along to Fremantle."

Breslin warned Brennan that on the *Georgette*, he "was to be a stranger" and stay away from Breslin and Anthony, whom Breslin would introduce as "the guest of Mr. Collins." Although Brennan agreed, the other two worried that he would prove incapable of playing his part.

Soon after the *Georgette* steamed from Bunbury and hugged the coastline north toward Fremantle, Anthony was introduced by Breslin to the ship's commander, Captain Grady. The two mariners hit it off instantly, and throughout the overnight voyage, Anthony entrenched himself, at his peer's invitation, in the steamship's pilot house, where the American questioned Grady about "the coast, the courses, and bearings." Because it was Anthony's first foray into Australian waters, Grady thought nothing of answering every query, even when Anthony "gave particular attention to the coast outside Rockingham and the positions of Rottnest and Garden Islands."

The *Georgette* raised Fremantle at noon of April 2, 1876. As with everyone arriving in the harbor for the first time, Anthony stared at the shimmering white walls of The Establishment, which hovered "like a sentinel" above the town.

But another sight shocked Anthony and Breslin. At the far end of the jetty, a warship flying the Union Jack was moored. To the plotters, the vessel, H.M.S. *Conflict,* bristling with cannons, posed the worst threat possible. Anthony immediately sized up the gunboat as "a fast sailer."

According to Anthony, he and "Mr. Breslin exchanged significant glances as they saw her." Both men understood that the warship's appearance could wreck the plot.

Part 4
This Chance Can
Never Occur Again

Let No Man's Heart
Fail Him

A nthony met King, McCarthy, and Walsh in Breslin's suite at the Emerald Isle on Sunday night, April 2, 1876, and was impressed with the caliber of all three. For the first time, Anthony also met Desmond, who had driven down the twelve-mile track from Perth to Fremantle to get his orders from Breslin for the imminent escape. Anthony flatly stated that if the H.M.S. *Conflict* still sat in port on Thursday, April 6, or was patrolling anywhere close to the waters where the *Catalpa* would await the prisoners and the rescuers on that date, the plot must be postponed. Under full steam and light sails, the warship could not sink the whaler with its cannons, but could easily catch the "duller-sailing ship" in a pursuit. Desmond grimaced as he relayed information gleaned in Perth: "The gunboat had come to Fremantle on an annual visit, and might remain for a week or ten days, then proceeding to Adelaide and Sydney."

For the rescuers, a delay that long could ruin everything. Anthony and Smith were already experiencing difficulties with their men. Breslin wrote, "[Anthony's] crew were in a very discontented state, and attempting to desert the ship. Four of them took a boat forcibly and made off to the bush. Three of these were brought back and put in irons onboard, and the fourth was confined in the Bunbury lockup." The longer the *Catalpa* sat in Bunbury, the greater the prospects that others in the crew would try to desert. Still, the plotters had no choice but to proceed, hoping that the *Conflict* would depart earlier than expected.

Although Brennan sat in on the meeting and heard such concerns, he was only concerned with the seeming lack of any key role for himself. He fumed as the others gave him little more than cursory attention. In response to Breslin's request that he stand ready for action when the moment came, Brennan stomped from the suite muttering and vowing to let Goff know how "Devoy's men" were treating him. Breslin prayed that the headstrong Brennan would do as he was told and sit still for a few days.

On Monday, April 3, 1876, King and Breslin spoke to a number of the *Conflict's* crew on the jetty and in several dockside pubs, culling corroboration of Desmond's assertion that the warship would remain in Fremantle for nine or ten days. Having no choice but to continue preparations, Breslin then hired a trap and drove Anthony, Desmond, and King south to Rockingham Beach on Monday afternoon, the twenty-mile trip, as Breslin had assured him, taking no more than two-and-a-half hours. He wanted to show them the rendezvous spot he had picked for Anthony.

Anthony walked along the firm sand beneath a searing sun and stared out at the densely wooded rises of Garden Island, approving of the way that the island shielded much of the beach from passing ships.

"Now, this is the place," said Breslin, "where we propose to bring the men, and where we expect you to meet us with a boat."

Nodding, Anthony picked up an old piece of a ship's joist or driftwood and jammed it deeply into the sand, but high enough to be easily visible above high tide to an approaching whaleboat.

Anthony turned to Breslin, Desmond, and King. The captain said, "Let it be understood that this is the place where I will meet you with my boat if God spares my life."

Back at the Emerald Isle that night, "thoroughly fatigued," they stayed late to craft a new code for the telegram messages of the days remaining before the escape. Anthony planned to leave for Bunbury on Thursday, April 6, the aborted escape date; he would wait in port until he received a wire from Breslin the moment that the *Conflict* steamed out of Fremantle. If Breslin telegraphed that "Your friend N has gone home," it meant that Anthony must wait another few agonizing days, as the British gunboat would be able to cut off the *Catalpa*'s escape route if promptly alerted. Conversely, "Your friend S has gone home" gave Anthony the news that the *Convict* was headed to Adelaide and the *Catalpa*'s course was clear.

Breslin had set up a coded message that he would get to Wilson at the proper moment: "Get ready; we start tomorrow morning." In their cells at Fremantle that week, the prisoners lay in their sweat-stained hammocks in the dark evening hours and prayed that the message would come, their fear and frustration swelling.

In a different manner, fear also struck the man the prisoners were counting on for deliverance. Before Captain Anthony left for Bunbury on April 6, 1876, he and Breslin were sent an invitation to dinner with Governor Robinson in Perth. Anthony had no desire to go, but did not want to offend the governor or raise suspicions in any way, as local officials were friendly enough to American whaling men, yet wary of them since O'Reilly's escape years back.

Surrounded by the colony's top legal, police, and naval officials, Anthony bantered with them in his laconic, likable manner during the gathering at the governor's mansion. Then, as the men took their seats at the table, one of Robinson's aides came up to the captain and clamped his hand on Anthony's arm.

"Excuse me, sir," the official said, "but what is your name and business and what are you doing here?"

Anthony, terrified that Robinson had discovered the rescue plot, gaped for a moment. Breslin, near Anthony, laughed and told Anthony that in this part of the country, blunt questions were the way in which men often greeted newcomers. Anthony replied that he was about to sail for the New Zealand whaling grounds, and the official walked away. Anthony later told Pease that he [Anthony] "received such a shock that he failed to thoroughly enjoy the dinner."

Anthony could not get back to Fremantle fast enough the next day, but when he did arrive, he walked straight to the port's hydrographic office and asked to buy a coastal chart. Though it was nowhere near as detailed as the naval chart from the *Hougoumont*, Anthony sought every scrap of updated information about reefs and depth soundings of the waters off Rockingham just in case any of the markings on the *Hougoumont*'s chart were now inaccurate.

A clerk scowled at the American and fired volleys of questions about his business, his intentions, and Anthony himself. Finally, the man took Anthony's money and handed him the chart. Shaken, Anthony, with $250 in gold that Breslin had given him to pay the *Catalpa*'s refitting and provisions bills, caught the Bunbury mail coach on April 6, 1876, for the long, sultry, dust-choked ride back to the *Catalpa*. Thirty-two hours later, the exhausted mariner reached his ship.

The grating rasps of a saw and the thuds of a hammer rose from the *Catalpa*'s forecastle. Under the quizzical glances of the crew, Dennis Duggan was constructing several new cabins.

Now all Anthony could do was to wait for word from Breslin.

Fearing that his frequent trips to the Bunbury telegraph office might arouse suspicion, the captain sent Sam Smith ashore each day to check for any telegrams from Fremantle. "Worn with anxiety," Anthony slept little. He watched his crew constantly, as desertions at this point would gut the rescue, and told them that the cabins were for several American businessmen paying to be dropped off at New Zealand.

In Fremantle, Breslin strode down to the jetty early on Tuesday, April 11, 1876. He rushed over to the shipping bulletin board and read that the warship *Conflict* had left for Adelaide—she posed no threat now to the *Catalpa*. At 9 P.M., as soon as the telegraph office opened, he stepped inside to wire a message to Anthony: "Your friend S has gone home. When do you sail? J. Collins"

When Smith picked up the message around noon, he dashed back to the *Catalpa* to deliver the news to Anthony. The captain rowed to the jetty and walked as calmly as possible into the Bunbury Customs House to request clearance to leave port. He intended to send a wire to Breslin as soon as the clearance papers were signed. Meanwhile, as required, port officials sent customs officers and water police to the *Catalpa* to search the vessel for stowaways and contraband. Anthony was not concerned, as Smith could handle that end of things. Or so the captain thought.

Anthony left the Customs House and walked to the telegraph office. Before he could compose a message, he was accosted by a port official who stated that the *Catalpa* had been seized because of failure to pay a duty on a barrel of pig feed. Anthony returned to the ship to find water police holding Sam Smith in his cabin. By the time Anthony and officials sorted out the minor infraction, Anthony paying the fee, he had lost the tide on which he needed to set sail and the telegraph office was closed.

As soon as the office opened on Wednesday, April 12, 1876,

Anthony wired Breslin: "I'll sail today. Good-bye. Answer, if received. G. S. Anthony"

Shortly after the note was sent, the Bunbury office's wires clattered, and a clerk handed Anthony a message: "Your telegram received. Friday being Good Friday, I shall remain in Fremantle, and leave for York on Saturday morning. I wish you may strike oil. Answer, if received. J. Collins"

Anthony understood from Breslin's words that since the prisoners were confined to their cells on religious holidays and most of the time on Sundays, Good Friday could not be the escape date. He was instructed to have the *Catalpa* ten to twelve miles off Rockingham on Saturday, April 16, 1876, and to be waiting on the beach with a whaleboat at first light.

On the evening of Thursday, April 13, a storm hit and continued to pound the coast through Friday morning. Anthony rushed ashore to wire Breslin: "Wind ahead and raining. Sail in the morning. Goodbye."

Immediately Breslin got a message, either through Father McCabe or some other means, to Wilson. The escape was set for Saturday, April 16, so it was up to Wilson and the other prisoners to be at the prearranged rendezvous site to meet Breslin, King, Desmond, and Brennan, who would have carriages and horses ready for the dash to Rockingham.

All Friday, the storm drove sheets of rain and fierce gusts against the coast, and the prisoners worried that with the gale, their last chance of escape might vanish as the *Catalpa* might just sail off. If they had met Anthony, that fear would not have troubled them.

Anthony was facing trouble of another type on Good Friday. The storm's fury dragged the *Catalpa*'s anchors along the floor of Bunbury Harbor, and the ship lurched toward a sandbar. At the helm, Anthony nudged her "through expert seamanship" into deeper waters near the harbor's mouth, but any chance of a Friday departure had gone. He sent an urgent telegram to Breslin: "It has blown heavy. Ship dragged both anchors. Can you advance more money if needed? Will telegraph again in the morning. G. Anthony"

Anthony's message launched Breslin into several frantic errands. Father McCabe had delivered a note to him that "the men were ready." First Breslin told McCarthy and Walsh not to cut the telegraph lines on Saturday. Then the Clan na Gael man rushed to Father McCabe and caught a fortunate break as Martin Hogan was in the rectory on an errand from the prison. When Breslin delivered the bad news, the tough, careworn ex-dragoon nearly burst into tears. Then he warned Breslin that a new road project had been announced and that the prisoners were about to be assigned to distant work camps.

Without knowing if Anthony could sail the ship from Bunbury in the next day or two, Breslin told Hogan he would give him a signal at Father McCabe's Easter morning Mass, Sunday, April 17. If Breslin placed a finger alongside his nose and moved it along his right cheek, the escape was on for "Easter Monday," [a local holiday for many] April 18, 1876.

Breslin then raced from the rectory and down to the telegraph office. He ran inside minutes before it closed. A message from Anthony greeted him: "I shall certainly sail today. Suppose you will leave for York [Rockingham Beach] Monday morning. Goodbye."

From the telegraph office Breslin ran to the Port Hotel, found King, and sent him galloping off to Perth to tell Desmond to be at the rendezvous with horses and a carriage on Monday morning. Then, as Breslin left the hotel, he had another stroke of luck—Wilson was working in a prison gang on the wharfs. Strolling past the grunting, sweating convicts, who were unloading a ship's cargo, Breslin caught Wilson's eye, and as he ambled past the ex-soldier, mouthed a single word: "Monday."

With warders all around the dock, Wilson gave no hint of recognition to Breslin beyond a quick glance that would not have aroused a glimmer of suspicion among the guards. But Breslin knew that the convict had understood the message.

Wilson relayed the news to his comrades in The Establishment that Saturday night. In muted tones, they vowed that no matter what happened on Monday, they would never return to the prison. After ten years in British jails, Cranston, Darragh, Harrington, Hassett, Hogan, and Wilson swore that they would be free on Monday—either aboard the *Catalpa* or lying dead in the road or on Rockingham Beach.

As the warders locked the military Fenians in their cells for the night, the heavy iron doors clanged shut as they had so many times over the past eight years. The men would hear that sound just one more time, Easter evening, if all went according to plan. All Saturday night and Sunday, the six prisoners reflected on a message from Breslin to Wilson earlier in the tumultuous week: "We have money, arms, and clothes; let no man's heart fail him, for this chance can never occur again."

The Supreme Test of My Courage

T he crisis has come," said Captain George S. Anthony on Easter Sunday, April 17, 1876. He rose from his high-backed captain's chair, its Moroccan-leather cushions worn from his endless hours of poring over unreliable nautical maps, and glanced one more time at the British naval chart splayed across the oak table. Rubbing his eyes with his left hand, he extended his right to First Mate Sam Smith and shook, Smith's grip as calloused as Anthony's from hard duty. Anthony caught a glimpse of himself in the shaving mirror dangling from a beam just behind Smith; the hollow-eyed, gaunt visage staring back startled the captain.

"If all goes right," Anthony said above the metallic groans of the *Catalpa's* dragging anchor chain, "we should take the Irishmen off the beach about ten o'clock tomorrow morning." He paused. His dark-blue eyes, rimmed with red, narrowed, and he released Smith's hand. "If I do not come back, you must use your best judgment. Go whaling or go home, as you like."

Smith's fissured, sun- and wind-burnished features tightened. He blinked back tears, unable to reply.

Running his hand back through his thick, dark hair, Anthony

glanced around the low-ceilinged captain's cabin. His map-strewn table barely left room for his bed, a box-bunk chained to an overhead beam. Beneath the man's boots lay a once-thick but now frayed Chinese carpet, whose jade and scarlet surface was bleached out by salt spray and sodden from storm waters that had sloshed through seams in the stern's planks. "Sam," Anthony said, smiling tersely, "this might all be yours by tomorrow evening."

Smith simply nodded.

Anthony grabbed his visored cap from a wall peg and pulled it low on his brow. Slowly, he picked up his long, navy-blue great-coat from his unmade berth, slung it over his shoulder, and managed a wan smile. "If we're caught by the British, Sam, I think that you and the crew will get off scot-free." The captain hesitated again. Then he added, "As for me, well, I reckon that Fremantle prison has a lot of cells."

The two men stepped from Anthony's cabin and climbed the ladder to the *Catalpa*'s quarterdeck, a light westerly breeze ruffling the whaling bark's worn topsails, gulls wheeling and darting around the topgallants in the azure skies. Twelve miles to the southwest lay the Australian coast, flanked by jagged coral reefs and scrub-choked islands. The tang of salt air carrying musky hints of that strange coast's vegetation vied in Anthony's nostrils with the reek of whale blubber that permeated every inch of the ninety-foot-long *Catalpa*. Smith whistled softly at the sight of white spray kicking up near one of those shadowy islands. "Breakers," he muttered. Anthony nodded, noting that "one errant bit of navigation on my part and we would drown in the surf."

As Anthony and Smith descended the four steps from the quarterdeck to the main deck, five crewmen waited in front of a thirty-foot whaleboat whose copper-sheathed hull glinted in the sunlight. They had stored their coats beneath the yellow oak benches of the craft, as Anthony had ordered that morning, Easter Sunday of 1876. The rest of the *Catalpa's* men were arrayed near the bow in their bare feet, in stark contrast to the chase boat crew, who, on Anthony's orders, had donned shoes. Unless "whalemen" were going ashore, they rarely wore shoes in warmer climes, their calloused feet surer than leather or rubber soles amid the slick mix of whales' blood and blubber coursing across the decks.

None of the crew said a word as they waited for their orders, with "no idea of the mortal hazards that awaited."

Anthony had carefully selected his oarsmen: the "cool-headed third-mate, Mr. Sylvia, a New Bedford Portuguese"; Tobey, "a colored, our finest boat-steerer"; Lewis, "a strong-backed Portuguese"; and two Malays, Mopsy and Lombard, who had "proven their mettle at the oarlocks." Worried that the chase boat would be overloaded and hard to keep above the surf once the Irishmen piled into it, Anthony had chosen rowers between five-foot-five and five-foot-seven, with wiry, lithe frames, except for the burly, six-foot Sylvia.

As Anthony looked at the taciturn, even surly faces of the other crewmen, anxiety tore at him. "I could trust only Smith and the men in my own whaleboat," he knew. "I had three men in irons belowdecks because they tried to jump ship. I can tell you, my crew was near mutiny." As if reading the captain's thoughts, Smith muttered: "Leave them to me, Captain. Just bring those Irish back here."

As if on cue, Dennis Duggan slipped "quick and deadly as a mongoose" alongside Anthony and Smith. The Dubliner's thin-lipped expression was impassive, his lank red hair plastered by salt spray to his forehead. His pale green gaze swept from one crewman to the next. All of them quickly averted their eyes from the Fenian assassin's silent challenge, taking stock of the holstered Navy Colt revolver on Duggan's right hip and the sheathed dragoon's saber on his left.

Captain Anthony cast a long look down the *Catalpa*'s main deck, harpoons and line stowed neatly amidships, the foredeck chase boat secured to its stanchion and covered with an oilskin tarpaulin. His eyes lingered on the six makeshift cabins that Duggan had constructed near the bow, canvas hammocks slung for the Fenian's fugitive comrades. In Anthony's own cabin, a chest of clothing and shoes awaited them, along with a Fenian cache of pistols hidden in a locked seaman's trunk.

The captain strode over to the whaleboat, tossed his coat into it, and pointed to several kegs of water, one of rum, a boiled ham, and a sack of hard-bread, all piled in front of the craft. "Stow them," he barked to Sylvia and the others.

Anthony reached for his silver pocket watch. He glanced at the bold black Roman numerals beneath the glass casement and marked the time—1 P.M. Before snapping the lid shut, he read its simple inscription, "My love, Your Emmie."

"Sam," the shipmaster said in a strong voice, betraying no hint of his fear, "we should raise you long before dark tomorrow." Anthony then leaned to Smith and whispered, "If it goes wrong, when you get home, tell Emmie what happened—everything."

Ordering the men into the whaleboat, Anthony clambered in behind them and sat behind the tiller, in the stern of the freshly caulked craft. "Lower away!" he shouted. The stanchion ropes hissed through the hooks and pulleys, and the whaleboat slowly descended and nestled twenty-five feet beneath the *Catalpa*'s gunwales into the shimmering turquoise waters of the Indian Ocean.

Anthony looked up at the mainmast, where the gold-trimmed ship's-agent pennant of his father-in-law unfurled in a sudden breeze to reveal the name "J. T. Richardson" in deep-blue script upon a white background. Above the banner, the Stars and Stripes billowed.

"Pull away!" snapped Anthony. The oarsmen bent to the task, their strong, rhythmic strokes soon putting distance between them and the *Catalpa*.

Anthony turned his head, taking in the contours of the New Bedford whaler, bow to stern, hull to mainmast. She rode under short canvas that was yellowed and torn in spots from a year's worth of Atlantic and Indian Ocean gales. Against sails stained black in places from the smoke of the foredeck's tryworks, the white canvas patches, "reefers' darning," stood out starkly. "She required a new mainsail and topgallant," Anthony noted, "but there was no time."

The *Catalpa* also stood in need of fresh black and yellow paint all along the hull, made of sturdy New England oak. Wincing at spots where salt-streaked wood showed through peeling copper paint and at several corroding copper hull fastenings, Anthony shook his head imperceptibly. There had been no time for repairs in Fremantle or Bunbury, only time for Duggan to fashion the "guest cabins" near the bow. As the whaling bark ebbed from view, Anthony "thanked fortune that I could leave my vessel in the hands of Sam Smith, a brave man who could be trusted, no matter the emergency to come."

Having moved to the canopied wheelhouse at the *Catalpa*'s stern, Smith waved once to Anthony.

For a moment, as the splashes of the oars carried him closer to the Western Australian shore and to "my desperate errand for those Irish prisoners," Anthony wondered whether he would ever see the *Catalpa* again. He took a last look at the bark. "If the Royal Navy caught us in territorial waters with the Irishmen," Anthony would say, "those Stars and Stripes would avail us not at all." An even more anguishing thought assailed him: "The possibility that I might never see my wife, Emmie, or my infant daughter was hard at me."

As he automatically adjusted the tiller to each hint of a swell, Anthony reflected that "the crisis at hand would be the supreme test of my courage."

Guiding the whaleboat past shoals whose razor-sharp fissures glinted lethally just below the blue-green surface three miles from the *Catalpa*, Anthony's fingers relaxed for a few moments on the tiller. He took a deep breath, relieved that his recently acquired British chart appeared accurate. With open water for the next few miles, he battled his "disconcerting thoughts."

Anthony wondered: "Whom will I meet on the beach? Might not the Irish conspirators have failed in carrying out the land end of the plot? Possibly the plan has been discovered, and the authorities are awaiting my arrival on shore to take me in custody and seize the *Catalpa*."

With the traditional self-discipline of New Bedford whaling masters, Anthony tightened his grip on the polished but well-worn oak surface of the tiller, tamped down his fears, and concentrated on landing the whaleboat in one piece at that still-distant rendezvous point, a desolate stretch of Rockingham Beach.

At a soft splash to the starboard gunwale, Anthony inclined his head. A dark-gray dorsal fin slashed through the sun-dappled waters for a few seconds and just as suddenly disappeared. Anthony grimaced—a shark. The man-eaters infested the waters all around the whaleboat. He looked to the west, where the next landfall lay nearly five thousands miles away, eastern Africa or Madagascar.

As a favorable onshore breeze began to swirl, Anthony ordered the crew to "ship oars" and to run up the whaleboat's "leg-o'-

mutton" sail. The patchwork canvas stiffened, billowed slightly, and pushed the boat in the direction of "the secret beachhead." With the sun starting to beat down, the crew, sweat glistening on their brows and bare shoulders, leaned against the gunwales and rested, some of them soon dozing. Their trust in the seamanship of the man at the helm was implicit; he had earned it in the wheelhouse of the *Catalpa* amid the fierce winds and towering waves of storms in the open ocean.

In the late afternoon, Anthony spotted his first landmark, the southern tip of Garden Island, a dense expanse of dark brush and forest clotting the edge of a beach so starkly white that Anthony had to shade his eyes. He ordered the sail furled "to lessen the boat's visibility from shore."

While the whaleboat carved the waters around Cape Peron and the southern rim of Cockburn Sound, Anthony scanned the scene in every direction with his two-foot-long, folding brass telescope, the gift of his father-in-law, and found no sign of red-coated Royal Marines or bayonets' silvery glint on the shore. No telltale smoke clouds of Royal Navy steamers H.M.S. *Conflict* or H.M.S. *Georgette* smeared the horizon. So far, Anthony's luck was holding. Still, he could not chase away thoughts of the warships' black cannon muzzles poking through their gunports as the vessels rode anchor in Bunbury Harbor three days ago.

Around 7 P.M., as the whaleboat slid abreast of Collie's Head, Anthony's hand suddenly tightened on the tiller—"a noise as loud as thunder crashed just beyond the boat's prow."

Third Mate Sylvia cried, "Breakers ahead!"

Whitecaps churned twenty feet high out of otherwise placid waters. Anthony had no time to lament that his charts had shown neither reef nor shoal near Collie's Head. "Trail oars!" he shouted above the near-deafening peal of the breakers. "Trim this damn boat!"

As the whaleboat was sucked into the "boiling foam," three massive waves gathered behind the vessel and rocketed toward it. Anthony and his men ducked, clutching oars and gunwales, Sylvia praying in Portuguese. The first two waves slammed into the boat and nearly swamped it, the craft spinning backward as the third wave rushed upon it. The "green and white wall of water" burst against the careening chase boat and flung it into the air. Blinded by the dense salt spray, retching as seawater forced its way into eyes and nostrils, all the crew could do was hang on and hope that the whaleboat landed "bottom-down."

For several endless seconds, the craft was suspended at a sharp angle above the wave, the men's shouts muffled by the roar of the surf. Then the craft plummeted into the wave's trough. The dive nearly catapulted Anthony overboard from the tiller, but Sylvia, clutching an oarlock with one massive hand, clamped his other on the captain's left forearm and held on. The boat smacked bow-first into the water, skidded back into the air, righted itself and was hurled past the breakers into the smooth, sheltered waters of Mangles Bay. In a long, graceful arc just two miles away stretched the deep, alabaster-hued sands of Rockingham Beach.

Anthony, his arm throbbing from Sylvia's life-saving but talon-like grip, panted and coughed up water for several minutes, amazed that the whaleboat had not capsized or broken apart. No one spoke. Miraculously, not even the water casks and food lashed to the benches had fallen into the water.

Anthony broke the silence with his command that the crew "ship oars." He did not dare land before nightfall, fearing that mounted police patrols "might still be about." In the coming twilight, he trained his telescope back and forth along a line of sand dunes framed by massive eucalyptus and soaring stands of gum trees and hardwoods. He was searching for an ancient giant of a gum tree whose gnarled trunk had been seared white by a blast of lightning. He had noticed it on his scouting trip to the beach with Breslin. "Our boat jogged on in the gathering darkness," Anthony wrote, "until little light remained."

Around 8:15 P.M., Anthony pointed toward the beach. The men immediately dipped the oars and began to pull, the surf choppier as they headed inshore. Because Anthony still had to peer at the darkening coast for the driftwood stake that he and John Breslin had set up in the sand in front of the gum tree more than a week earlier, he had yet to pick a landing spot. Finally, around 8:30 P.M., the captain spotted what he hoped was the right tree trunk. Choosing a gentle swell, he waited for just the right moment to "ride her in." The whaleboat shuddered slightly and then shot shoreward until it hissed to a halt in the sand.

Anthony leaped from the boat and, after helping his men haul the craft beyond the high-water mark and to camouflage it with grass and bush, strode over to the sprawling gum tree. "I had not walked more than three hundred feet," he said, "when my foot struck the stake I had set up as a mark on my previous visit."

He rushed back to where his men huddled in the sand near the boat and informed them that they had best find a place in the beach grass and grab a bit of sleep. "I told them there would be no cookfire," Anthony related. After a dinner of cold boiled ham and hard-bisquit washed down with rum and water, the exhausted crew crawled into the waist-high beach grass. Their snores soon rose from the beach. Not even the rustlings of strange, unseen creatures in the adjacent woods nor the shrieks of nocturnal birds woke them.

As the men slept, Anthony paced the shoreline, sweating in the warm air. He stared both at the ocean, where moonlight flitted across the foam-flecked bay, and at the clear sky, "a gleaming canopy of stars." Beyond the long, low mass of Garden Island, whose high grass and tangled brush looked "the picture of gloom" to Anthony, the *Catalpa* weighed anchor some twelve miles distant in international waters. Beyond his crew's rude campsite, thick vegetation and forest stretched inland toward the white limestone walls of Fremantle Gaol, where he tried to picture the Irish prisoners anguishing in their fetid cells over the morning to come.

Sleep would not come for Anthony that long night. He walked the beach, his hands clasped and unclasped behind his back, his "mind and heart filled with disquieting thoughts and longing for the day."

Near midnight, Anthony started at the sound of soft footsteps in the sand—Sylvia was headed to the bushes to relieve himself. He passed Anthony wordlessly, both men nodding at each other. Anthony went back to his pacing.

Around 2 A.M., Anthony rousted his men from sleep because the tide was creeping in toward the whaleboat. He told them to haul the boat farther up the beach and conceal it again with brush. Grumbling, they carried out the order and "soon dropped asleep again in careless sailor fashion."

Anthony made no attempt to sleep. Of one thing he was certain as he fretted back and forth along the shore: "There were many anxious hearts in Australia that night, and as I paced the lonely beach, I was not alone in my sleepless vigil."

At the first faint streaks of dawn on Easter Monday, white cockatoos darting from the fragrant eucalyptus and the lofty gum trees began yammering to one another. Gulls and terns soon added their cries to the din. Captain George Anthony listened to the clamor for a moment, rubbed his bleary eyes, and felt a surge of energy course through him despite his sleepless night. He was "even more impatient to know the fate which awaited me."

As the sun began to ascend, roseate and gold streaks illuminating the horizon and flickering across the whitecaps, Anthony reached into one of the casks to splash water on his face. He straightened up and noticed that there was a slight hint of cool, moist air. Wondering if a squall could be moving in later that day, he shoved aside the fear for the moment. He strode over to his men and nudged them awake with his foot. They lurched to their feet, rubbing sand from their eyes and combing dry beach grass out of their hair with their fingers, and waited for their captain's instructions. What would their reaction be, he wondered, when the fleeing Irish prisoners appeared? If they appeared.

Twenty miles to the north, dawn broke across the white houses and businesses of Fremantle. Breslin called for a bellboy at 5:30 A.M. and asked him to carry his luggage to the trap and team he had hired at nearby Albert's Stable.

As Breslin headed down to the lobby of the Emerald Isle, McCarthy shouldered a bundle tied to a stick and tramped south down the Bunbury Road. Inside the bag was a set of wirecutters. Walsh, the other IRB agent, headed north from Fremantle on the road to Perth. He, too, carried a hidden pair of wirecutters.

At 6 A.M. Thomas Brennan climbed into a wagon whose canvas tarpaulin hid clothing and a small cache of rifles, carbines, and revolvers, and rattled away for Rockingham Beach.

"Mr. Collins" settled up his bill with Patrick Maloney, told him that he was off to Perth on business and for the annual Easter Monday Regatta, wished him a heartfelt farewell, strode out the lobby door to High Street, and walked over to the the stable to find a team of fine horses harnessed to a lightweight, four-wheeled trap. He turned to find Tom Desmond alongside, nodded, and told him to take his own trap and team by a side street and several turns and drive up onto the Rockingham road. Desmond left as quickly as he had appeared.

As he inspected his horses, Breslin was pleased to have such a good team, for he had feared that all of the better horses had been hired out to people driving up to Perth for the regatta; Desmond had only been able to hire a pair of second-rate horses at Perth. At least, Breslin thought, any of the local police, prison, and naval officials who had hired the good horses and rigs would be at the regatta and nowhere near the scene of the morning's coming events.

Breslin had ordered John King, who had somehow gotten his hands on a fine mount, to remain in Fremantle for an hour or so to see if "the alarm had been given" and then race for Rockingham.

Breslin climbed up into the trap, reached for the reins, and nudged the old horses onto High Street. Breslin would write:

> At half past 7 A.M., I drove slowly up the principal street and, turning once right, walked my horses by the wardens' quarters and Pensioner [Guards] barracks. The men were beginning to assemble for parade. I had arranged with our men [the prisoners] that I would have the traps in position on the road at a quarter to eight and would remain so, the [position] being within five minutes run of the prison, until 9 A.M.
>
> Being ahead of my time I drove slowly along the Rockingham road and Desmond, coming up shortly after, drove by me. Coming to a shaded part of the road, we halted and having divided the hats and coats [for the Fenians], three of each to each trap . . . time five minutes to eight.

Breslin and Desmond also placed a trio of "six-shooters" and ammunition in each trap. Then, in the shadow of the gum trees, the pair waited, the sky a deep blue, seabirds and cockatoos wheeling overhead. Breslin and Desmond stared at the white walls and towers of The Establishment.

Behind those walls, Thomas Hassett and Robert Cranston, assigned to the prison storehouse but allowed to walk outside the walls when their boss, the prison accountant, ate breakfast, walked up to Warder Lindsey at the main gate. Today, they told him, they had been assigned to dig potatoes at the clerk of works' garden in town. Since neither man had ever given him any trouble, he waved them through, expecting them to return as usual. Hassett walked off to the potato beds, where Darragh was working. Meanwhile, Cranston headed straight for Fremantle's south jetty, where Harrington sweated in the gathering heat as he cut and dragged stone blocks to repair the dock. Strolling up to Warder Booler, who treated the prisoners with a modicum of decency, Cranston said that the superintendent wanted Harrington to help move furniture at the governor's house, on Hampton Road. Booler sent them on their way.

Wilson, working in the prison chaplain's stable, outside the prison walls, slipped out and half-walked, half-trotted away from his detail.

Shortly after 8 A.M., Cranston and Harrington met up with Wilson, and the three men worked their way to the potato gardens. As soon as Hassett and Darragh spotted their comrades, the pair slung their spades over their shoulders and trailed them at a slight distance. Only Hogan was left.

Darragh and Hassett halted at the Fauntleroy house, where Hogan, paintbrush and can in his hands, saw them. He quickly joined them, still holding brush and pail. Praying that the guards perched atop The Establishment's towers would still be recovering from their Easter celebrations and not as vigilant as normal, the two squads of prisoners moved fast toward their roadside rendezvous.

Breslin and Desmond spied three men running toward them—Breslin recognized Wilson, Cranston, and Harrington. Their faces flushed with sweat and perhaps tears, they obeyed instantly as Breslin waved them toward Desmond's wagon, where Harrington flung himself into the back with a shout of "Ireland forever!" The other two jumped in behind him.

Desmond tore down the Rockingham road as the three Fenians ripped off their convict-arrowed garments and put on the clothes and coats—long linen dusters—that Breslin and Desmond had laid out for them. The click of bullets being slipped into six-shooters' chambers told Desmond that the ex-soldiers had found their weapons.

Within minutes of the first wagon's departure, Darragh, Hassett, and Hogan ran toward Breslin shouting and waving their arms. Breslin's horses started, and as Darragh drew near, he grabbed the bridles to calm the creatures. The three Fenians changed into their new clothes, leaped into the trap, and shoved their revolvers into the dusters' pockets as Breslin followed Desmond down the Rockingham road.

On Rockingham Beach early that Easter Monday, Anthony could only hope that matters in Fremantle had gotten off to a good start.

"Start a small cookfire, lads," Anthony said, reckoning that the tiny flames would not be easily spotted in daylight. "But snuff it soon as you cook. No rum this morning."

Spearing slices of ham with their "line-cutters," eight-inch, wickedly hooked knives, the men broiled the meat and stamped out the fire. Anthony, munching on a piece, walked a few paces to the north, where a veil of haze was lifting. He stiffened—"How could Breslin and I have missed it?" he would always wonder. Just a half-mile away, a long jetty painted on its landward side with the words "Jarrah Timber Company" jutted from the shore.

Five lumbermen, whose grunts and oaths now reached Anthony, were hauling a huge wagonload of square-cut wood along the quay, which meant one thing—the workers were readying a load of lumber for a ship that would dock at the jetty. That vessel could be a British warship.

Alarm filled Anthony, but he managed to hide it from his men. One of the lumbermen clambered down from the rough stones of the jetty and splashed along the waterline toward Anthony.

In his dark-blue greatcoat and with his shipmaster's cap pulled down nearly level with his brow and hooding his eyes, Anthony fingered the Navy Colt revolver concealed in the coat's right hip pocket. He ordered his men to stay put and walked up to the stranger. Both men halted within "hand-shaking distance."

"My name's William Bell. I'm the crew chief," the sinewy, fiftyish man snapped at Anthony. Hooking his thumbs into his belt, Bell demanded: "What's going on here?"

Anthony uncocked his revolver and pulled his hand from his pocket. "I am bound to Fremantle for an anchor to replace the one I lost in Friday's storm." Scratching his salt-encrusted beard, Anthony scrutinized the other man.

Bell peered back and said, "I believe you're no master of a ship, but Kenneth Brown—you ran after killing your wife in Perth."

Anthony shook his head and pointed at his crew. "Look at them—Portuguese, Malays—we're whaling men. Behind them in that grass, you can see our chase boat."

Folding his arms, Bell stared at the men. "Maybe you're whalemen as you say." He flashed a gap-toothed grin. "But, lad, you and those"—he pointed at the crew—"have hooked it [deserted] from some ship."

Still grinning, he added: "I'm an ex-prisoner myself, and I advise you to get out. This is no place to lay." He gestured at the jetty, where the other lumbermen stood in a knot at the dock's side and, gesticulating at the strangers, watched their foreman. Anthony grasped the man's meaning: Royal Navy vessels "laid to" at the dock, as Anthony had suspected upon seeing "the saw-cut load of timber," used for ships, planks, and houses' walls and floors.

The warning led Anthony to hope that Bell "seemed disposed to assist us." Feeling out the lumber-crew chief further, Anthony quickly learned that he was right: "To my relief, the man had no love for the authorities, for if he had started to alert his companions, I would have been alarmed to an extent which might have made it necessary to resort to desperate means for his detention."

Admitting that this was his first time in Australian waters, the New Bedford shipmaster asked Bell "the best way to get out with a boat."

Bell answered without hesitation, "Be sure and keep close to Garden Island. There is a dangerous reef farther out." He wagged a knobby finger in its direction. "And it would be sure destruction to your boat to attempt to go out that way."

Startled, Anthony responded, "But that's the way I came." He pulled his telescope from his coat pocket, focused the lens on the spot that Bell had indicated, and in the now-brilliant sunlight, saw giant breakers cascading in sprays of white foam across the coral reef. Anthony, who had paced the beach confident that his seamanship had in large part brought them safely through last night's surf, suddenly understood that he "must have been carried completely over it [the uncharted, unseen reef] by the blind rollers the previous night and realized that our escape had been providential."

Bell's next words proved anything but "providential" to Anthony: "You should leave soon. We're getting that cargo of timber ready for the *Georgette*."

Anthony's stomach churned, and he struggled for a deep breath.

"When is the *Georgette* coming?" he croaked.

Smirking at the seaman's clenched expression, Bell answered, "Why, she's coming now."

Far to the northwest, a dark wisp of smoke smudged the "gun-metal blue horizon." The H.M.S. *Georgette,* with twelve-pounder cannon and Royal Marines, was steaming to the Jarrah loading station. Measuring the distant smoke and gauging that the *Georgette* lay four to six hours away, Anthony determined that he could wait three hours at most for the prisoners; even then, any chance of a successful escape would have decreased significantly. He checked his pocket watch—7:35 A.M.

Bell offered his hand to Anthony, who clasped it and decided that detaining the man would only raise further suspicion. The crew chief strolled back to the jetty, and Anthony ran to his men, all with "perturbed countenances."

"Captain, does that man think we're deserters?" asked Mopsy, whose eyes darted from Anthony to the others.

"No," Anthony replied. "None of you men are going to be thrown in jail."

As several of the men glanced toward the jetty, Anthony decided "a little of the truth might be well-used now." He told the crew that they were taking on passengers, "prospectors" who would pay cash for passage to America. At his command, the sailors dragged the whaleboat from the grass and to the waterline, bow seaward, and sat with backs against the copper-wrapped hull. He allowed them "a bit of rum to wash the sand down."

Anthony stood nearby, tracking the smoke on the horizon, straining to hear any hint of horses galloping through the bush or of gunshots "that would mean a running battle with police and soldiers." He checked his watch again and again, the dragging minutes broken only by the sounds of a faint breeze wafting through the gum trees, the ongoing screeches of the gulls and cockatoos, and the occasional shouts of the men stacking timber for the *Georgette.*

As Anthony opened his watch yet again at 10:30 A.M., one of the Malays stood and yelled, "Wagon come!" Anthony whirled toward the Rockingham road to find a foam-slathered horse drawing a two-wheeled trap up the sandy track "on the gallop" and veering directly at him. At the reins was a brawny man sporting a long beige "duster-coat" and a broad-brimmed "bush hat." He reined in just a few paces from Anthony. At the same instant, Bell, who had rushed back from the jetty to see "what was up," appeared alongside Anthony and gaped at "the luggage and rifles and revolvers piled high in the trap."

Thomas Brennan, tossing down the reins from his right hand and hefting a whip in his left, glowered down at Bell. "Who is that man, Anthony?"

The captain, acutely aware of the lantern-jawed, mustachioed Fenian's reputation as "a man accustomed to killing," responded in an even tone, "He's no problem. Just the crew chief on the jetty."

Brennan pulled a Colt from his belt and leveled it at the wide-eyed Bell. The Irishman said, "We must shoot him."

Stepping between Brennan and Bell with arms outstretched, Anthony glared at the Irishman, now standing in the wagon, still aiming at the ashen-faced lumberman. "Brennan, I'm in command here—not you, not Breslin. There will be no shooting yet."

For another moment, Brennan brandished his revolver and peered at Anthony, who held his gaze. Then Brennan shrugged, slipped the Colt back into his belt, leaped down from the seat, and began piling the valises, which belonged to John Breslin, John King—on their way to the beach—and himself, onto the sand.

"Where are the others?" Anthony asked as he motioned for his crew to stack the luggage and weapons in the whaleboat.

Brennan grunted, "Close behind." He scowled again at Bell, who remained transfixed.

All three men suddenly turned as a single rider raced up and halted. Thirty-year-old John King, his handsome features caked with sweat and dust, gasped, "They're fifteen minutes away." He wheeled around and galloped back to "urge Breslin, Desmond, and the six escapees on" with the news that the rescue boat was waiting and to pass on Anthony's warning that the *Georgette* was steaming for the jetty.

As King sped off, Anthony assembled his crew, "apprehensive of the proceedings," by the whaleboat. "Do not be afraid—whatever happens," Anthony said.

"The poor fellows looked at me [Anthony] and at the frightful Brennan and then at each other with consternation." Anthony ordered "each man to stand by the side of the boat, each abreast his thwart."

Fifteen interminable minutes passed, the sun slipping behind an expanding but still distant bank of swollen gray clouds, Anthony checking the *Georgette*'s smoke trail. With vague relief, he discerned that the steamer could not have made much progress in the last hour, a sign that she was in no great hurry—for the moment.

Finally, a clatter of hoofs and a rattling of iron-rimmed wheels along the loose, sandswept stones of the Rockingham road, echoed along the beach. Two more traps burst out of the bush. Anthony immediately recognized the tall and wide-shouldered John Breslin at the reins of one carriage. Breslin, whose full-bearded face was flushed and whose expensive light suit was now stained with sweat, yelled at the other driver, Desmond, to pull up. The six Fenian prisoners jumped from the carriages, and their long linen coats provided by their rescuers blew open, revealing their new civilian garb with "unusual accompaniments of English belts that each contained a pair of six-shooters."

For a full minute or two, the Fenians stood in the sand, blinking, "seemingly paralyzed from their first two hours of freedom." The prisoners stared at Anthony, the chase boat, and the crew and looked to Martin Hogan to make the first move. "To the boat, boys!" he shouted.

The Irishmen seized rifles and armfuls of cartridges from the traps and dashed for the boat. As the Fenians loaded their rifles on the run without a misstep, Anthony's first "brief look at these men proved that there was no turning back and that they would all die before spending another day in that prison . . . they handled those weapons with the skill of the professional soldiers they still were."

Anthony's crew gaped at the disheveled men bearing down on them with rifles and revolvers. At the sight of Hogan, who ran at them with an explosive burst of speed and "hard blue eyes shining," several crewmen jumped away from their posts, on the verge of running for their lives. None thought of plunging into the surf—they too had seen the shark's fin the previous day. For a few seconds, the crew "stood immobile, for they thought they were about to be attacked." Then a Malay oarsmen drew his gleaming line-cutter from its sheath.

Anthony bellowed to his men in Portuguese, English, and "broken Malay" to "lay back" as the rest pulled out their knives or brandished oars. At the same time, Hogan, the former Royal Dragoon sergeant with the jagged facial scar, cried, "Hold fire, boys!" His five comrades—as well as Brennan, Breslin, and King—obeyed but pulled up several feet from the crew with gun barrels still pointed at them.

Anthony shouted for his crew to shove the whaleboat into the

surf and man the oars. Because the Irishmen had lowered their
weapons, the crew warily but reflexively obeyed Anthony. As the
ten Irishmen splashed up to the boat, Anthony ordered them to
stow themselves as low as possible in the bottom of the craft. He
bellowed, "Give us room to row!" He positioned Breslin, King,
and Desmond in the stern, hopped aboard on top of the stern
sheet, and manned the tiller.

At the first dips of the oars, the boat barely stirred. Waves lap-
ping the gunwales, the boat swayed under the weight of sixteen
men and their gear. She drifted broadside to the surf as waves
swept over the sides, saturating the men.

"Pull as if you were pulling for a whale!" Anthony urged the
crew. The men, Breslin marveled, "obeyed with enthusiasm to
the accompaniment of Anthony's rallying cries: 'Come down,
Mopsy! Pull, Tobey, pull! Give them the stroke, Mr. Sylvia! What
do you say, men! Come down all together! Pull away, my men,
pull away!'"

As Anthony roared encouragement, his crew, muttering oaths
in their native tongues, dug their oars hard into the tide and
pulled the craft seaward. Sylvia leaned toward him and said,
"Captain, we thought they [the Irishmen] were officials who
thought you were smuggling." Anthony was relieved that "my
crew had determined to fight if necessary to prevent the arrest of
their captain."

Despite the labors of his grunting oarsmen, the vessel made
but tortured progress, for a wind had risen up from the west and
was racing onshore, slowing the whaleboat's path to open waters.
Anthony scowled at another impending problem—the dark bank
of clouds crawling in from the same westerly track. For the
moment, he urged his men on and alternately scanned the beach
for "any activity" and the northwest horizon for the *Georgette*.

Anthony could still see William Bell standing on the shore

and staring at the pitching whaleboat and speculated that the timber worker was "dumbfounded at the spectacle and aware of his good fortune that Brennan or one of the prisoners had not blown off his head." The horses, with their traps, wandered about the sand.

As the whaleboat spun in the surf, no more than a half-mile from the beach, a flash of white—a crew of pensioner guards— was spotted on the Rockingham road, accompanied by shouts and thudding hoofbeats. Within a few minutes, the pensioners and Territorial Mounted Police, clad in black tunics and black bush hats, streamed onto the beach. Bell ran up to them and pointed at the sea.

Alongside Anthony, ex-Sergeant Hogan lifted his head above the gunwales, and Anthony pointed at the shore, which was full of guards and police wielding carbines and rifles, and at an equally chilling sight: "They [the British] had brought along a band of trackers, aboriginal Bushmen who play the role of human bloodhounds. They wore short *bokas,* or cloaks of kangaroo skin, with belts of twisted fur around their naked bodies. These natives are attached to the prisons to follow the trail of absconding con- victs, and they are wonderfully adept in running down a prisoner and cutting his throat as the British look on. If they had found us before we reached Rockingham, we were dead men."

For several minutes, the cavalry and the police stood by their mounts as the officers conferred. According to most accounts, the police held their fire. But Wilson would claim that some of the guards fanned out with spurs jangling and rushed to the water- line. Hogan grabbed Anthony's right arm, yanked it, and shouted: "Firing line—everyone down!"

Anthony and the others ducked as carbines flashed in several synchronized volleys, and the rounds kicked up tiny spouts of water behind the boat.

The soldiers then ceased fire and milled along the beach. Wilson's account, however, would receive no corroboration from the other men in the boat.

The rowers, driven on by terror, finally began to pull away to Anthony's cries of "Down together! That's the stuff!" By 11:30 A.M., the craft lay two miles from the beach, and cheers erupted from the boat as the soldiers and police mounted up and vanished into the bush.

Breslin, his blue eyes fixed upon Anthony, reached into one of his coat's sodden pockets, removed a piece of folded oilskin, gingerly unwrapped it, and pulled out a sheet of blue notepaper. Then, as the six escapees from The Establishment sat upright, he cleared his throat and read:

Rockingham, April 17, 1876

To His Excellency the British Governor of Western Australia,

This is to certify that I have this day released from the clemency of Her Most Gracious Majesty Victoria, Queen of Great Britain, etc., etc., six Irishmen, condemned to imprisonment for life by the enlightened and magnanimous government of Great Britain for having been guilty of the atrocious and unpardonable crimes known to the unenlightened portion of mankind as "Love of Country" and "Hatred of Tyranny"; for this act of "Irish Assurance" my birth and my blood being my full and sufficient warrant. Allow me to add that:

I'm taking my leave now, I've only to say,
A few cells I've emptied (a sell in its way).

I've the honor and pleasure to bid you good-day.
From all future acquaintance, excuse me, I pray.

> In the service of my country.
> John J. Breslin

By letter's end, the gaunt prisoners—still cradling rifles—
were weeping. Breslin fought to control additional emotions: he
had sent Mary Tondut to her parents home in Perth to await both
the passage money to America he intended to send and the birth
of their child. On Easter Monday, her father, Charles, was winning races at the regatta in his yacht, the *Frenchman.*

Although the oarsmen looked on in bemusement at the
Irishmen, Anthony was moved by "the audacity and courage of
those long-suffering men."

The six military Fenians had left behind two others, whose suffering would continue. With Thomas Delaney, the escaped prisoners could not have taken the chance of bringing an alcoholic
into the scheme, fearing that while drunk he might blurt out the
details of the escape plan to a warder or an informer.

Such was not the case with James Keilley, of the 53rd Regiment, a Fenian sentenced to life servitude. At Dartmoor and Millbank, his Fenian comrades suspected that he had turned informer
in hopes of a future reduction of his sentence. Married and the
father of two when he was sentenced in June 1866, Keilley had
tried to hang himself at Millbank. Even if Wilson and the others
had some sympathy for him because of the desperation that
clutched him, they also reviled him, as his relationship with Acting
Comptroller-General Fauntleroy and the official's family crushed
any chance that the others would take him into the plot. They
remained suspicious of a Fenian handyman so well-liked by the
Fauntleroys that he was often allowed to stay at the house until 9

P.M. or later before returning to his cell. Wilson had bluntly told Breslin that Keilley was out.

As the rowers pulled the whaleboat ever farther from shore, Breslin rewrapped the letter in the oilskin packet, pulled a small piece of wood from his pocket, and bound it to the waterproof package. Then, as Anthony and the others watched, he "launched [the] tiny craft shoreward with the wind and tide full ashore."

Turning to Anthony, Breslin said, " 'Tis done, Captain. . . ."

His hand clamping even harder around the tiller, Anthony nodded. But he knew it was far from done as the whaleboat began to rise and fall. "We headed into lengthened swells which were rolling in from the ocean with increasing violence," he noted.

A gale was gathering, and somewhere to the northeast lurked the *Georgette*. A deadly race against the Royal Navy and the elements loomed.

From Perth to Fremantle, a race to catch the escapees and their helpers began. When prison officials tried to send a telegram to Albany, in King George's Sound, to dispatch the H.M.S. *Conflict* in pursuit of the convicts, the lines were dead in every direction. McCarthy and Walsh, who would soon head east and catch a steamer for Ireland, had done their work of disabling the telegraph lines.

An onlooker to the frantic scene in Fremantle during the first hours after the escape wrote: "They [the escapees] were not missed for about an hour and a half, and then there was a scene of the wildest excitement, officials running here and there, mounted policemen flying with orders and dispatches, and finally two mounted policemen and a native black man, a tracker. . . . There will be hard times for the officials and lots of dismissals. . . . I need hardly tell you that the Irish people here are in the very highest state of jubilation at the escape of the prisoners."

When mounted police raced into Perth with the news,

Governor Robinson rushed from the regatta to Fremantle. He found Water Police Superintendent Stone with a fistful of copies of all the telegrams between "Collins" and Anthony. The *Catalpa*, Stone declared, had left Bunbury that weekend and was the only American whaler that had put out in that time frame.

By early afternoon, the telegraph lines had been repaired, and messages began flying back and forth from Fremantle, to Perth, to Albany, and to the Royal Navy Station at Sydney. The Fremantle Police Occurrence Book for Easter Monday, April 17, 1876, recorded that warders from the prison sounded the alert at 10 A.M. "that six men had made their escapes from various working parties; their names and numbers were given and it was realized that all were Irish political prisoners."

As soon as the telegraph to Perth was working again, Fremantle Police Sergeant Joseph Campbell wired the detective bureau in Perth. Detective Sergeant Thomas Rowe replied with a telegram at 10:30 A.M. urging Campbell to dispatch men to Rockingham Beach, but it was too late. After William Bell was brought to Fremantle and gave his account of the morning's drama at Rockingham Beach, Sergeant Campbell telegraphed Rowe again: "Prisoners gone in boat. All armed. Got agents. Send assistance. Recommend steamer to follow."

Rowe dashed off another message asking for details about the escape boat and its crew. In answer, Campbell wired: "Good whaleboat, coloured crew. Would be out of sight in an hour. Water police gone in pursuit, but will never catch them. Much needed reinforcements arrived from Perth at half past one, they included Constables White and Donovan and the native assistant Harry. Corporal MacKay and Constable Truslove just left the station to join the water police pursuit."

At 1:30 P.M. Stone had sent a police cutter to scour the waters for both the whaleboat and the *Catalpa*.

As mounted police gathered at the waterfront and warders at the prison locked all the prisoners in their cells, Sergeant Campbell received orders from Stone to muster a heavily armed contingent of police to go aboard the *Georgette,* which was steaming to Fremantle from Champion Bay. Campbell asserted to Stone that pensioner guards should also be packed aboard the steamer. Rowe would recall: "This met with approval, and he [Campbell] was advised to apply to Sergeant Latimer for rifles and ammunition."

As the pensioners began to assemble along the dock, Perth Detective Corporal James Archdeacon, like Rowe a former warder on the *Hougoumont* and familiar with the escaped Fenians, rode up to the jetty with another constable and two native Aborigine trackers. Though it was too late for trackers, Archdeacon could identify the prisoners if the police and troops had to board the *Catalpa.*

Campbell received another telegram from Perth minutes after Archdeacon's arrival: "Sergeant McLarty and two constables have just left to go . . . from Fremantle in the *Georgette.* Keep Perth men for the present . . . to be employed as the occasion requires. Have rifles ready to go onboard on arrival of Sergeant McLarty."

At 4 P.M., Campbell was instructed by Stone that McLarty was to take command of the pensioner guards who would go with the *Georgette*—not an order that would sit well with the soldiers, who would resent obeying a "mere" police sergeant. Stone also ordered Campbell to advise the shipmaster, Captain O'Grady, to "have everything ready to sail immediately."

As soon as McLarty rode into Fremantle shortly after 4 P.M., he inspected the gathering police and pensioners.

Sergeant Campbell was glad to see Detective Rowe, arguably the best in Western Australia, emerge from the mail van that ran

from Perth to Fremantle and leap down "to relieve the station sergeant of some of the responsibility for this unusual and alarming
operation." Rowe immediately sent a telegram to Sub-Inspector
Finlay at Albany, asking if there was even a chance that H.M.S.
Conflict might still get up enough steam to turn around and take
a run at the *Catalpa*.

The reply officially left the *Georgette* as the only pursuit ship:
"No, left yesterday morning."

While the *Georgette* steamed for Fremantle, Robinson and
Stone debated just how far they could go in hunting down the
prisoners and attacking the *Catalpa* if her captain refused to
hand them over to the British. Great Britain and the United States
had been engaged for several years in hot debate over ships'
freedom to operate in any manner in international waters. The
governor and the water police commander debated whether they
could not only chase the whaleboat and the *Catalpa* in international waters, but also destroy them if the crews resisted.
Robinson and Stone went back and forth, knowing that they
would have to give Captain O'Grady his orders.

Of one thing they were certain: their determination to catch the
Irishmen and punish the rescuers—or, if they resisted, use all
force at the *Georgette*'s disposal.

Governor Robinson prepared to send a telegram to every naval
station and port in Australia: "Detain, by force if necessary,
American whaling barque *Catalpa*, George Anthony, Master.
Arrest said Anthony, his officers and crew, and any passengers
who may be aboard."

The Open Boat

As police, pensioners, and excited onlookers clotted the Fremantle waterfront in the late morning and throughout the afternoon of Easter Monday 1876, Captain Anthony guided the whaleboat and its fifteen other occupants toward the *Catalpa*, sixteen miles to the southeast. At 12:30 P.M., Anthony navigated the boat past the reefs that had nearly capsized it the previous night. He would reveal that when "he saw the menacing reef upon which the water was foaming and breaking, it seemed impossible that he had gone over it the night before."

Anthony ordered his crew to hoist the leg-o'-mutton sail and steered southeast to the seaward of Garden Island. By 4 P.M., he had not spotted the *Catalpa* and, with the wind still blowing to the southeast, ordered the crew to take in the sail and row due west. Smiling confidently at the nervous Irishmen, he assured them that the ship would soon come into view.

Anthony had no doubt that they were nearing the whaler, but was concerned by the longer swells and churning whitecaps, which would make it harder for lookouts on the *Catalpa* to spot the whaleboat as it rose and dipped. As he scanned the western horizon, the dark clouds were gathering and moving quickly toward Anthony and his comrades. He knew what was coming.

At 5:30, with the sky turning from gray to black, the boat bobbed on frothing waves that grew higher and fiercer as they crashed against the overladen boat. Suddenly, Tobey cried out and pointed to the west. Fifteen heads turned at the same moment and squinted at the faintest outline of a vessel on the rim of the dark horizon, some four miles off. The *Catalpa*, Anthony told the Irishmen.

The rowers did not need any urging from Anthony to pull as hard as they could, their grunts and twitching fingers punctuating their efforts. Slowly, the whaleboat began to gain on the *Catalpa*, and by 6:30 P.M. Anthony could discern her topsails above the crests of the huge waves directly ahead.

According to Pease, Anthony noted, "The wind was blasty, but hauled a little in the boat's favor, so that [he] ordered the little sail set and told his companions if he could head in the way he was now going, the ship could be raised in an hour."

Anthony hoped he was right. Breslin wrote: "At this time the weather had been gloomy with rain squalls and we were all pretty thoroughly soaked. The boat made good headway under sail, and we were rapidly overhauling the ship, carrying all sail and the whole boat's crew, sixteen men in all, perched on the weather gunwale, with the water rushing from time on the leeside. . . ."

Anthony could see the fright on the other men's faces, even those of his own crew, as the storm began to hit. He recorded: "The fury of the wind and sea now poured upon the boat, and darkness was coming on. . . . The sky grew blacker and the sea grew steadily heavier. The boat began to jump and jar until it seemed that she might lose her spar or her mast-step."

"I've been in worse, boys," Anthony said. In truth, he reflected, he had never been in worse. He ordered the Irishmen to bail, Hogan and Cranston slopping water from the boat with particular urgency. With sixteen men in the boat, designed for no more than six to ten, the craft rode low in the water—so low that the gunnels sat bare inches above the thrashing sea.

Anthony would tell Pease: "A crisis had arrived, and any risk was preferable to a night on the ocean in such a storm as was imminent. The boat leaped forward at a spanking rate, and the spray flew like feathers; and the water rose in mimic mountains, crowned with white foam which the wind blew in mist from summit to summit. Miles away the *Catalpa* was seen, barely discernible at moments when she rose on the crest of a larger wave than common, thrusting her bows in the air, surrounded by foam, and apparently ready to take flight from the sea."

Anthony took a risk by keeping the sail up in winds threatening to crack the mast in two, but felt he had no choice. At all costs, they needed to reach the *Catalpa*. But Smith's first responsibility, as Anthony knew, was to the whaler, not the little boat floundering in the sea.

Sometime between 7 and 8 P.M. a crack pierced the shrieking gusts, and the men in the whaleboat gaped as the mast snapped off close to its base and toppled over the side, splashing into the sea. Rigging, the sail, and halyard went over with the mast and started to tip the boat to one side. With only minutes before the weight of the debris sank the whaleboat, Sylvia seized a hatchet and chopped the sail's shrouds loose. Then as other hands helped, he dragged the tangled ropes and canvas back aboard. The boat righted itself, but still pitched only inches above the sea. Several of the escaped prisoners retched and groaned, too seasick to be of any more use. Hogan and Cranston kept on bailing like soaked, ashen-faced automatons.

As Anthony and Sylvia worked to cut and rig the salvaged mess into a "jury mast"—a sail attached to the midship oar and jammed into the stand—the boat nearly overturned several times to the windward side. One of the passengers remembered: "But the captain threw her head to the wind, and the magnificent efforts of the crew kept her afloat. Monstrous seas now rolled into her, threatening to overwhelm the craft. She was almost water-logged, and shipped water over bow and stern alternately, as she rose and fell. The crew bailed vehemently and desperately. The rescued men were very sick, and lay in the bottom of the boat, a wretched heap of miserable humanity."

Sometime after 10 P.M., Anthony and the others saw the faint image of the *Catalpa*, outlined by the yellow glow of her lanterns, vanish. Smith was tacking her farther offshore, as was wise, Anthony thought. The first mate would take no chance of the gale driving the whaler onto the shoals near Garden Island. If Anthony could keep his small stricken craft afloat until the storm subsided, he knew that Smith would return. As the captain ordered his rowers to "ship oars," which "accomplished nothing more than holding the boat on her course," he calculated that his odds of guiding the craft through the gale until morning were ebbing fast.

Again, he assured the Irishmen and his crew of their chances—he had seen worse, he lied once more.

Breslin remembered, "We then hoisted the jib on an oar and steered the course we supposed the vessel had gone."

As the hours trudged on, the waves broke across the boat, and the men kept bailing, their arms numb but their minds racing with fears of drowning. To toss more water from the craft, Anthony ordered the crew to break open the lids of the few food and water casks that had not been washed overboard, dump the contents over the side, and bail with the larger containers. Every now and then, however, the Irishmen would ask Anthony for some sort of encouragement. One asked, "Captain, do you think we will float through the night?"

Anthony managed a tight smile and replied again, "Oh, yes.

I've been out on many a worse night." He kept his real thoughts hidden: "[I] would not have given a cent for the lives of the entire company," himself included.

Hunger and thirst began to gnaw at the men in the black gloom of the first hours of April 18. Anthony was on his knees by the jury mast most of the time, steering with each blast of the storm. He recalled that often the sea rose to his armpits. "The men were groaning," he would tell Pease, "and it was so dark that he could not see his crew."

To the east, the storm also lashed the jetty at Fremantle, but the *Georgette* was making ready to put out to sea despite the wind and waves. The police and the pensioners, under the command of Major Finerty, marched aboard in the driving rain as a crowd of citizens braved the gale to watch. A huge twelve-pounder cannon was dragged aboard the steamer, the weapon easily able to sink the whaler. Superintendent of Water Police Stone was ordered by Governor Robinson "to go alongside the *Catalpa* and try to find out whether the prisoners were aboard, and if they were, to demand their surrender, warning the captain of the consequences of his act if he refused to give them up."

With sails furled and smoke belching from its funnel, the *Georgette* pulled away from the jetty at 9 P.M. on April 17, 1876, and jolted southwest against the giant waves and surging gusts.

Captain Anthony somehow continued to steer the whaleboat in the storm, employing every bit of seamanship he knew, but at 2 A.M., he was preparing himself for death. He believed that "the boat must swamp before long." Surely no measure of his skill could prevent that.

Before 3 A.M., a sudden shift in the wind caught his attention. The gusts had slackened slightly. The waves still rushed at the whaleboat, but not as frequently and not as high. In an instant

Anthony realized that the gale was ebbing and that he could keep the craft afloat.

The storm lingered at dawn, but was dying. Anthony noted: "Daylight was welcome after the awful night. The sea had now gone down, and there was the prospect of a fair day. The sea came aboard less frequently, and courage and hope returned."

At 6:45 A.M. on Tuesday, April 18, 1876, they spied the *Catalpa* "standing in toward the land" several miles off. A cheer erupted from the shivering, sodden men in the whaleboat. The crew shipped oars and rowed for the *Catalpa* in the still-choppy sea. With her lower sails set, she progressed toward the whaleboat although Smith's lookouts had not yet located the small craft.

Breslin turned to look behind the whaleboat. A dark smudge rose against the clearing skies to the east from the direction of Fremantle. With a shout to Anthony, Breslin pointed at the sooty cloud. Anthony's eyes grew wide, and he ordered the rowers to pull with all they had.

You Are Firing on the American Flag!

Shortly after 7 A.M. on Tuesday, April 18, 1876, Breslin recognized the vessel beneath the dark cloud of coal smoke. The *Georgette* appeared to churn on the exact course as the whaleboat.

Breslin held out hope for a moment that the steamer might be on her normal run to Albany with the Colonial mails. "For a short time," he would say, "we were in doubt whether she was in pursuit or going on her regular trip. A little further observation convinced me that she was too far out of her regular course to be going to Albany, and a slight alteration in her steering decided the question, showing us that she was making for the *Catalpa*, which she must have seen before we did."

Anthony ordered the crew to run up the sail, man their oars, and pull for the *Catalpa* in a desperate hope that they could beat the steamer to the whaler.

On the *Catalpa*'s quarterdeck, Sam Smith scanned the waters to the east, the landward side. The outline of the coast distorted his view in conjunction with the still-surging swells, and he did not see the whaleboat. Then he spied the *Georgette* and turned the whaler to the southwest. Although the winds blew against the *Catalpa*, she still lurched farther from the whaleboat. Breslin agonized: "However we still struggled on the course, the *Catalpa* was sailing . . . fast receding from our view, and some of our crew called her the phantom ship as the more we tried to approach her the farther off she appeared to sail."

Guessing that the British steamer had not yet spied the whaleboat bouncing on the fading but still high swells, and hoping to become as invisible as possible, Anthony took down the sail, barked at the crew to stow their oars, and ordered everyone to lay down as best they could in the overcrowded craft.

As the *Georgette* approached, the six escaped prisoners, plus Breslin, King, Desmond, and Brennan, grabbed rifles and revolvers, emptied the weapons' sodden cartridges, broke open the cartridge boxes that the ex-soldiers had clung to throughout the storm, and reloaded. All ten vowed that they "would fight until the last man was killed." Anthony had no doubt that they meant every word.

As the *Georgette* appeared less than a half-mile away, Anthony inclined his head slightly. He saw an officer standing on the bridge and peering through a pair of field glasses at the waters leading to the shoreline. Then the steamer slogged past the whaleboat and veered toward the *Catalpa.* Anthony figured that from the half-mile distance, the *Georgette*'s lookouts had mistaken the whaleboat for a large piece of driftwood. He also reckoned that the heavily armed vessel had, like the men in the whaleboat, spotted the *Catalpa* and was bearing down on her.

Now, Anthony took a gamble. Calculating that the *Georgette*'s lookouts would be focused on the *Catalpa* and not looking to the steamer's stern, he told his crew to put out their oars and row in the steamer's wake, which would help pull the whaleboat forward.

Breslin wrote: " We now plied oar and sail to reach the ship, but it soon became apparent that the *Georgette* was gaining too fast on us and would fetch the ship much sooner than we could.

She was also coming close enough to catch us under sail, so we determined to take down the sail and lie to, taking the chance of her passing by without seeing us. The *Georgette* passed without having seen our boat, steering direct for the *Catalpa*, now distant about five miles. As soon as he had passed far enough ahead we pulled after her wake, judging it to be the safest position we could occupy if she was in search of us, also bringing us nearer to the ship. . . ."

Anthony's crew strained at the oars even with the aid of the steamer's wake, making labored but steady headway in the heavy seas. As they came within closer view of the *Catalpa*, they saw the *Georgette*—at least twice as large as the whaler—stand to alongside her. They could neither see nor hear the confrontation erupting between Smith and the *Georgette*'s officers.

From the deck of the steamer, Superintendent Stone of the water police shouted out a question to Smith: "Where is the boat missing from your cranes?"

Smith shouted back that his captain had taken it to Fremantle.

"What for?" cried Stone.

In reply, Smith offered that the captain had left to buy an anchor to replace one damaged by the previous night's gale.

Stone yelled that he intended to board the *Catalpa* and search for "Irish prisoners."

Smith grabbed a harpoon and brandished it at Stone. "You try it and you'll be goddamned good and sorry!" the first mate roared. "What the hell did we lick the pants of you damn Britishers in 1812 about? You don't own the goddamn ocean!"

As the red-faced Stone mulled whether to storm the whaler, Captain Grady told him that the steamer's coal was running low and that they had to run back to Fremantle to replenish the ship's coal bunkers. Stone hesitated. But when Grady assured the police official that the *Catalpa* was going nowhere for the next day or so with the prevailing winds, Stone agreed to head for port. He counted on a second go at the insolent Yankee officer and his ship.

The *Georgette* came about and sailed away from the whaler—and back in the direction of Anthony's boat. Once again he and the other fifteen men lay as flat as they could, one atop the other, and the steamer passed so close that Anthony and Breslin saw the ranks of pensioner guards and the glints of their bayonets on the ship's main deck. She swept by without spotting the whaleboat and tacked toward the coast.

After waiting for the *Georgette* to fade, Anthony ran up the jury sail and ordered his crew to pull for the *Catalpa*.

On its way back to Fremantle, the *Georgette* heaved to along-side the water police cutter that had been dispatched earlier, and Stone ordered Coxwain Mills to search for the missing whaleboat and cut off her route to the *Catalpa*. Grady and his officers believed that as the storm had intensified the whaleboat had returned to the shore somewhere, but was now out the water. The cutter, a wide craft with a pair of mutton-leg sails and jammed with thirty to forty police officers, set out immediately to search for the whaleboat.

In the early afternoon, Desmond glanced to the north from his position on the whaleboat and spotted a vessel. Then he cried, "My God! There's the guard boat, filled with police! Pass out those rifles!"

Anthony had to make another snap decision: to stay where they were, hope the cutter did not see them, and then make a run for the whaler as the police boat started away; or row for the *Catalpa* now, and clamber aboard before the police spotted the whaleboat wide open in the water.

With a shout of "Pull harder!" Anthony set his rowers into fierce motion. As the whaleboat and the cutter steadily closed the distance to the *Catalpa* from opposite directions, the whaler suddenly tacked away from the police cutter and headed under full sail straight for Anthony's boat. Sam Smith had seen them, and just as Anthony had hoped, the first mate had decided to get to them before the police could. Just to be sure, Breslin yelled at Wilson to grab a blue signal flag from the deck and wave it from the bow. The *Catalpa* continued straight for the whaleboat.

Smith's action set the men on the cutter into intensified motion, the officers running up their sail hoops. With three or four men at each of the masts' sweeps, the police boat rapidly gained on the *Catalpa*.

A three-way race continued as the whaleboat and the cutter dashed toward the *Catalpa*, and Anthony's crew rowed desperately. If the cutter got there first, it was over for the prisoners—one way or the other. The Irishmen grabbed at the oars to try to help pull faster, but Anthony bellowed at them to leave the crew alone and lie down. They obeyed, faces taut, clutching their rifles and revolvers. The whaleboat, with a shorter distance to the *Catalpa* than the cutter, was going to get there first. As the two ships neared and the cutter closed the gap fast, Anthony stood and shouted to Smith, "Hoist the ensign!"

One of the *Catalpa*'s crewmen ran the Stars and Stripes up the mainmast. Moments later the whaleboat thumped against the yellow hull of the whaler. Anthony and Sylvia seized the tackle lines lowered from the *Catalpa* and secured the whaleboat. The six prisoners, followed by the rest of the boat's sodden occupants, scrambled up the sideboards by the grip rope, still clutching their rifles and revolvers. Quickly, the crew hoisted the whaleboat onto its davits, and Anthony, the last man up, climbed over the rail just seconds before the water police cutter swept a hundred yards away from the *Catalpa*'s bow, kicking up a great spout of foam.

In his account of those moments, Breslin remembered:

> At three o'clock P.M. we ran up to the ship on the weather side the police boat being close up on the lee quarter and scrambled onboard in double quick time. As soon as my feet struck the deck over the quarter line, Mr. Smith the first mate called out to me "What shall I do now Mr. Collins? What shall I do?" I replied "hoist the boat and stand out to sea" and never was a maneuver executed in more prompt and seamanlike manner. The stars and stripes were flying at the perch, our boat was hoisted and in its place at the davits the ship wove and was standing on her course inside of two minutes. The police boat was dropping alongside. As we went past, I stepped to the rail and kissed my hand to the gentlemen who had lost the race. Their boat dropped astern. . . .

Coxwain Mills reported: "The Water Police saw the Absconders get onboard from the whaleboat to the *Catalpa;* the master of the *Catalpa* with his speaking trumpet in his hand, on the deck of the *Catalpa,* was recognized to be the man in charge of the whaleboat which left Rockingham; . . . saw and recognized two of the Absconders in the forepart of the *Catalpa.*

The "absconders" stood at the rail of the *Catalpa,* brandishing their rifles and yelling at the police. On the cutter, Mills had no choice but to sail back to Fremantle: he had no orders to board the whaler and dared not do so on his own initiative.

According to Anthony and Breslin, Mills picked up his speaking trumpet and shouted, "Good-morning captain."

Through his own trumpet, Anthony called back, "Good-morning."

With that, the cutter made for shore.

Their hair wet and matted with salt, their skin as deeply burned as that of sailors, Cranston, Darragh, Harrington, Hassett, Hogan, and Wilson wept, laughed, hugged each other and the crewmen, who were baffled by these gaunt men who sounded like Duggan, the ship's carpenter. Duggan embraced the new passengers, the stoic IRB man fighting back tears of his own. Several times the Irishmen burst into cheers for Anthony and Smith.

Breslin wrote: "After 28 hours in an open boat with a liberal allowance of rain and sea water, cramped for want of room and cheered with a glorious uncertainty as to whether we should gain freedom or the chain gang, a suit of dry clothes, a glass of New England rum and a mug of hot coffee were just the things to be put 'where they would do the most good' and they were put accordingly."

John King described: "Then the prisoners felt that they were free at last, and they gathered around Breslin and fell on the deck. . . . We were all overwhelmed with thanks, and it certainly was a relief. . . ."

From his many conversations with Anthony, Pease related:

> If Captain Anthony, Mr. Breslin, and the others had been reprieved from a death sentence they would have felt no greater joy and contentment. Captain Anthony and Breslin complimented Mate Smith, and the former called the steward.
>
> "Get up the best dinner the ship can afford," he said. "We're hungry."
>
> The steward succeeded admirably. There were canned chickens and lobsters, boiled potatoes, canned fruits, tea and coffee, and it was the most memorable dinner in the lifetime of the men who assembled.

> Messrs. Breslin, Desmond, and King dined with the captain, and the rescued men ate in the steerage.

The fact that the six prisoners ate their first dinner as free men in more than a decade in the steerage reflected no slight on Anthony's part. His cabin was too small to accommodate everyone, and he figured that after all the six Irishmen had endured, they would want to spend those first hours in freedom with each other.

After dinner, Captain Anthony instructed Smith to tell the men who had rowed the whaleboat that they were excused from duty the next day and could sleep as long as they wanted. He gave his cabin that night to Breslin and assigned Desmond and King to berths in the forward cabin. Before the exhausted captain settled down on a chair in Smith's cabin, he went on deck to check the wind. The ship's sails sagged from the yards, the faint offshore breeze not enough to stir the canvas. He told Smith to work off shore if possible, but the ship did not move her own length during the entire night.

Dismayed but too weary to ponder the problem for long, Anthony reeled to Smith's cabin and sank into the chair. He still had one more task, the day's entry in the ship's log. His laconic or weary phrases made it sound like just another day at sea: "At 2 P.M. wore ship and headed more northward. At 2:15 raised the boat N.N. by E. Kept off for her, and at 3 P.M. she came alongside with eleven passengers [a hint of Anthony's exhaustion—there were sixteen in the whaleboat]. The coastguard boat was in sight. She hoisted her flag and we hoisted ours, and wore ship. The coastguard boat was alongside of us, and her captain wished us good-bye."

With that, George Anthony fell asleep.

Of that night aboard the *Catalpa*, Breslin remembered: "After supper we walked about the deck and enjoyed what we supposed to be a last look at the shores of Western Australia. All hands except the watch on deck, relieved for the night at about 9 o'clock P.M., slept soundly."

If they had possessed any inkling of the events to come the next day, no one aboard the *Catalpa* would have slept soundly.

At daybreak Smith shook Anthony awake—the *Georgette* was approaching under full steam. Anthony ran to his cabin and woke Breslin, and they scampered onto the deck. Smith stormed along the rail, glaring at the coming steamer, cursing. "Damn him, let him sink us. . . . I'll never start sheet or tack for him!"

As the steamer swept closer, everyone on the *Catalpa* stared at the black cannon on the *Georgette*'s top deck. On the main deck, pensioners were arrayed, "a forest of bayonets glistening in the morning sun."

Anthony noticed not only the the man-o'-war flag the steamer flew, but also a vice admiral's flag—the *Georgette* meant business. Whoever was standing on the British vessel's bridge had the full authority to take action against the whaler.

Ordering that the Stars and Stripes be raised to the highest masthead, Anthony, with his crew gaping at the onrushing ship and then back at him, realized that a dose of the truth was necessary. He tersely informed them that the British were coming for the six Irishmen and that if the *Georgette* captured the whaler, every man would be thrown into the prison from which the Irishmen had escaped. As the crewmen gaped, he then armed them with harpoons and blubber-cutting spades, knowing that they would fight rather than be dragged away to a prison. At the same time, Smith and several crewmen dragged grindstones and heavy spare spars from the hold to the main deck; if the British tried to put a boarding party in a longboat, Smith planned to drop the stones and spars on the attackers.

Smith was not finished. He had a harpoon gun mounted amidships with a stack of explosive cartridges and leveled the weapon at the approaching steamer.

Belowdecks, Breslin armed the escapees with rifles and revolvers, with Anthony's blessing but his admonition that the six Irishmen remain out of sight. Cradling rifles and pistols, Breslin, King, Duggan, and Desmond climbed on deck.

Mounting the poop deck in full view of the British, Anthony noticed a wind picking up—and blowing westward. Captain Grady, on the bridge of the *Georgette,* also noticed. Then he ran up a signal flag ordering the *Catalpa* to heave to and take in her sails. Anthony ignored the flag.

Peering out the thin windows of the ship's mess, Cranston, Darragh, Harrington, Hassett, Hogan, and Wilson waited with their rifles and revolvers, ready to die before spending another second in The Establishment. The bombastic Brennan, who Anthony wanted nowhere near the main deck, was with the "absconders."

Superintendent Stone barked an order. The cannon roared and a solid shot streaked just over the *Catalpa*'s bow. Anthony watched as the ball "ricocheted along [and] the water flew as high as the masthead."

At the same time, the *Catalpa,* with all sails set, started to surge to the west. The *Georgette* stalked her.

Stone raised his speaking trumpet and shouted: "Heave to!"

Through his trumpet, Anthony called out, "What for?"

"You have escaped prisoners aboard that ship."

Anthony called out, "You're mistaken. There are no prisoners aboard this ship. There are none but free men aboard!"

Stone retorted, "I see the men aboard the ship now."

"You're mistaken, sir," returned Captain Anthony. "Get up, men, and show yourselves."

Anthony's crew lined the rail, mainly Malays and Portuguese. "You can see for yourself they are my crew," he yelled.

Stone screamed, "I have telegraphed the American government, and have orders to seize you."

Anthony said nothing.

"Are you going to heave to?" asked the colonel.

Calmly, though his heart was racing, Anthony responded, "No sir!"

The *Georgette* lay on the leeward side of the whaler.

"Don't you know you have violated the colonial laws?" asked Stone.

"No, sir," answered Anthony.

The words sent Stone blustering about the deck for several moments.

Again, he threatened: "I'll give you fifteen minutes in which to heave to! If you do not, I shall blow the masts out of you and sink you!"

Stone turned and gestured at the cannon, which pensioners were swabbing and preparing to reload. This time, if they decided to rake the *Catalpa*'s deck with grapeshot, they could tear apart Anthony's crew—and he knew it.

For a moment, Captain Anthony scanned the cannon, the soldiers and police poised to board, and the British battle flag that stirred in the gathering wind. He knew that belowdecks, the military Fenians were counting off the minutes, measuring how long they might have before their last fight. Darragh, Hogan, and Harrington had known many such moments in the service of the Crown. Now they experienced it for Ireland, an emotion they had never had the chance to feel in the collapse of the Fenian rebellion a decade earlier.

Wearing his battered cap and the salt-streaked, dark-blue greatcoat, Anthony stood nearly motionless for several minutes.

His crew's eyes darted back and forth from their captain to the British ship. Standing near him, Breslin, King, Desmond, and Duggan, all of whom had seen George Anthony's courage and coolness firsthand, waited for his next move.

Anthony glared out across the water at Stone. Then, the New Bedford shipmaster raised the speaking trumpet to his lips again and pointed up at the mainmast, at the Stars and Stripes.

"This ship is sailing under the American flag, and she is on the high seas," Anthony shouted. "If you fire on me, I warn you that you are firing on the American flag!"

Silence hung between the two vessels for several moments.

Stone then blurted, "But if there are escaped convicts onboard, your flag won't protect you in that."

Coolly, Anthony said, "Yes it will in international waters."

"I intend to board your ship, sir!"

In the *Catalpa*'s mess, six men's hands tightened around their rifles.

None of the Irishmen would ever forget Anthony's next words to Superintendent Stone: "I don't care what you do."

"Then your government will be communicated with—after you take the consequences," Stone called out. "You have fifteen minutes."

While Anthony's comment about the American flag did "make the British pause," Stone could make a case that the *Catalpa*'s mission was "itself an act of war against Great Britain."

Eighteen miles off the Australian coast, Anthony risked all by "running the *Catalpa* inshore to gain the wind and then turn about for open water." If the *Catalpa* sailed too far to the east, Stone and Captain Grady could seize her in "British territorial waters." The *Georgette* trailed the whaler, Breslin agonizing that a blast of canister would ravage the *Catalpa* at any moment.

Anthony feared the same, but continued his course toward

shore. Tracking the whaler through his glass, Grady thought that he had won the standoff when Anthony "unexpectedly hauled up the clews on the mainsail, hauled down the head of the spanker, and let the gaff topsail run down" and slowed the *Catalpa* to a near stop. Grady "hove to" in the belief that the *Catalpa* was surrendering.

In an expert maneuver, Anthony suddenly "spun the wheel up," and the *Catalpa*'s sails filled with an offshore wind and launched the whaler back toward open ocean—and straight at the *Georgette*. The British seamen, soldiers, and police cringed for "the ramming." But the *Catalpa* veered past. Her jibboom, Anthony would note, barely cleared the *Georgette's* rigging.

For the next hour, the steamer trailed the whaler. Breslin expected the British ship to steam alongside the *Catalpa* at any moment and unleash a blast of grapeshot or solid shot. Then, around 4 P.M., the *Catalpa,* her sails starting to fill with an increasing breeze to the west, appeared to be putting distance between herself and the steamer. Anthony fixed his telescope on the *Georgette*. She had stopped.

When the *Catalpa* increased the distance, Captain Anthony summoned Cranston, Darragh, Harrington, Hassett, Hogan, and Wilson on deck. Anthony gestured at the *Georgette* and looked at the six Irishman.

"Boys," he said, "take a good look at her. Probably you'll never see her again."

Of the man who said those words, George Anthony, Henry Hathaway had said to Devoy over a year ago: "The man who engaged to do this will keep that engagement, or he won't come out of the penal colony."

Later, in Ireland, the *Kilkenny Journal* would chide: "Every credit is due the *Georgette*. She steered off in magnificent style. As it turned a stern lookout upon its foe, the banner of Britain displayed its folds, and the blazoned lion, shimmering in the sun, seemed to make a gesture of defiance with his tail, by curving it between his heels."

Still, with over ten thousand miles of two oceans to America, Anthony worried that they might well see other warships flying the Union Jack. So, too, he would learn, did the "Fremantle Six."

Part 5
The Furor and
the Fallout

Rolling Home

As the *Catalpa* sailed west across the Indian Ocean and when the *Georgette* steamed back empty-handed to Fremantle, finger-pointing and rage swept through official circles in Western Australia and spread to London. In response to fiery criticism that ignited within hours of the *Georgette*'s return, Governor Robinson received a staunch defense from the editors of the *Fremantle Herald*: "The Governor . . . was not to be led into committing a breach of international law, to ratify a feeling of resentment against the cool effrontery of the Yankee."

In his official report to the Colonial Office, Robinson took the same tack with his contention that sinking the *Catalpa* "would not justify me in involving Her Majesty's Government in an undesirable conflict with the Government of the United States."

From Perth, to Fremantle, and Bunbury, Detective Sergeant Rowe and other officers began to backtrack and piece together how the plot had materialized under the collective noses of the authorities. Rowe unmasked too late the successful charade that "Mr. Collins" had pulled off on everyone from Governor Robinson to Superintendent Joseph Doonan. In one report, Rowe revealed the relationship between Breslin and Mary Tondut: "Mary Tonduit [*sic*] a Roman Catholic of this Colony, late servant at the Emerald Isle Hotel, where Collins was lodged, was seduced by Collins and is now enceinte [pregnant]. She left this Colony in the Northern Light. Her expenses were paid by Collins through Maloney. She is to be accouched in Sydney, where further arrangements are promised to be made to take her to Collins."

The role of Patrick Maloney, ex-Dublin constable and proprietor of the Emerald Isle, in the plot would remain murky. He was brought in for several lengthy interrogations about his seemingly all-too-cozy relationship with Collins/Breslin. In official police records, Rowe and other detectives suspected that Maloney knew far more than he let on to them, for obvious reasons. Whenever Breslin had needed an introduction to officials he could dupe, Maloney had often proved the conduit for "the Yankee." Everyone from Fremantle to Perth and Bunbury knew that Maloney had struck up friendships with many civilian Fenians who had been amnestied and remained in Australia. No one could connect him to the six military Fenians, but the police suspected that Maloney had been in on the escape plot from the start. They just could not prove it. A police officer recorded: " But Mr. Patrick Maloney, County Clare, had not been for some time in the constabulary [in Ireland] . . . without having acquired enough of that rare adroitness earned by commerce with such service, to be a match for any policeman in the antipodes [Australia]."

At the Port Hotel, Fremantle police hauled in Walsh and McCarthy for questioning by the savvy Thomas Rowe. The Scotland Yard detective had no doubt that the two were IRB men and had played a part in the plot, but as with Maloney, Rowe could not break down the pair. Several weeks after the *Catalpa*'s escape, a large crowd of local Irish gave McCarthy and Walsh a rousing send-off as they boarded the *Georgette* for their journey back to Ireland and eventually to America. Walsh was far from finished in rebel circles. He would help found The Invincibles, a radical band of Irish rebels who would murder Frederick Cavendish, the Chief Secretary for Ireland, in a savage assault with "long knives" in Dublin's Phoenix Park in 1882.

Detective Rowe also made the "America connection":

Collins was in fact John Breslin, a leading Fenian. In association with Fenian sympathizers in America, and John Boyle O'Reilly, he had masterminded the escape plan before coming to Western Australia as a man of business.

Some help had been given by people in the immediate vicinity of Fremantle to a man named Collins but only as casual visitors at Public Houses as regards stranger who have arrived in the Colony an entry in my occurance [sic] book dated 14th December 1875 shows as follows "Stranger Noticed in Perth" an American working at Mr. W. Sloans as a Wheelwright name Thomas Johnson is a native of Illinois, U.S.A. he arrived at Albany on the 2nd November 1875 . . . this man was working regularly at Sloans, and nothing appeared suspicious in his conduct until the escape of the six Fenians.

James Collins arrived in this Colony about last November and stopped at Maloney's Hotel ostensibly as a commercial traveler mixing with the best society frequenting Maloney's Hotel . . . he had expressed his intention of going pearling at the north west coast in consequence of which rumour no suspicions were aroused from the fact of his purchasing clothing and a rifle with ammunition.

Jones [King] arrived at Albany from the eastern Colonies on the 2nd March last. . . . and put up at the Maloney Hotel, Fremantle, on the 5th of March. No intimacy was noticed between Collins and Jones more than is usual between persons stopping at the same hotel. There was nothing in his conduct or manners to excite suspicion. . . . There is no doubt that the men seen with the escaped prisoners were Collins, Jones, Johnson. . . .

I beg to state that my principal observations were confined to Fenians at large as I believed the Fenian Prisoneres [*sic*] were under strict surveillance inside the prison.

Thos. Rowe
Det. Sergeant

Within days of the escape, Governor Robinson sanctioned a commision of inquiry to place blame for the furor. The scapegoating quickly led to the superintendent of Fremantle Gaol, Joseph Doonan, the man so gulled by Collins as to have personally given the man a tour of The Establishment. In turn Doonan reported to Acting Comptroller-General Fauntleroy that Warder Lindsey, who had waved Cranston and Hassett through the main gate without permission on Easter Monday, bore a large share of culpability. So, too, Doonan contended, did Warder Booler for having allowed Cranston to remove Harrington from the dockside quarrying crew.

The commission dismissed the two warders from the penal service. Booler left the colony, reportedly carrying two hundred pounds sterling supplied by Patrick Maloney. Lindsey, however, would be reinstated after tempers cooled. He had not technically slipped up on Easter Monday, as Cranston and Hassett had been allowed to leave the prison itself when the accountant of stores ate breakfast.

Acting Comptroller-General Fauntleroy scapegoated Doonan and convinced the commission to suspend the superintendent of The Establishment. Shortly afterward, Doonan suffered a mental breakdown. On July 16, 1876, he slashed his throat with a razor and "hovered between life and death." He survived, and for the rest of his life, he wore high collars to hide the scar.

Doonan was granted an invalid's pension in September 1876, his appeals for reinstatement by the Home Office and the Colonial Secretary eliciting no sympathy. Eventually, he opened a dry goods store in Fremantle.

With each mile that the *Catalpa* put between the rescued prisoners and The Establishment, the more the furor gripping Western Australia spread. The first to suffer for the six Irishmen's daring escape were the Fenians left behind, and not merely Keilley and Delaney. In a letter sent to a friend in Virginia City, Nevada, an Englishman living in Fremantle wrote:

> You cannot imagine the excitement caused by this escape. . . . It seems that the Governor was extremely annoyed. . . . One thing this escape has been the cause of which I regret—those unfortunate men who were out of prison by what is called a "ticket of leave" had their tickets revoked, and those others who were employed about the town in gangs are now kept within the prison wall in close confinement. . . . it is an act worthy of a slave driver. . . .
>
> The public appear to be in favour of the escapes, and not even the worst enemy [of the Fenians] amongst us does not wish for the capture of the prisoners, but merely for the sending back of the "notorious Collins,"

the supposed leader of the expedition. Opinions even as regards him are divided, some being for hanging and others—amongst them the ladies—for letting him escape.

Suffering the most were those "unfortunate men," six soldier Fenians who had either completed their sentences or had tickets-of-leave and now found themselves back inside The Establishment, Delaney and Keilley, of course, among them.

The Tory papers and leaders of Australia ranted for "vengeance" and for people to take the blame and to accept responsibility. In the pages of the *Perth Enquirer*, an editor opined: "It seems humiliating that a Yankee, with half a dozen coloured men, should be able to come into our waters and carry off six of the most determined of the Fenian convicts—all the unreleased of the military prisoners—and then to laugh at us for allowing them to be taken away without securing them."

The *Enquirer* added: "It would appear that there was a desire to obtain correct legal information on international law, for about the time of Captain Anthony's visit to Fremantle, Johnson [Desmond] called upon Mr. Howell, the solicitor in Perth, and asked him several questions as to the limit of neutral waters, from which we would infer that the Captain [Anthony] knew what he was about when he told Mr. Stone that his flag protected him where he then was against misdemeanour or felony either."

In a final note, the editor urged "Her Majesty's ships give full chase to the whaler and bring the fugitives back to their cells."

The *Melbourne Argus* similarly demanded that the Royal Navy comb the Indian and Atlantic Oceans for the *Catalpa*.

From the *Melbourne Advocate* came a grudging nod to the audacity of the prisoners and the plotters: "The feeling of irritation at this whole business is very strong in Fremantle and naturally so, for it is no trifle that men who were rebels while they wore the uniform of the Queen, and whom her Majesty's ministers refused over and over again to recommend to her clemency, have taken French leave of their jailers; and it is still more irritating that an accomplice of their flight, standing under the United States flag, and relying on it as a protecting aegis, defied an English vessel, legally commissioned, to capture the fugitives by force."

The news of the escape took nearly two weeks to reach London—someone had cut the telegraph cable between Australia and Java. According to Devoy, IRB agents had done the work some forty-five miles from Darwin, Australia. Whether that was the case or some fortunate—for the *Catalpa*—natural mishap had taken out the cable would remain an open question. In a letter to Devoy on April 29, 1876, some ten days after the breakout, Dr. William Carroll, a prominent Philadelphia Clan na Gael leader and a man in on the *Catalpa*'s rescue mission, wrote: "Yours of yesterday is just to hand. I hope your surmise as to the cause of 'the cable' being 'broken' is correct. If so, and all goes well with our friends, it will electrify our people the world over."

Not until June 6, 1876, would Parliament and the Queen receive full details of the six military Fenians' escape. On May 22, 1876, Tory Prime Minister Benjamin Disraeli had condemned and blocked a Labor Party initiative to free the military Fenians of Australia on humanitarian grounds. He intoned, "I am bound to say that I am not prepared to advise Her Majesty to release the prisoners referred to. . . ."

In Parliament that day, no one listening to Disraeli's diatribe against the military Fenians knew yet that the six were already free and far from Fremantle. Thomas Mooney, the London correspondent of the *Irish World*, a New York newspaper, wrote: "The expression of his [Disraeli's] whole person, face, mouth, and eyes, at the supreme moment when he sat down declaring against the prisoners' release, was one of royal contempt towards the Irish nation, its martyrs and its advocates."

Disraeli's contempt was about to turn to shock.

On June 6, 1876, a copyboy raced up to John Boyle O'Reilly in the offices of the *Boston Pilot* with a cablegram from London: "London, June 6—A dispatch from Melbourne, Australia, states that all the political prisoners [an error—six was the number] have escaped on the American whaleship *Catalpa.*

O'Reilly, nearly euphoric, wired Devoy at once: "Grand glory and complete success. Ireland triumphs. London dispatch admits all our men safe aboard *Catalpa*. Watch your cables for more details. Erin go Bragh."

O'Reilly sat down to break the news in the pages of his newspaper, knowing that newspapers from all over the nation would soon be wiring him and sending reporters to the *Pilot*'s offices. In his piece, O'Reilly was careful to omit the name of the whaler, its captain, and the plotters. He handed the proofs to Denis Cashman and ran to catch the afternoon train to New Bedford with his original handwritten draft of the article in his pocket.

Two hours later, O'Reilly waded through the crowd at the New Bedford depot and, with a long look at the masts and spars of whalers rising along the wharves, strode to a tidy wood-frame house on Second Street. An attractive young woman stood in the yard, hanging clothes as a toddler clambered around her petticoats and played with wooden clothespins from the woman's wicker basket. O'Reilly went over to introduce himself to Emma Richardson Anthony, smiling at little Sophie.

According to Leon Huggins, the man who would one day marry Sophie, the handsome O'Reilly gently told Emma: "He will be back soon. The moment I learn when the *Catalpa* will reach

America, I shall be in touch with you by telegraph. The whole world will be awaiting him, I assure you."

Emma invited O'Reilly inside, where they talked for an hour before he had to catch his train and prepare for the coming public fenzy over the escape.

As O'Reilly had anticipated, the news sparked front-page coverage throughout the United States. Although he had tried to hide many of the escape's details for the moment, the New Bedford papers found out that the *Catalpa* and Anthony were involved and ran the names.

O'Reilly, the ex-Hussar, had written:

> To see their comrades forgotten and left to rot in their dungeons was enough to make the Irishmen of the [British] army abjure their nationality and accept the English dominion in Ireland.
>
> This has been averted by the rescue. The soldiers in the English army will read the news with a deeper thrill than any other Irishmen. It has a larger meaning to them than to others. "Now," they will say, "now, at last, we are a part of the Irish people. Our red coats do not separate us from our countrymen; and if we suffer for their cause, they will be as true as steel to us in the day of trial."

Throughout America, even newspapers opposed to Fenianism and Clan na Gael applauded the rescue and, to the fury of the British government, recognized the six military Fenians as political prisoners. In Irish communities from coast to coast, impromptu torchlight processions to celebrate the news were held.

The *New York World*, no friend of the Irish, stated: "The news of the escape . . . with the friendly help of an American whaler, will be very generally received. . . . In this country everybody will be cordially pleased."

In Devoy's paper, the *New York Herald,* publisher James Gordon Bennett offered: "This carefully prepared plan to rescue a number of sentenced prisoners . . . shows that they were estimated by their brethren for their sacrifices as much as for their personal value, and the demonstration of this alone will, doubtless, stimulate the anti-English sentiment among the mass of Irishmen opposed to English rule. The affair will bring little credit to Mr. Disraeli, who so recently refused to remit the penalities of these men."

The *New York Times* ran similar opinions, speculating that O'Reilly was somehow involved with the rescue.

In London, "some high and holy Tory anger" exploded. The *Daily Telegraph* fumed that "the Yankee captain" had hurled a humiliating insult at Britain and that the Queen and Disraeli must "insist . . . on redress in some form for a violation of our sovereignty."

The *London Times* railed: "When the whaler comes into an American port and lands her passengers, the British authorities, it seems, might have very good ground for interference, and it is difficut to see how the United States could avoid giving up the prisoners and punishing the vessel and, if they can be found, those engaged in the rescue."

The *New York World*'s rebuttle to the *London Times* reflected the stance that President Ulysses S. Grant and Congress espoused, grounded in ongoing Federal rancor toward British aid on the high seas to the Confederacy during the American Civil War:

> The complaint of the *London Times* in regard to the assistance rendered by Americans in the escape of the Fenian prisoners from West Australia was not

conceived in good taste, and has been brought forth in very bad temper. . . .

English volunteers never hesitated out of reverence to "the public justice of a friendly State," to take a hand in aid . . . of Jefferson Davis or of any other man, patriot or conspirator, who happened to be striking at the existing order of things in his own country. . . . It is rather cool of England, then, to be annoyed when other nations adopt her own opinions in regard to baffled revolutionists and political prisoners generally. . . . We venture to say that no vessel flying the British flag would refuse upon the high seas to receive fugitives escaping from the political prisons of any other nation. Technically, the American ship which rescued the Fenians has done no more than this, *and all talk about demanding redress is mere nonsense.*

The *Catalpa* may have gone to the Australian coast with the design of rescuing the Fenian prisoners, but she kept on the high seas, and in no way compromised her flag. The men who planned the escape, and effected it at their own proper risk, were doubtless Irishmen—partakers, it may be, in the conspiracy for which the prisoners were suffering. In their eyes the convicts were not criminals, but martyrs.

. . . They owed neither courtesy nor comity to the British government, at the hands of which the greatest favor they had to expect would be a commutation of the death-penalty into penal servitude for life. They did owe something to the comrades whom they had perhaps originally helped to lead into danger, and they quitted themselves of their obligation like good men and true. The only part, so far as yet appears, which any American took in the affair, was one which eminently befits an American, that of receiving under the Stars and Stripes fugitives whose greatest crime was their uncalculating and foolhardy zeal for their native land.

Nations which find it necessary to fill penal colonies with political convicts must not insist upon the sympathy and help of other countries in the task of guarding them. If it was a legitimate employment of English capital for English shipowners to make a regular trade of running the blockade with supplies to the Confederates during our Civil War, it certainly is fair enough for New Bedford whalers, if they are paid for the business, to stand off and on twenty to thirty miles from the coast of West Australia and pick up political prisoners, who may swim or row out to them, as John Boyle O'Reilly did formerly, and as Wilson and his compatriots have now done. . . .

The New York *Irish World* spoke for most of America's Irish with the following sentiments: "Easter Monday was the day of days for them [the escaped Fenians]. They had heard the glad alleluiah in the chapels, telling that Death had been conquered, and the Grave made to give up its dead. They were dead—was there to be a call to life sped to them, even there in the dark Sepulchre of Slavery, amid the corruption of sin and crime? . . . They pass from Fetters to Freedom."

On the Indian Ocean, the *Catalpa* ran into another gale her first night after the standoff with the *Georgette*. Anthony used all his skills at the helm and with the sails to turn the gusts to the ship's advantage, and she was four hundred miles from Australia within two days.

Anthony ordered his crew to retreive two chests of clothing—

whalemen's "slops"—and said to the Irishmen: "Go in and help yourselves. Take all you care for, and you'll need the thickest, for you'll see some cold weather before you reach America." The escapees, as well as Breslin, Brennan, Desmond, and King, took two suits of clothing each and an ample supply of woolen underclothes.

In the cabins built by Duggan, the passengers were supplied with "bedding, seats, and tables . . . and a boy from the forecastle was assigned to attend to the men."

Anthony steered northward for weeks to catch the southeast trade winds, which launched the *Catalpa* across the Indian Ocean at a brisk clip, the whaler making over two hundred miles a day. Allowed to roam the ship at will, the prisoners reveled at first in their newfound freedom. Breslin put his sentiments to words in a poem he entitled "Rolling Home":

Right across the Indian Ocean, while the trade-wind
  follows fast,
Speeds our ship with gentle motion; fear and chains
  behind us east.
Rolling home! rolling home! rolling home across the
  sea;
Rolling home to bright Columbia; home to friends and
  liberty

Through the waters blue and bright, through dark
  waves and hissing foam,
Ever onward, with delight, we are sailing still for home.
O'er our pathway, in the sunshine, flies the wide-
  winged albatross,
O'er our topmast, in the moonlight, hangs the starry
  Southern Cross.

By the stormy cape now flying, with a full and flowing
  sail,
See the daylight round us dying on the black breast of
  the gale!
See the lightning flash above us and the dark surge roll
  below!
Here's a health to those who love us! Here's defiance to
  the foe!

Now the wide Atlantic clearing with our good ship
  speeding free.
The dull, "Cape of Storms" we're leaving far to east
  ward on our lee.
And as homeward through the waters the old *Catalpa*
  goes,
Ho! You fellows at the masthead, let us hear once more,
  "She blows."

Next by the lonely St. Helena, with a steady wind we
  glide
By the rock-built, sea-grit prison, where the gallant
  Frenchman died,
With the flying fish and porpoise sporting 'round us in
  the wave,
With the starry flag of freedom floating o'er us bright
  and brave.

Past "The Line" and now the dipper hangs glittering in
  the sky.
Onward still! In the blue water, see, the gulf weed
  passing by.
Homeward! Homeward to Columbia, blow you, steady
  breezes, blow,

'Till we hear it, from the masthead, the joyful cry,
"Land ho!"

On May 8, 1876, a more somber note was sounded aboard the ship. Second Mate Farnham died suddenly of a heart attack, and with Anthony presiding and the entire ship's company in attendance, including the Irishmen gathered at the rail, Farnham was buried at sea the following day. Anthony would tell Pease: "He [Farnham] had been a faithful man, and there was sincere sorrow throughout the ship's company."

Anthony grew wary at the prospect of British warships as he took the *Catalpa* south of Madagascar and, with the help of the trade winds, rounded the Cape of Good Hope and headed into the Atlantic.

"Naturally," he would recall, "the bark gave the island of St. Helena a wide berth, since the neighborhood of a British possession was to be avoided."

Pease added: "Subsequently it was learned that an English warship awaited the *Catalpa* at this point. There is an English naval station at Ascension, and Captain Anthony was likewise shy of a near approach to the men on this day."

Heading for the Atlantic whaling grounds, Anthony intended to stay there long enough to catch a few more whales and return to New Bedford with bigger profits. "Now is just the season," he said to Breslin, "for whaling on the Western Grounds. We are well enough fitted, excepting that we lack small stores, and we have plenty of money to buy from other vessels. I know the whaling grounds, and by hauling up to the northward we are almost certain to pick up a few hundred barrels of oil, and the voyage can be made as successful financially as it has been in other respects."

Breslin concurred as Anthony laid a course north by east. The prisoners, told that they were to land at Fernandina, a Florida town where several notable Fenians had settled, recoiled at the thought that Anthony was going to stay at sea and risk the threat of a British warship stopping the *Catalpa.*

Brennan now encouraged the ex-soldiers to demand that Anthony sail immediately not for Florida, but to their friends in New York. Breslin wrote: "We had not been at sea for a fortnight when I was informed by one of the prisoners that Brennan meant to do me all the mischief he could, and I shortly after learned that Duggan and he combined for that purpose."

Still seething at what he considered poor treatment by Anthony and Breslin, Brennan found a willing accomplice in Duggan in convincing the escaped prisoners that every extra moment they spent at sea placed them in jeopardy from British warships. Duggan, who all along had been supposed to go ashore at Fremantle to aid Breslin, had been incensed when Breslin replaced him with King on "the land end" of the rescue. Ever the loyal Fenian and unwilling through a fit of pique to risk the chances for his imprisoned comrades to escape, Duggan helped Smith keep the *Catalpa*'s crew in line throughout the rescue. Although the saturnine Duggan had come to like and respect Anthony, the Irishman grabbed at Brennan's plan to, in some measure take over the ship's course, if not the ship itself.

When Brennan began telling the ex-prisoners that he, not Breslin, was the man who held real authority in Clan na Gael and had been the "true" architect of the escape plot, Duggan endorsed Brennan's lie. The word of Duggan—like Breslin—a rescuer of Stephens and renowned for his at times cold-blooded commitment to Irish freedom—carried a great deal of weight with the six former soldiers.

Duggan and Brennan stoked the Fenians fears of recapture and also their health concerns. Harrington suffered from the lingering effects of dysentery, and Wilson from chronic chest pains.

All six men endured digestive woes brought on by their prison work-gang diets, Hogan complaining to Breslin that he [Hogan] needed boiled onions to settle his stomach agony. On the *Catalpa*, a stimulant called "Pain Killer" was given to him from the ship's medical stores, but he claimed to need rum or brandy, which Anthony kept under lock and key.

In late July 1876, Wilson confronted Breslin: "We ought all to be on shore long ago, and might have been only for you."

Desmond, trying to mediate, suggested to the six ex-soldiers that they put their concerns in writing to Breslin and Anthony. On July 27, the captain and Breslin received the letter:

> We the undersigned do hereby request that this ship be brought into port without delay for the following reasons:
>
> 1st. Owing to the inutritious [*sic*] quality of the food, the ex-prisoners believe it injurious to their health.
>
> 2nd. Owing to the ill-health of some of the ex-prisoners it is deemed dangerous to prolong the voyage.
>
> 3rd. The ex-prisoners consider themselves not actually free men until placed on American soil.
>
> 4th. By complying with the above we believe it will be satisfactory to all parties interested in this undertaking.

All six of the former prisoners, plus Brennan, Desmond, Duggan, and King signed the appeal.

Breslin was furious. Anthony pondered the appeal for two days; then, unwilling to go whaling with ten tough, capable, and desperate men on the edge of mutiny, and able to understand their fears of recapture, he acceded. He turned the *Catalpa* toward New York City.

At 2 A.M. on August 19, 1876, the battered whaleship, her copper sheathing cracked and barnacles encrusting parts of her keel, slipped into New York Harbor about a mile from the Battery. A pilot came aboard, and the craft's captain "was greatly surprised to find the destination to be New York, inasmuch as the vessel was a whaleship." The pilot guided Anthony to an anchorage off Castle Garden, where she waited for a tug.

A tug pulled alongside the whaler at 6 A.M., and the tow's captain offered to take the *Catalpa* to an anchorage in the harbor for $250. Anthony scoffed at the price and talked the man down to $90.

Anthony and Breslin went ashore in one of the *Catalpa*'s whaleboats at sunrise and went to 182 Chatham Square, the hotel of Fenian leader O'Donovan Rossa, who was away on business. But Rossa's son and the the emaciated, coughing Will Foley were in the lobby, shocked to see them in New York but warmly welcoming them. One look at Foley's waxy pallor and loose skin told both men that the gallant ex-soldier did not have long to live. As if to confirm the sad fact, Foley, overcome with emotion and illness, fainted at the news that his fellow "graduates" of The Establishment were in the harbor. After reviving him, Rossa's son and Breslin rushed off to send messages and telegrams to friends in New York and all over the country to proclaim the news that the *Catalpa* had arrived. Meanwhile, Anthony walked alone in midmorning to the Customs Office and obtained a permit to land his passengers.

By the time he returned to the *Catalpa* in the late morning, small boats packed with the press and cheering Clan na Gael men surrounded the ship, and as he climbed on deck, he was swarmed by reporters who had boarded the whaler and had already begun interviewing the escapees.

"Men," Anthony called to the "Fremantle Six," as reporters

had quickly dubbed them, "I have a permit for you to go ashore, and you are at liberty to go when you please."

Shortly before noon on August 19, 1876, Thomas Darragh, the grizzled soldier who had served on so many of the Queen's battlefields and had developed almost a touch of hero worship for the New Bedford captain, marched over to Anthony and looked at him for a long moment. His dark-hollowed eyes moist, Darragh said, "God bless you, Captain, you've saved our lives."

On their way to a waiting boat packed with Clan na Gael men, each of the Fremantle prisoners clutched Anthony's hand. Breslin harbored some anger at all of the freed prisoners except Darragh, believing that their threatened "mutiny" had been an insult to Anthony and all that he had risked for them. Anthony, however, held no resentment whatsoever against the military Fenians for the events of late July. In their position, he believed that he would have felt the same dread of recapture by a British warship. He also knew that if a Royal Navy vessel had stopped them on the high seas, they might well have arrested Anthony, too, and defied the United States government to do anything about such a move.

Now, as the six Fenians, men aged far beyond their years by a decade of suffering, shook Anthony's hand and met his gaze, few words were spoken. Few were needed.

At 1:30 A.M. on August 20, 1876, Anthony opened his logbook and, with a tinge of humor, wrote: "Went to City Wharf. Made her fast. So ends this day a *pleasant* voyage for J. T. Richardson."

The Bold Fenian Men

John Devoy, running a fever and hacking away from cold at Dr. Carroll's home in Philadelphia, climbed out of bed and rushed to the station to board a train to New York shortly after he received Dennis Rossa's telegram. Clan na Gael had brought the escaped prisoners in carriages to Rossa's hotel and had turned that establishment into the site of celebration, hundreds of people gathering inside 182 Chatham Square and in the street outside to give "the bold Fenian men" a heroes' welcome. With the prisoners safely landed, all that British officials could do was to file protests in New York and Washington, D.C. The appeals were ignored. The *Irish World* reported: "Rossa's hotel, on which the green flag was hoisted immediately on the arrival of the news, became the centre of attraction for nationalists. A constant stream of visitors kept pouring in throughout the day, and the 'Catalpan Six' would have been quickly tired out but that the satisfaction at being free men and compatriots did not allow any other feeling to affect them. . . . All were in the garb of sailors, provided them onboard the *Catalpa*.

When Devoy arrived, he nearly sobbed at the sight of the human scarecows who had been such robust men back in the days of Curran's and Pilsworth's when he had met with them so often. He brought them all into a private room to talk. Devoy went slack-jawed as all, but Darragh launched into diatribes against Breslin and praised Brennan as their "deliverer."

Devoy replied that Brennan was a liar and a troublemaker and that the escaped prisoners owed their lives to Breslin. Still, the bitterness stoked in them by Brennan and Duggan lingered, and Devoy wrote that he "never succeeded in removing the feeling of positive hatred, not to speak of ingratitude, which they entertained for Breslin." Already embroiled in a feud with Goff over Brennan and the finances of the rescue, Devoy would hold Goff greatly responsible for robbing Breslin of his full due in the mission.

Back near the *Catalpa*, people continued to row out to see the now-famous whaler and her captain. Anthony's thoughts, however, had turned north, to New Bedford, where his wife and his daughter waited. On Tuesday, August 22, 1876, he telegraphed Richardson that the *Catalpa* was coming home. Anthony wrote in his logbook: "This day commences with fresh breezes from the W. and clear, pleasant weather . . . took a tug and started for New Bedford. . . . "

With Sam Smith beside him in the covered wheelhouse, Anthony took the *Catalpa* into New Bedford Harbor on the afternoon of Thursday, August 24, 1876. He gaped at the hundreds of people jamming the main dock. Their cheers carried out across the water to the oncoming bark as they waved and shouted "to welcome home one of the bravest that ever lived of New Bedford's sons."

As the *Catalpa* neared its mooring, Anthony nearly wept at the sight of Emma, Sophie, the Richardsons, and Hathaway waiting for him in the front of the throng. Suddenly the crash of artillery echoed above the seaport—a seventy-one-gun salute for every state in the Union and every county in Ireland.

A short while later, as Anthony stepped onto the dock, his family and friends stared for a moment at him.

Pease wrote: "They were shocked at the changed appearance of the captain. When he left New Bedford, sixteen months before, he weighed 160 pounds and his hair was black as coal. The months of worry and intense excitement had worn upon him to such an extent that his weight was now reduced to 123 pounds and his hair was sprinkled with gray."

The crowd closed in around Anthony, Smith, and the astonished crew and informed them that the following evening, a gala reception would be held for the men of the *Catalpa* at New Bedford's Liberty Hall and that John Boyle O'Reilly would address the gathering. As Anthony climbed into a carriage with Emma and Sophie and the rig clattered up the cobblestoned hill to Second Avenue, a sudden and bittersweet thought hit him: here he was acclaimed as a seafaring hero, but never again would he command a ship on the high seas. From this moment on, he was subject to arrest in any port where the Royal Navy docked, in any sea where the Queen's fleets patrolled—in short, everywhere except the territorial waters of the United States. He had no choice but to obey his once-broken pledge to Emma that he would "abandon the longboat forever."

George and Emma Anthony walked into Liberty Hall on Friday evening of August 25, 1876, to a tumultuous wave of applause and cheers from the hundreds of friends, family, reporters, and Clan na Gael men who jammed every nook of the auditorium. Escorted to the stage, over which hung the Stars and Stripes and the green, white, and orange banner that Irish nationalists hoped to fly over their land in the near future, the Anthonys were seated in the "spots of honor" next to the speaker's dais. Sam Smith, looking somewhat uncomfortable in a suit, also took his place on the stage.

As George Anthony nodded at the beaming John Boyle O'Reilly, the captain suddenly spied a haggard, sunburned face smiling at him from next to O'Reilly. Anthony blinked at Thomas Hassett, who had traveled up from New York to honor him.

Pease would write:

> O'Reilly's address on this occasion was one of his most eloquent efforts, and it is to be regretted that it is not preserved in its entirety. The summaries which were printed in the newspapers do him very inadequate justice.
>
> He said that it was not with ordinary feelings that he had come. He owed to New Bedford no ordinary debt, and he would gladly have come a thousand miles to do honor to New Bedford whalemen. Seven years of liberty, wife, children, and a happy home in a free country were his debt of gratitude . . . his debt to New Bedford might be grown too heavy to bear.
>
> They were there, he said, to do honor to Captain Anthony, to show their gratitude to the man who had done a brave and wonderful deed. The self-sacrifice and unfailing devotion of him who had taken his life in his hand and beached his whaleboat on the penal colony, defying its fearful laws, defying the gallows and the chain-gang, in order to keep the faith with the men who had placed their trust in him,—and this almost beyond belief in our selfish and commonplace time.
>
> There were sides to this question worth looking at, he continued. To Irishmen it was significant in manifold ways, one of which was that these men, being soldiers, could not be left in prison without demoralizing the Irishmen in the English army, who would not forget that their comrades had been forsaken and left to die in confinement, when the civilian leaders of the move-

ment had been set free. But the spirit that prompted their release was larger and nobler than this, and its beauty could be appreciated by all men, partaking as it did of the universal instinct of humanity to love their race and their native land.

England said that the rescue was a lawless and disgraceful filibustering raid. Not so, said Mr. O'Reilly. If these men were criminals, the rescue would be criminal. But they were political offenders against England, not against the law, or order, or religion. They had lain in prison for ten years, with millions of their countrymen asking their release, imploring England, against their will to beg, to set these men at liberty. Had England done so it would have partially disarmed Ireland. A generous act by England would be reciprocated instantly by millions of the warmest hearts in the world. But she was blind, as of old; blind and arrogant and cruel. She would not release the men; she scorned to give Ireland an answer. She called the prisoners cowardly criminals, not political offenders.

After the ship sailed and there was a long time when no tidings came, O'Reilly said that doubts and fears came, as they were sure to do; but Captain Hathaway said once and always of Captain Anthony: "The man who engaged to do this will keep that engagement, or he won't come out of the penal colony."

After describing some of his own experiences in Australia, Mr. O'Reilly pointed to the bronzed and worn face of Mr. Hassett, one of the rescued prisoners, and said: "Look at that man sitting there. Six years ago he escaped from his prison in the penal colony and fled into the bush, living there like a wild beast for a whole year, hunted from district to district, in a blind but manful attempt to win his liberty. When England said the rescue was illegal, America could answer, as the anti-slavery men answered when they attacked the Constitution, as England herself answered in the cause of Poland: "We have acted from a higher law than your written constitution and treatise—the law of God and humanity." It was in obedience to this supreme law that Captain Anthony rescued the prisoners, and pointed his finger at the Stars and Stripes, when the English commander threatened to fire on his ship.

"The Irishman," concluded Mr. O'Reilly, "who could forget what the Stars and Stripes have done for his countrymen deserves that in time of need that flag shall forget him."

Then Mr. Hassett described the bravery of Captain Anthony, and pictured him as he held the steering oars on the night of the gale, risking his life for the men. He could never amply express his gratitude to Captain Anthony, he said, and he was sure that New Bedford never produced a braver sailor.

Just a day or two after the gala, Henry Hathaway strolled into his office in the New Bedford Police station for the night shift and found a letter perched on his desk's blotter. He picked it up, and as he saw the postmark, his eyes widened. It was stamped with the words "Perth, Western Australia" and was addressed to "The Officer in Charge of Police Department, New Bedford, Massachusetts, United States, America."

He unsealed the envelope and removed a sheet of paper emblazoned with the letterhead "Police Department, Chief

Office, Perth, Western Australia." The letter was dated April 18, 1876—the day after the escape:

> Sir,—I beg to inform you that on the 17th instant [Easter Monday] the imperial convicts named in the margin absconded from the convict settlement at Fremantle, in this colony, and escaped from the colony in the American whaling bark *Catalpa*, G. Anthony master. This bark is from New Bedford, Massachusetts, U.S.A. The convicts were taken from the shore in a whaleboat belonging to the *Catalpa*, manned by Captain Anthony and six of the crew. The abettors were Collins, Jones [King], and Johnson.
>
> I attach the description of each of the absconders, and have to request that you will be good enough to furnish me with any particulars you may be able to gather concerning them.
>
> I have the honor to be, sir,
> Your obedient servant,
> M. A. Smith, Supt. of Police

In the Western Australian authorities' desperate attempt to recapture the prisoners, they had unwittingly sent a letter to the very man who had handpicked Captain Anthony as "just the man for the job" of commanding the *Catalpa*. Beyond showing the letter to Anthony and Richardson for their amusement, Hathaway did nothing with the request.

For several months following the reception at Liberty Hall, Hassett joined his fellow escapees at crowded receptions thrown in their honor by Clan na Gael chapters across the country with donations raised for the "Prisoners Fund," to help them start their new lives in America. The men appeared in groups of two or three at the events, at which admission fees for the fund were charged. At the end of the "*Catalpa* tour," some fifteen thousand dollars, less travel expenses, was divided among the *Catalpa* Six.

With the ex-prisoners safe and the *Catalpa* docked in New Bedford, Devoy now turned to settling up with the whaling men who had risked their lives in a cause that was not their own. "We wanted to deal generously with all the men who had enabled us to carry out the rescue, to make a good impression that would be of service in future enterprises."

The net cost of the mission to the Rescue Committee rang in at $25,858.02, and a faction of Clan na Gael leaders led by Goff tore into Devoy because Anthony had sailed the *Catalpa* straight to New York after picking up the Fenians rather than continue whaling and turning a profit. Goff conveniently overlooked that his man, Brennan, had hamstrung any additional hunting in the Atlantic.

In February 1877, Clan na Gael, with Goff haranguing Devoy every step of the way, authorized Devoy, Breslin, and William Cannon to settle with the New Bedford men. The three used the *Whaleman's Shipping List,* the bible of the industry, to figure out the whalemen's "lay." Anthony received $2,165.63 for "share of voyage" and a $1,000 "gratuity for rescue," for a total of $3,165.63. Sam Smith's lay totaled $1,443.75, with a rescue gratuity of $200. Affixing a market value of $6,000 to the *Catalpa,* Clan na Gael gave her to Anthony, Richardson, and Hathaway, but when the three men sold the whaler, her battered condition— she needed new copper sheathing, among many other costly repairs—knocked down the sale price. Clan na Gael did not record the selling price. Still, Devoy often expressed uncertainty that the New Bedford men, especially Anthony, had been fairly compensated, as a profitable whaling voyage would have netted more for the captain. None of the men complained, however, proud to have played their parts in such a noble adventure.

For Clan na Gael and for the Irish, from "the old sod" to everywhere emigration had sent them, the rescue of the six military Fenians from The Establishment sent a surge of pride and renewed purpose through nationalists. Less than a decade after the Fenian uprising fell apart, Devoy, Breslin, and the Rescue Committee had proven that an Irish organization could strike a political blow against "the old oppressor, Britain." Despite the feud between Devoy and Goff, despite financial problems, Clan na Gael had converted the contributions of washerwomen and judges alike into a rescue that jolted the British Empire and set off celebrations wherever the Irish lived. In June 1876, when the news of the rescue appeared in Irish newspapers, up to a hundred thousand people marched in a wild torchlight parade in Dublin to honor the *Catalpa* Six and their rescuers. All across America, the celebrations continued for weeks after the *Catalpa*'s arrival in New York City.

Flushed with the success of the rescue, Clan na Gael saw its membership and money swell. In his scholarly study of the Fenian movement and the *Catalpa* rescue, Dublin historian Seán O'Luing assessed:

> Thereafter, Clan na Gael extended its sinews from New York westwards to 'Frisco, northwards to Boston and points beyond, and southwards to New Orleans, until camps flourished in every territory, state, and city of the American Union. It became the inspiration and the great unseen driving force behind the combination of the Land League and Parnellite movements [the political pushes for fair agrarian laws and social equality in Ireland in the 1880s and spearheaded by once-impris-

oned civilian Fenian Michael Davitt and Charles Stewart Parnell]. . . . The hard resolute sinews of the organization extended wherever the Irish had settled in the United States, and caused revolutionary activity to flourish in hundreds of centres.

John Devoy would emerge as the driving force of Clan na Gael, and John J. Breslin would remain a prominent player in the organization he had once balked at joining. Devoy would take every public opportunity to make sure that Breslin, not Brennan, received the credit for the land end of the rescue. Chiding Goff's contention that Brennan was "the honest man" onboard the *Catalpa,* Devoy wrote in the *Gaelic American* newspaper in 1904, ". . .the man who won the victory in the crisis [the land end of the rescue] was John J. Breslin, and no decent Irishman will try to rob him of it."

In Boston, John Boyle O'Reilly, editor of *The Pilot,* a publication closely tied to the Catholic Church, which denounced Fenianism and Clan na Gael, never joined the organization and was decried by some nationalists as a "turncoat." Still, Devoy and other Clan na Gael leaders often sought O'Reilly's counsel, and as Devoy always noted, without O'Reilly and his path to the sea, the voyage of the *Catalpa* would never have materialized.

By 1900, Devoy stood as the acknowledged head of Clan na Gael, and as the fires of Irish rebellion ignited once again, Devoy and his organization funneled money and arms to the Gaelic League, Sinn Fein, and the rejuvenated IRB as rebels readied to take on the British Army yet again. When the Easter Rising erupted in 1916 in Dublin, Devoy's hand was all over it. Nearly sixty years after British troops and police had hauled him from Pilsworth's, he had played his part in the rebellion that would finally lead to a free Irish republic. The men who formed that republic would never forget Devoy and his relentless, lifelong battle against the Crown.

In many ways, that battle had slowly begun to turn in Devoy's and his compatriots' favor when a weather-beaten New Bedford whaler had slipped into New York Harbor in the gray hours before dawn on August 19, 1876. As her Yankee master stood at her helm and guided her through the murk, six haggard Irishmen huddled at the rail. The long voyage of the *Catalpa* had ended with "none aboard but free men."

Epilogue

On August 6, 1896, thousands of Irish citizens and Irish Americans poured into Philadelphia from all over the United States for the annual Clan na Gael celebration. They milled about the vast grounds of Rising Sun Park, where "the green flag of Ireland, entwined with the Stars and Stripes, floated proudly over the main entrance."

The *Philadelphia Times* reported: "The grounds were decorated possibly on a more elaborate scale than on any former occasion. Exclusive of what the track and field provided in the way of amusement, there were pastimes for the younger and older folks, such as tenpin alleys, merry-go-rounds, baseball, and swings. There were several bands of music. . . ."

In the afternoon, throngs of people took seats or stood at the main pavilion, where a flag-draped platform was crowded with politicians and Clan na Gael leaders. At first glance, a stocky middle-aged man with thick gray hair and a well-groomed mustache looked little different than the other men wearing sober suits and sitting on the platform's chairs. Near him sat three men he had not seen for nearly two decades, men who looked far older than their years. As shared memories washed over all four men, the stocky man, his bronzed skin attesting to years spent at sea, clutched a folded flag in his hands and waited.

Luke Dillon, president of the Irish American Club, stepped to the podium and called for silence. Then he introduced Captain George Anthony. As cheers exploded from the crowd, Anthony walked up to the podium and, with Dillon's help, attached the flag to a temporary pole. As the band on the platform broke into the "Star Spangled Banner" and over four thousand men, women, and children rose to their feet, "the old Stars and Stripes were unfurled to the breeze."

With the final notes of the anthem, two volleys from the Clan na Gael Guards cracked through the air in salute of the flag and Anthony.

The *Philadelphia Times* stated: "The great feature of the day's exercises, and that which attracted the most attention, were the introduction of Captain George S. Anthony and the presentation by him to the Clan-na-Gaels of the flag which floated from the masthead of the whaling bark *Catalpa,* which had onboard the political prisoners rescued from the penal settlement of Western Australia, when it was overtaken by a British gunboat."

Dillon returned to his seat, and Anthony remained at the podium, enveloped in the applause. As he waited for the din to wane, three of the men he had plucked from The Establishment sat close by—Martin Hogan, Thomas Darragh, and Robert Cranston.

Cranston had married soon after his arrival in New York and had settled down there, working as an aide to O'Donovan Rossa. Hogan had headed to Chicago, also remaining active in Fenian affairs. In Rhode Island, James Wilson had married and raised a family, but had been unable to attend the convention, his heart problems dogging him. Michael Harrington and Thomas Henry Hassett had passed away in the early 1890s, their health ruined by their years in prisons from Dublin to Fremantle.

Martin Hogan initially had trouble adjusting to his new life after so many years in prison. On New Year's Eve of 1876, the ex-dragoon, carrying a small bag and reportedly drunk, sat down in New York City with Breslin and Devoy and charged that Devoy had shortchanged the *Catalpa* Six by paying them less than the agreed-upon five thousand dollars per man from the Prisoners Fund. Devoy's truthful statement that he had paid them all he could from what was raised—fifteen thousand dollars less travel expenses for the ex-prisoners—only enraged Hogan further. The two men argued, their voices swelling. Hogan suddenly sprang out of his chair, pulled two revolvers from the bag, and tossed them on the table.

The former dragoon roared, "There's only one way to resolve this!"

Before Devoy could grab one of the pistols and as Hogan lunged for one, Breslin scooped up the weapons. Hogan came at Breslin, and Breslin slammed a pistol butt against Hogan's head. Still, perhaps with all the anger, fear, and resentments of his long years of suffering boiling out of control, Hogan kept fighting. Several police officers were called to the scene, and they carted Hogan to a cell to cool off. Hogan, recovering his composure by morning, was released. He would not spend another day of his life behind bars.

Many others who had played parts in the rescue mission of the *Catalpa* had also died in the years since Easter Monday of 1876. Early in the morning of April 10, 1890, forty-six-year-old John Boyle O'Reilly—acclaimed as a novelist, poet, editor, and journalist nationwide—worn down by a brutal workload and perhaps tormented by his prison sufferings, was found by his wife Mary, slumped in a chair in his Hull, Massachusetts, home. His left hand rested on a book opened on the table in front of him, and his lips were clamped around a cigar. When she tried to wake him, he did not move. She sent a servant racing for a doctor, and when he arrived, O'Reilly stirred for a moment—then sagged back in the chair and died. Some believe he mistakenly took too large a dose of a sedative meant to help him sleep.

Dennis Duggan, who had built the berths for the *Catalpa* Six, had returned to Dublin and continued his IRB activities, always one step ahead of the police and British soldiers. He died of natural causes on September 9, 1884, and twelve thousand people accompanied the Fenian hero's cortege to Glasnevin Cemetery, where a memorial to him would be dedicated at his grave in 1938 by the Republic of Ireland that he had fought for but had never lived to see.

Also gone was Peter Curran, who had died in New York on December 30, 1881. Five of the *Catalpa* Six had known his public house well in the 1860s, and Curran's New York address, which James Wilson had spotted in a smuggled newspaper in The Establishment, was where the prisoner had sent the first desperate appeal for help from "our friends in America."

Will Foley, the genial ex-soldier and ex-Fremantle prisoner who had risked his ticket-of-leave to carry Breslin's messages to the *Catalpa* Six, died in a New York Hospital within a few months of the whaler's arrival in America. November 2, 1876, Devoy wrote to Reynolds: "Poor Foley is dead and will be buried Sunday. Will any of the boys come in?"

Now, on August 6, 1895, on the Clan na Gael stage, the man whom those friends had placed in the *Catalpa*'s wheelhouse addressed the throng:

> The flag which floated over the *Catalpa* on that April day in 1876—the Stars and Stripes which protected the liberated men and their rescuers—I have preserved and cherished for twenty years as a sacred relic. I would fain keep it and hand it down to my children as

a family heirloom, but I am confident it will be safe in the keeping of those who were associated with me in an enterprise of which we have all reason to be proud. Your countrymen have ever been loyal to the flag of the United States and ever ready to shed their blood in its defense. I, therefore, present you with this flag of the *Catalpa* as a memento of our common share in a good work well done and a token of the sympathy of all true Americans with the cause of liberty in Ireland. I know you will cherish it as I do, and that if the interests of that flag should ever again demand it your countrymen will be among the first to rally to its defense.

John Devoy had planned to accept the *Catalpa's* flag and deliver a speech in Anthony's honor, but had fallen ill with a heavy cold. In Devoy's place, Clan na Gael notable Michael J. Ryan read the address Devoy had composed:

Captain Anthony, old friend and comrade, I accept this flag on behalf of the organization which fitted out the *Catalpa,* selected you as her commander, and which shared with you the credit for the work of humanity which she was the chief instrument in accomplishing. I accept it with pride as a memento of a noble deed, and I promise you it shall be cherished by us while life is left us, and handed down to future generations, who will love and cherish it as well. It is the flag of our adopted country, under which Irishmen have fought side by side with native Americans on every battlefield where the interests and honor of that flag were at stake, from Bunker Hill to Appomattox. It is the flag which symbolizes the highest development of human liberty on this earth, and in the future, as in the past, the men to which we, to whom you present this flag, belong, will stand shoulder to shoulder with yours in its defense and in the maintenance of its proud and glorious record.

You recall to our minds to-day memories of events in which native American and Irishmen were closely associated; in which Irish enthusiasm and Yankee coolness, grit, and skill in seamanship effected a combination that won a decisive victory for humanity over the forces of oppression. The battle of human freedom has not yet been won, and the combination of which you formed such an important part may serve as an example worthy of imitation and enlargement in the future.

Your part in that work was noble and disinterested throughout. I went to New Bedford twenty years ago, knowing not a soul in the city, bearing a letter of introduction from John Boyle O'Reilly to Henry C. Hathaway, who has done noble work in aiding the poet-patriot to escape from the Western Australian prison to the land of the free. He entered heartily into the project with which the Clan-na-Gael had entrusted me, and introduced me to you and your father-in-law, Mr. Richardson. Without any promise of reward for your services, or compensation for the risks you would run, you undertook to carry out the work of liberation. You sailed away to the southern seas, you carried out the work you pledged yourself to accomplish, you incurred new risks which had not been asked of you, you defied the British commander who threatened to fire on the Stars and Stripes, and brought the six Irishmen rescued from a British prison in safety to America. In all this you bore yourself proudly and gallantly, like a true American sailor, and you placed the Irish people under heavy obligations to you.

Devoy next paid homage to another man, who had died in 1887: "Our chief regret to-day is that the man most closely associated with you in the rescue, John J. Breslin, the man who commanded the land force of the expedition, and to whose skill and courage its success was wholly due, is not here to receive this flag from your hands. As he has gone to his last account, the honor of taking his place has been assigned to me, although I was only concerned in the management of the American end of the enterprise."

In the years after the rescue, Breslin had proven a force in Clan na Gael. He was deeply involved with John P. Holland, of County Clare, in the building and testing of the "Fenian Ram," a submarine intended to lauch underwater attacks against British warships. While it never did, Holland's underwater craft would become the prototype for the U.S. Navy's first underwater squadrons.

Mary Tondut, Breslin's lover in Fremantle, gave birth to a son in December 1876 in Sydney, Australia. She named him John Joseph, but never came to America even though Breslin had left her ample money with Patrick Maloney. As for her reasons to stay in Australia, no one, outside her family, perhaps, would ever know. In 1880, she married a Sydney watchmaker.

After paying homage to Breslin, Devoy's speech ended with a paen to Anthony: "Many of those who took part in the rescue and two of the men to whom you helped to give liberty are here to do you honor and to thank you in the name of the Irish race for the gallant feat you accomplished nineteen years ago and for your generous gift of this historic flag. Others still are in their graves, while some live too far away to participate in this day's proceedings, which recall an event of which we are all proud. Captain Anthony, in the name of Clan-na-Gael, I thank you for the *Catalpa*'s flag, and wish you a long and happy life.

Another key man in the rescue mission, "*Catalpa* Jim" Reynolds, who risked his home and business to pay for the whaler and without whom the vessel might well have never left New Bedford, would hold a seat on Clan na Gael's executive board, and would endure much tragedy in his personal life. Four of his five children died before he did. In 1897, he passed away in New Haven, and his friends, including Devoy and Goff, helped unveil a stately Celtic cross over "*Catalpa* Jim's" grave in 1904.

The whaler that Reynolds had mortgaged his house for came to a sad end. Richardson, Hathaway, and Anthony sold her to another shipping agent, and the rugged bark set out on three more voyages to the world's whaling grounds. For the men of New Bedford, however, the golden age of whaling was ending, sperm oil replaced by petroleum. The *Catalpa* was sold to a consortium in Central America in 1884, and her last journeys were as a coal barge. Sometime in the 1880s, she was abandoned and burned on a beach at Belize, in British Honduras.

On December 1, 1876, the *Georgette,* the vessel that had challenged the *Catalpa* and lost, ran into a storm off Western Australia and was wrecked, the waves and wind tearing apart the steamer.

Tom Desmond went on to serve as the elected Sheriff of San Francisco and remained immersed in Clan na Gael affairs for the rest of his life. He died of natural causes on October 23, 1910, and was eulogized by *The Gaelic American*: "In his death Ireland loses a devoted and faithful son, and the Clan na Gael one of its truest and staunchest members."

Of Desmond, John J. Breslin noted too modestly: "I now believe that if Desmond had been sent [alone to Australia], the rescue would have been as successfully accomplished. . . ."

Sam Smith, the man who had refused to let the water police and pensioner guards board the *Catalpa* when the *Georgette* confronted her the first time, was granted his shipmaster's papers shortly after the *Catalpa* returned to New Bedford. He married Amy Chase, of Edgartown, Martha's Vineyard, Massachusetts, in 1883 and hunted whales until his death at the age of sixty-three in 1909. On his gravestone, at Edgartown, is the chiseled image of an achor.

Father Patrick McCabe left Western Australia several years after the rescue and was assigned to a quiet parish in Waseca County, Minnesota, where he would live out his days. He and O'Reilly remained in contact throughout their post-Australian years, and in early 1890, O'Reilly, on a nationwide lecture tour to raise funds for the cause of Home Rule for Ireland, stayed with Father McCabe in a St. Paul, Minnesota, hotel and promised to visit McCabe at his parish the following fall. Father McCabe would never see the ill-fated O'Reilly again. The priest who helped O'Reilly and his six soldier comrades to find their path to the sea would be buried in his snow-shrouded parish, one so different from the sun-baked bush he had once roamed with his trap and team.

In 1920, Eamon De Valera, one of the heroes of the Easter Rising in 1916 and President of the Irish Republic, toured the United States, and in Boston in late June, over forty thousand people jammed Fenway Park to hear him speak. On his swing through New England, De Valera met in Pawtucket, Rhode Island, with an eighty-one-year-old man. Despite his heart problems, James Wilson had lived long enough to see Ireland on the verge of independence. The man who had penned "The Voice from the Tomb Letter" was the last surviving member of the *Catalpa* Six. Within a few months after the meeting, James Wilson would join the other five.

De Valera had one last stop in mind before he left New England. He traveled to New Bedford to lay a wreath on the grave of Captain George Smith Anthony. Anthony had died of pneumonia at the age of sixty-nine on May 22, 1913. After the *Catalpa*, he worked for a number of years as a manager in several New Bedford mills. Eventually, he landed a more fitting position for a mariner when he was appointed as a customs inspector for the Port of New Bedford. Until the last few days of his life, he would walk to the docks where he had set out as a cabin boy on his first whaler and had landed the *Catalpa*, his final voyage, in triumph. As New Bedford's whaling days ebbed and ended, Anthony's exploit faded from the minds of many locals.

De Valera never forgot the saga of the Yankee captain who had challenged the "British Lion" for the sake of six men he had never seen and for a cause that had not been his own. Flanked by Emma Richardson Anthony, Sophie Anthony Huggins, and Captain Henry Hathaway, the tall, bespectacled De Valera laid a wreath and the tri-colored flag of the Irish Republic upon George Anthony's grave, where his beloved Emma would be laid to rest in November 1935.

A man who risked his own freedom for that of strangers, George Smith Anthony remains the embodiment of the quiet hero.

Acknowledgments

I had come across the saga of the *Catalpa* in various forms over the years, but it was not until Mark R. Day, a gifted documentary filmmaker and good friend who asked me to appear in his award-winning documentary *The San Patricios* when I was working on a book entitled *The Rogue's March: John Riley and the St. Patrick's Battalion, 1846-48*, asked if I'd like to lend a hand with his new project, a documentary about the *Catalpa*. A few summers ago, he sent me a copy of a rare book published in 1897. Only a few hundred copies of *The Catalpa Expedition* were published; it is the story of the whaling ship's rescue mission and its valiant captain, George Smith Anthony, who sat down with writer Z. W. Pease to tell it from the viewpoint of the man who stood at the *Catalpa's* helm throughout the daring and perilous mission to rescue six Irish political prisoners from a hellish imprisonment in Western Australia in 1875-76.

As I read Captain Anthony's account, the sheer audacity of the plot and the sheer adventure of it—there were twists and turns that any first-rate novelist might have a hard time conjuring—compelled to research and write what has become *The Voyage of the Catalpa*.

The course of my research led to a wide number of libraries, museums, archives, and people who shared their time, their insights, and their material with me. At the New Bedford Whaling Museum, Massachusetts, the staff graciously allowed me access to the *Catalpa's* logbook and their files of firsthand and secondary source material about the ship and its mission. This museum is a wonderful institution whose staff truly preserve the seafaring heritage of New Bedford, and personifies the term "living history."

The collections of the Kendall Whaling Museum, in Sharon, Massachusetts, have since been acquired by the New Bedford Whaling Museum. At the Kendall, Erik Larson and Michael Dwyer opened their resources and their knowledge about America's whaling days and about the

Catalpa to me. Tina Furtado, of the New Bedford Public Library, provided access to the library's amazing collection of whaling history sources.

In Ireland, Michael Kenny, Director of the National Museum, Dublin, has been a friend and resource for both the book and the evolving documentary. Also in Dublin, Elizabeth M. Kirwan and other librarians and archivists at the National Library, Kildare Street, provided inestimable help for me. In Australia, the Battye Library, Perth, is a tremendous resource not only for material about the *Catalpa*, but also the penal history of the Fenian prisoners and Western Australia.

My thanks go out to Jim Gallagher, of New Haven. He provided me a wealth of material about two of the story's principal players: John J. Breslin and "Catalpa Jim" Reynolds.

I also want to mention my neighbor Jack Forbes, who generously lent me not only his copy of John Devoy's *Postbag*, but also welcome material about Tom Desmond, a pivotal figure in the story of the *Catalpa*.

Professor Robert O'Neill gave me free rein to explore the John Boyle O'Reilly Collection at the Burns Library, at Boston College, Chestnut Hill, Massachusetts. The Burns's Irish collections and Boston College's Irish Studies programs are world-class, as is the staff at the library.

At the Thomas Crane Library, in Quincy, Massachusetts, Mary Clark and Linda Beeler patiently helped me track down a number of 19th-century volumes necessary to this work.

My special thanks go out to musician and historical sleuth Brendan Woods, of Perth, Australia. Brendan's tremendous CD and show "Cashman's Diary" present the saga of the military Fenians of Western Australia and the *Catalpa* to vivid life in story and song. Brendan, currently working on a project to preserve both the legacy of the military Fenians and that of Fremantle Gaol, "The Establishment," the Australian prison from which six military Fenians escaped aboard the *Catalpa*, shared with me his treasure trove of documents and knowledge about the prison, the prisoners, their warders, and the "land end" of the *Catalpa* rescue. I am in his debt, and hope that his proposal for a living history project at Fremantle Gaol comes to fruition.

This book would not have been possible without the support, skill, and savvy advice of my literary agent, Frank Weimann, of the Literary Group International, New York. To Philip Turner, Executive Editor at Carroll & Graf, I'm indebted for his tireless help, insights, invaluable advice, patience, and superb editorial skills. My gratitude, also, to Keith Wallman, assistant editor at Carroll & Graf, for his forbearance and editorial talent.

Linda Kosarin, Art Director at Carroll & Graf, also deserves my thanks.

Ed Forry, publisher of the *Reporter Newsgroup*, and Bill Forry, managing editor of the *Dorchester Reporter*, opened up their resources to me, and I'm deeply grateful for their help.

I want to extend my thanks to my own "Fenian circle": Peg Stevens, Karen Stevens, Greg Stevens, Valerie Doran, and Paula and Joe Axelrod. Without their help and support, *The Voyage of the Catalpa* might never have left port, so to speak.

Finally, I want to express my gratitude to Jim Ryan, of New Bedford, Massachusetts. The grandson of Captain George Smith Anthony, Jim has preserved his valiant ancestor's story, and Jim's words to me about Captain Anthony's motive in having risked his life and his family's future by signing on for the *Catalpa*'s perilous and audacious mission still linger: "Captain Anthony knew it was the right thing to do."

About the Author

The news and features editor of the *Boston Irish Reporter*, Peter F. Stevens is a journalist and author whose books include *The Rogue's March: John Riley and the St. Patrick's Battalion, 1846-1848; The Mayflower Murderer and Other Forgotten Firsts in American History; Notorious and Notable New Englanders;* and *Links Lore: Dramatic Moments and Neglected Milestones from Golf's History.*

Among the national and regional magazines in which his work has run are *American Heritage, American History, America's Civil War, Military History, Great Battles, Early American Homes, British Heritage, True West, Yankee,* and *The World of Hibernia,* and *The New York Times* has syndicated many of his articles to newspapers nationwide.

Much of his work has dealt with Irish-American and Irish history. Stevens lives in Quincy, Massachusetts.